YOUNG PEOPLE AND MENTAL HEALTH

YOUNG PEOPLE AND MENTAL HEALTH

edited by

PETER AGGLETON, JANE HURRY and IAN WARWICK
Institute of Education, University of London, UK

JOHN WILEY & SONS, LTD
Chichester · New York · Weinheim · Brisbane · Singapore · Toronto

Copyright © 2000 by John Wiley & Sons Ltd,
Baffins Lane, Chichester,
West Sussex PO19 1UD, England

National   01243 779777
International   (+44) 1243 779777
e-mail (for orders and customer service enquiries):
cs-books@wiley.co.uk
Visit our Home Page on http://www.wiley.co.uk
                    or http://www.wiley.com

Other Wiley Editorial Offices

John Wiley & Sons, Inc., 605 Third Avenue,
New York, NY 10158-0012, USA

WILEY-VCH Verlag GmbH, Pappelallee 3,
D-69469 Weinheim, Germany

Jacaranda Wiley Ltd, 33 Park Road, Milton,
Queensland 4064, Australia

John Wiley & Sons (Asia) Pte Ltd, 2 Clementi Loop #02-01,
Jin Xing Distripark, Singapore 129809

John Wiley & Sons (Canada) Ltd, 22 Worcester Road,
Rexdale, Ontario M9W 1L1, Canada

Library of Congress Cataloging-in-Publication Data

Young people and mental health / edited by Peter Aggleton, Jane Hurry
    and Ian Warwick.
        p.   cm.
    Includes bibliographical references and index.
    ISBN 0-471-97678-4 (alk. paper)
    1. Youth—Mental health.   2. Adolescent psychopathology.
I. Aggleton, Peter.   II. Hurry, Jane.   III. Warwick, Ian.
RJ503.Y676   1999
616.89'00835—dc21   99-40027
                                                            CIP

British Library Cataloguing in Publication Data

A catalogue record for this book is available from the British Library

ISBN 0 471 97678 4

Typeset in 10/12pt Palatino by Dorwyn Ltd, Rowlands Castle, Hants.
Printed and bound in Great Britain by Bookcraft, Bath, Somerset.
This book is printed on acid-free paper responsibly manufactured from sustainable
forestry, in which at least two trees are planted for each one used for paper production.

CONTENTS

ABOUT THE AUTHORS

Peter Aggleton is Professor in Education, and Director of the Thomas Coram Research Unit at the Institute of Education, University of London. He has worked internationally in the field of health promotion for over twenty years and has a particular interest in young people's mental health. He is the editor of the journal *Culture, Health and Sexuality* and has written and edited over twenty books.

Sue Bailey is a Consultant Child and Adolescent Forensic Psychiatrist at Salford and Maudsley NHS Trust, and Senior Research Fellow at the University of Manchester. She is Chair of the Resource Network for Adolescents and Secretary of the European Association of Child and Adolescent Forensic Psychiatrists and Psychologists. She has research interests in the field of adolescent offenders, early onset psychosis, personality development in adolescents, children's rights, and issues of consent to treatment. She has recently set up training programmes to work with young offenders in Eastern Europe.

Jenny Corbett is Senior Lecturer in Special and Inclusive Education at the Institute of Education, University of London. She has worked in mainstream and special schools as well as in further and higher education. Her publications include (with Len Barton) *A Struggle for Choice: Students with Special Needs in Transition to Adulthood* (Routledge, 1992), *Bad-Mouthing: The Language of Special Needs* (Falmer, 1996) and *Special Educational Needs in the Twentieth Century: A Cultural Analysis* (Cassell, 1998).

John B. Davies is Director of the Centre for Applied Social Psychology (CASP) at the University of Strathclyde, Glasgow. He has worked extensively in the area of addiction and the problems of substance use/ misuse for over twenty-five years, carrying out work for the Scottish Office, the Home Office, the Scottish Prison Service, the Drugs Prevention Initiative and a number of health trusts. His publications include *The Myth of Addiction* (Harwood Academic Press, 1992, 2nd edition, 1997) and *Drugspeak: The Analysis of Drug Discourse* (Harwood Academic Press, 1997). He is co-editor of the international journal, *Addiction Research*, and a founder member of the Addictions Forum.

Jane Hurry is a lecturer in research methods at the Institute of Education, University of London. One thread of her work is concerned with mental health and adolescence. She has published widely in the area of adult depression and more recently has been involved in research into adolescent drug use and adolescent deliberate self-harm. In all of this work she has had a particular focus on service responses, both medical and educational, to mental health problems.

Andreas Karwautz is a psychiatrist and psychotherapist at the University Clinic of Neuropsychiatry of Childhood and Adolescence in Vienna, Austria. He is currently in receipt of a research fellowship awarded by the FWF (Austrian Science Foundation) for work on environmental and genetic risk for anorexia nervosa, and is working at the Eating Disorders Unit at the Institute of Psychiatry, London, UK.

Michael Kerfoot is Professor in Child and Adolescent Policy and Research, and co-director of the Mental Health Social Work Research Unit in the School of Psychiatry and Behavioural Sciences at the University of Manchester. He has conducted research into adolescent suicidal behaviour for over twenty years and has published and lectured widely both nationally and internationally. He is the author (with Alan Butler) of *Problems of Childhood and Adolescence* (Macmillan, 1988). During a secondment to the NHS Health Advisory Service he was co-author of *Suicide Prevention: The Challenge Confronted* (HMSO, 1994), *Together We Stand: The Commissioning, Role and Management of Child and Adolescent Mental Health Services* (HMSO, 1995), and *Voices in Partnership: Involving Users and Carers in Commissioning and Delivering Mental Health Services* (HMSO, 1997). He has twice been a visiting research associate at the Los Angeles Suicide Prevention Centre and is currently a visiting professor in the School of Social Work, Kiev Mohyla University, Ukraine.

Juliet Koprowska is a lecturer in social work in the Department of Social Policy and Social Work at the University of York. Her main areas of interest are mental health across the life cycle, and interviewing and communications skills in the caring profession. Her publications include (with T. Fisher) 'The teaching and learning of interview skills: developing reflective practice' in *Learning for Competence York Conference* (CCETSW, 1997), and (with C.-A. Hooper and U. McCluskey) 'Groups for women survivors of childhood sexual abuse: the implications of attachment theory' in the *Journal of Social Work Practice* (1997).

Davina Lilley is a group analytic psychotherapist and currently Director of the charity Just Ask Counselling and Advisory Service in central London. The charity provides long-term free psychodynamic counselling to young people who are homeless, unemployed or low waged. Throughout her career she has experience of training and supervising trainees and continues to practise as a clinician. Publications include *Let's Keep Madness in its Right Place* (ESCARTA, 1986). With Sally Baldwin, she has co-edited *A Transitional Space in Action* (1996), *Working with*

Diversity (1998) and *A Space to Think* (1998). She is currently examining how psychoanalytic theory can be applied to organisational structures and strategies.

Christine Oliver is a research officer at the Thomas Coram Research Unit at the Institute of Education, University of London. She has worked on a number of research topics which relate directly to questions of sexuality and discrimination. Her publications include *Charter for Lesbian Equality* (GLC, 1986), *Violence Against Gay Men* (Lewisham Safer Cities, 1994), and (with Peter Aggleton and Kim Rivers) *Young People, Sex, Sexuality and Relationships* (Health Education Authority, 1998).

John Pearce is Professor of Child and Adolescent Psychiatry and Head of Developmental Psychiatry at Nottingham University. Previously, he was a consultant child and adolescent psychiatrist at Guy's Hospital in London. He has worked clinically with young people and their families for more than twenty-five years and has a special interest in the development of emotional disorders. His MPhil thesis on the recognition of childhood depression was completed in 1974 at a time when there was doubt about whether or not children could become depressed. Subsequent work has confirmed the reality of depressive disorders in young people. He has written a number of books for parents and the general public concerning mental health problems in young people.

Martin Plant has been Director of the Alcohol and Health Research Centre in Edinburgh (formerly the Alcohol Research Group) since 1988. He is a sociologist engaged in research into alcohol, drugs, and a variety of health and social issues. He has also conducted studies of ethnicity, risk taking, HIV/AIDS, sexual behaviour, prostitution and violence directed against gay, lesbian, bisexual and transsexual people. He has worked as a technical adviser to the World Health Organisation and was recently a member of the Department of Health's Expert Committee on Cannabis. His books include: *Drugtakers in an English Town* (Tavistock, 1975), *Drinking Careers* (Tavistock, 1979), *Drugs in Perspective* (Tavistock, 1986) and *Risk Takers* (Tavistock/Routledge, 1992).

Mike Stein is Professor of Social Work and co-director of the Social Work Research and Development Unit in the Department of Social Policy and Social Work at the University of York. For the last twenty years, he has been researching the problems faced by young people leaving care and, more recently, street children and young people who go missing from care. His publications include (with Kate Carey) *Leaving Care* (Barnardos, 1990), *Leaving Care and the 1989 Children Act* (First Key, 1991), (with Nina Biehal, Jasmine Clayden and Jim Wade) *Prepared for Living* (National Children's Bureau, 1992), (with Nina Biehal, Jasmine Clayden and Jim Wade) *Moving On, Young People and Leaving Care Schemes* (HMSO, 1995), (with Jim Wade, Nina Biehal and Jasmine Clayden) *Going Missing: Young People Absent from Care* (Wiley, 1998), and *Leaving Care: Reflections and Challenges* (Blackwell, 1999).

David A. Thompson is a senior lecturer in education and Director of the Educational Psychology Programme in the Department of Educational Studies at the University of Sheffield. He has been involved in research on bullying and anti-bullying strategies in schools since 1987, particularly in the area of whole school policies to combat bullying. His publications include (Ed. with Peter Smith) *Practical Approaches to Bullying* (David Fulton, 1991), (with Sonia Sharp) *Improving Schools— Establishing and Integrating Whole School Behaviour Policies* (David Fulton, 1994) and (Ed. with Geoff Lindsay) *Values into Practice in Special Education* (David Fulton, 1997).

Janet Treasure is a psychiatrist at the Bethlem and Maudsley Hospital and works in the Eating Disorders Unit at the Institute of Psychiatry in London. The unit is active in research and development in all aspects of eating disorders. She is also vice-chair of a European project examining the effectiveness of treatment of eating disorders in over twenty countries. She has edited a number of texts on eating disorders including (with K. Hoek, and M. Katzman) *Neurobiology in the Treatment of Eating Disorders* (Wiley, 1997) and (with G. Szmukler and C. Dare) *Handbook of Eating Disorders* (Wiley, 1995). She has authored two self help books one (with U. Schmidt) on bulimia nervosa, *Getting Better Bite by Bite* (Psychology Press, 1993), and one for parents and teachers as well as sufferers themselves on anorexia nervosa, *Anorexia Nervosa. A Survival Guide for Families, Friends and Sufferers* (Psychology Press, 1997).

Ian Warwick is Associate Director of the Health and Education Research Unit and a research officer in the Thomas Coram Research Unit at the Institute of Education, University of London. He teaches social research methods to the MA in Health Education and Health Promotion at the Institute of Education, University of London. He has worked on a range of research projects concerned with young people and health promotion—most especially in the fields of sexuality and HIV and AIDS. Recent publications include: *Health Promotion with Young People. An Introductory Guide to Evaluation* (Health Education Authority, 1998) and *Playing It Safe. Responses of Secondary School Teachers to Lesbian, Gay and Bisexual Pupils, Bullying, HIV and AIDS Education and Section 28* (Terrence Higgins Trust, 1998).

Chapter 1

Introduction

Jane Hurry, Peter Aggleton and Ian Warwick

Adults with responsibility for young people may jokingly remark that
'mental health' between the ages of 10 and 20 is a rare phenomenon. The
popular depiction of Kevin, a greasy-haired, chaotic and unreasonable
teenager, in the British comedy series 'Harry Enfield and friends' (1997–
98) captures the essence of this cultural joke. However, behind the light-
hearted stereotype lies a complex web of issues. Stanley Hall (1904),
Anna Freud (1966) and Blos (1962) are among many to have characterised the period from about 12 to 20 years of age as adolescence, a
highly charged and tumultuous stage of development. For these theorists, puberty, the upsurge of hormones and the bodily changes that
occur at this time are the catalysts for emotional upheaval. It has
similarly been argued by some sociologists and social psychologists,
though from a different perspective, that adolescence is a period marked
by stress and conflict in the family (Davis, 1940; Rice, 1975; Clausen,
1986; Simmons and Blyth, 1987). They have emphasised the rapidly
changing social roles that confront young people and their families during adolescence: defining educational competence in high stakes examinations, developing intimate relationships outside the family, going to
work, and moving towards attaining financial and physical
independence.

However, much research in the last two decades has challenged this
view (e.g. Conger, 1981; Dusek and Flaherty, 1981; Holmbeck and Hill
1988; Brooks-Gunn, 1989; Hauser and Bowlds, 1990; Buchanan *et al.*,
1992; Offer and Schonert-Reichl, 1992). In particular, Offer and his colleagues, in a study of 6000 adolescents in ten countries (Japan, Israel,
Hungary, West Germany, Italy, Australia, Turkey, Bangladesh, Taiwan
and the USA), report that the majority of teenagers (approximately 80%)

Young People and Mental Health. Edited by P. Aggleton, J. Hurry and I. Warwick.
© 2000 John Wiley & Sons Ltd.

do not experience turmoil or psychological disturbance, but are able to cope well during this period (Offer and Boxer, 1991).

There are also those that caution against adopting a conception of adolescence at all, without a critical understanding of the degree to which it is a social and cultural construction. From this perspective it is argued that the notion of adolescence is a fairly recent one in the West (Hall and Jefferson, 1976). Prior to the twentieth century, children moved fairly rapidly into an adult lifestyle, taking on adult roles of wage earning in their early to mid teens or even earlier in some cases (Ariès, 1962). In many less wealthy countries it is still commonplace for children and teenagers to be responsible for child rearing, wage earning or being part of the community survival effort once they leave infancy behind.

Nonetheless, the mental health of young people described in the following chapters is situated within a contemporary, Western context. Twentieth century young people enjoy a relatively long transitional period between the dependency of childhood and the relative independence of adult life. During this time they must gradually but radically alter their lifestyles to become relatively independent of their families, physically, emotionally and financially. In this process they are seen by their community to emerge as formed personalities. The moratorium of childhood, where anything might be possible, where problems and weaknesses might merely be 'a phase', is left behind. The individual is revealed and the chrysalis becomes a butterfly. Here, too, we are dealing to some extent with social perceptions. Much of what we will become can be predicted from childhood, as discussed in the chapters concerning emotional disorders, eating disorders, serious antisocial behaviour and learning difficulties. It would be mistaken to assume that young people make their journey of transition alone. Those who live or work with them are intimately involved. For example, while there is a debate about the extent to which adolescence is a stressful time for young people, there seems to be less doubt about the stressful nature of the experience for parents (Montemayor, 1983; Small et al., 1983; Pasley and Gecas, 1984; Gecas and Seff, 1990). The majority of parents report that this is the most difficult stage of parenting, particularly due to issues around the loss of control and fears for safety as young people take increasing responsibility for their own lives (Pasley and Gecas, 1984). Perhaps as a result of this, research on marital satisfaction (Rollins and Feldman, 1970) and life satisfaction (Hoffman and Manis, 1978) finds that the parents of adolescents have the lowest levels of satisfaction.

It is tempting to conclude from this that the period of 'storm and stress' described by Hall (1904) is more a projection of adult fears than an accurate account of young people's experience. However, evidence presented in the following chapters does not support so radical an interpretation. While the majority of young people are mentally healthy, and while there is evidence that adolescent risk-taking behaviour is overly characterised as dangerous by adults (see Chapter 2), it is clear that as young people move into their teens the incidence of a range of mental health problems increases dramatically (see in particular Chapters 4, 5 and 7). Why this should be the case is, however, open to debate, as several of the authors represented here make clear. Individual, generational, cultural and societal factors all have a role to play in influencing the mental health of young people and the responses to which this gives rise.

THE NATURE OF MENTAL HEALTH ISSUES OR PROBLEMS

The book is divided into roughly two halves. The first half (Part I) examines different types of mental ill health including emotional disorders (Chapter 4), eating disorders (Chapter 5), serious antisocial behaviour (Chapter 6), suicide and deliberate self-harm (Chapter 7), drugs and alcohol use (Chapters 2 and 3). The second half (Parts II and III) looks at contexts of living which may be responsible for some of these problems—sexuality (Chapter 8), learning difficulties (Chapter 9), being looked after (Chapter 10), homelessness (Chapter 11), and bullying and harassment in and out of school (Chapter 12).

The types of mental health problems reviewed represent the traditional areas of concern for young people and they differ in some significant respects from similar reviews of childhood or adult mental health problems. As in this book, reviews of childhood problems are likely to include coverage of emotional disorders and antisocial behaviours or conduct disorders, but overall they tend to focus on behaviours which present management problems for *adult* carers, such as sleeping difficulties, temper tantrums, school refusal and bed wetting. Adult mental health tends to be more firmly sited within a medical and psychiatric framework where affective, obsessional and the major psychotic disorders are central, with antisocial behaviour, drug and alcohol abuse (rather than use), and personality disorders, taking a more peripheral position.

The focus for mental health in young people is influenced by the disorders that tend to rise or peak in frequency in the teenage years (Rutter and Smith, 1995). However, it is also consistent with the transitional nature of young people's experience, moving from a world that is defined for them by adults to their own definitions of themselves. Thus there is a greater emphasis on internally experienced problems than might be the case in a review of childhood problems, but the inclusion of drug and alcohol use (Chapters 2 and 3) reflects adult concerns about adolescent risk-taking as much as it does young people's problems.

The definition of what constitutes mental health problems in the young owes something to adult constructions of adolescence. For example, Davies in his chapter on drugs (Chapter 3) proposes that to a very real extent the 'drug problem' of young people is a socially constructed one. He argues that drug use in the young is showing signs of becoming statistically normal, and comments that in some research there is evidence that young substance users show better psychological adjustment than non-users. This is not to say that drug use presents no dangers but rather that the focus should be on the minimal yet real dangers rather than on adults' fears.

A recurrent theme in the book is the interlocking and complex nature of the mental health problems of young people, often going beyond what would sit comfortably in the domain of adult psychiatry to the murky area of problems with living or personality disorders. Lilley comments in her chapter on homelessness (Chapter 11) that health professionals find it hard to label the problems of the young within the standard diagnostic categories of DSM IV or ICD 10, falling back on terms such as 'personality disorder' out of desperation to try and give some meaning to the chaotic and complex picture often presented. Co-morbidity is discussed in the chapters on alcohol use (Chapter 2), emotional disorders (Chapter 4), eating disorders (Chapter 5), serious antisocial behaviour (Chapter 6) and suicide and deliberate self-harm (Chapter 7). As well as the expected associations between affective disorders and deliberate self-harm, there are frequently observed clusters between self-harm, bulimia, substance use and aggressive or antisocial behaviour, reminiscent of Jessor and Jessor's (1977) concept of 'problem behaviour' (see also Chapter 2).

Where in the adult context such 'problem behaviour' tends to be classified as 'bad', in the case of young people it is more likely to be seen as 'mad', as illness rather than deliberately antisocial action, deserving treatment rather than punishment. This again is consistent with the transitional nature of adolescence, where, like children, young people are not held entirely responsible for their own actions. Perhaps adult carers are reluctant to acknowledge that the socially unacceptable behaviour of young people may be a manifestation of their personality, something that has to be accepted and lived with. It may be preferable to see adolescent risk-taking behaviour, such as substance use and some aspects of sexual activity, as something that can be treated rather than as a dimension of young people's lives that is to some extent at least deliberately chosen. Also, as Corbett mentions (Chapter 9), the popularity of diagnoses such as attention deficit disorder without hyperactivity syndrome (ADDS) may be due to the opportunity they offer to present behaviour as a sickness rather than the fault of children or their parents.

The contexts of living associated with mental health problems in the young covered in the book include the important dimensions of the individual, the family, the peer group and the wider social and institutional setting. The chapter on sexuality and mental health promotion (Chapter 8) explores the psychological consequences of being part of a minority group subject to prejudice and discrimination. Bullying and harassment in and out of school (Chapter 12) similarly deals with the impact of being abused, in this case by peers. The chapters on homelessness (Chapter 11) and 'looked after' young people (Chapter 10) demonstrate the important role of the family in the mental health of young people, a theme which recurs throughout the book.

PREVALENCE AND INCIDENCE

It is clear that there is a dramatic increase in the prevalence of most of the mental health problems covered here as young people move into the teenage years. Alcohol (Chapter 2) and drug use (Chapter 3) emerge as fairly commonplace behaviours from 14 years of age onwards. The average time for the onset of anorexia nervosa is in the mid teens, and for bulimia in the late teens and the early adult years (Chapter 5). Suicide and deliberate self-harm are reportedly very rare before the age of 12 years and rise in frequency during the mid to late teens, suicide being the second most common cause of death for 15–24 year olds in the UK (Chapter 7). The reported prevalence of both anxiety and depression increases markedly during adolescence, the increase being particularly pronounced in girls (Chapter 4). Certain contextual factors associated with mental stress, such as sexuality and homelessness, also only emerge as young people reach the age of about 14 to 16 years.

Despite the contemporary tendency to reject the theories of turbulent adolescence, these prevalence rates suggest that there is something fairly significant happening in our internal worlds that roughly coincides with puberty. Explanations of what this might be vary. Pearce (Chapter 4) proposes that it is not until children reach the age of seven or eight that they have sufficient maturity and self-awareness to experience thoughts of hopelessness and worthlessness. Hawton (1986) offers a similar cognitive explanation for the relative rarity of suicidal behaviour in the under 12s, remarking that children may not develop a full awareness of the finality of death until around 12 years of age (Piaget, 1960; Koocher, 1974).

As already discussed, other theorists suggest that the hormonal changes associated with puberty are responsible for setting off a chain of events leading to rebellious and sometimes moody behaviour, while social psychological theory highlights the significance of the multiple role changes experienced by the young. However, whilst prevalence rates for a range of mental health problems show an increase from childhood, it is much less clear that they exceed those found in adult populations. This makes explanations that rely on pubertal or role changes associated with adolescence less persuasive. Developmental stage models such as those alluded to by Pearce, Hawton and the major child developmental theorists such as Piaget are more consistent with the evidence. The especially raised prevalence rates discussed in the chapters concerning contexts of living demonstrate that any explanation of mental health problems in the young which ignores social factors such as homelessness, being looked after or the experience of discrimination or bullying is likely to be limited.

There are, however, some issues surrounding the validity of the prevalence rates as measures of mental health problems. As mentioned above, the fact that young people are starting to take drugs and drink does not necessarily signify that they have a problem, though in some cases it does. Both Plant (Chapter 2) and Davies (Chapter 3) suggest that some of the hazards involved with substance use in the young are more akin to learning about a new experience than a manifestation of mental problems. An analogy could be drawn with road safety, where the peak age for accidents is around 11 and 12 years of age, when many children start to negotiate busy roads on their own for the first time. Of course road accidents are a problem that must be addressed, but in the case of road safety no-one has suggested preventing young people crossing roads. It is accepted that the transitional learning period must be successfully negotiated. As Davies points out, numerous studies have demonstrated the levels of drug and alcohol use in the young but there is very little data available on the levels of problem use or abuse or indeed what that might constitute. It seems likely that young people actually have lower overall rates of alcohol and drug abuse than adults.

The chapters by Pearce (Chapter 4) and Kerfoot (Chapter 7), dealing with emotional disorders and deliberate self-harm, discuss the problematic nature of prevalence rates of mental health problems. There is a notoriously wide range of definitions and diagnostic criteria for identifying the existence of affective disorders and many of the same difficulties surround the identification of suicidal thoughts, intentions and acts. In addition, as Kerfoot remarks, prevalence rates for deliberate self-harm are mainly derived from hospital presentations and it is known that there is a large hidden prevalence. Figures on the prevalence of eating disorders are subject to the same limitations. Finally, consistent with the theme of who perceives the problem, in the case of emotional disorders in young people and children, these are frequently assessed through an adult respondent, either parent or teacher. Puura and colleagues conclude from their recent review of the literature that parents are fairly insensitive to the inner experiences and emotions of their children, but more sensitive to external, challenging behaviour (Puura *et al.*, 1998). It is possible that variations in prevalence rates of these types of problem may in part be due to the respondent selected. Some of the low prevalence rates reported for childhood depression may be due to a failure on the part of parents or teachers to notice children's feelings of unhappiness.

RISK FACTORS, HEALTH PROTECTING BEHAVIOURS AND EFFECTIVE INTERVENTIONS

The factor of overwhelming importance in terms of both risk and protection is the quality of family support. There is tremendous individual variation in terms of young people's personalities, their genetic predispositions, their academic ability and their sexuality. All of these factors can place young people at risk or protect them from reacting negatively to social contexts. But families are cited in every chapter of this book as having an impact on young people's ability to cope with problems and are also identified as a major cause of mental health problems.

Families are frequently responsible for young people's referral to helping agencies, although the research of Brannen and Storey on young people's health practices shows that there is a gradual shift towards independence (Brannen and Storey, 1996). Arguably, young people are a relatively inaccessible group for effective health intervention because of this transitional status in their help-seeking behaviour. Perhaps for this reason, primary intervention in schools is a popular method of mental health promotion (see Chapters 2, 3, 5, 6, 7, 8, 12), despite the considerable problems associated with engaging teachers in health issues when their central concerns lie in academic areas. While there is relatively disappointing evidence concerning the effectiveness of school-based interventions in the long term, certain initiatives, for example in the area of bullying, have proved valuable.

Because of the central role of the family in the mental health of young people, interventions frequently involve the family. Kerfoot discusses in the context of deliberate self-harm how this influences the sort of therapy that might practically be offered. The families in question are frequently in crisis, and may find it difficult to sustain appointments over a protracted time period. For this reason, a brief and focused intervention has been developed for the families of young people who have harmed themselves. It is clear from the chapters on homelessness and looked after young people that where family relationships have broken down a sizeable minority of young people become psychological casualties. As a society we do not seem to be very successful in offering effective institutional support in the absence of the family. In response to this, some of the health initiatives described are aimed at producing good parents, or supporting parents rather than directly treating young people themselves.

CONCLUSION

Young people in our society occupy a special place, poised between childhood and adulthood. As we have discussed, this has a profound impact on many of the issues surrounding their mental health. What are considered problems in the young are caught between the dominant role of adults in defining childhood problems and the emerging assertion of the young to express their own concerns and experiences. The traces of childhood are also evident in a social will to free young people of blame for their actions. Rule-breaking behaviour can still be defined as illness and antisocial behaviour and chaotic lifestyle are accepted as mental health problems in the young where in adults they are more likely to be viewed as criminal or socially outcast. Ties with the family are still very much in evidence, both in terms of risk/protective factors and in terms of treatment.

There are dangers in the transitional nature of the adolescent's position. In particular, adults are beginning to hand over the responsibility of health care to the young people themselves. Yet young people are very inexperienced at seeking help for their own health problems, and in the socially taboo area of mental health it is likely that they will not seek the help that they need. Helping agencies are themselves very unclear about the position of the young. For example, if a young person aged between 16 and 18 years old presents at an Accident and Emergency clinic following an overdose, the hospital might classify him or her as either a child or an adult, depending on whether or not he or she is at school.

In some ways exploring the mental health issues of young people is like an anthropological investigation, stepping from the adult to the youth culture. The world of youth mental health care is largely defined by adults, but the voices of young people must still guide us.

REFERENCES

Ariès, P. (1962) *Centuries of Childhood*. Harmondsworth: Penguin Books.

Blos, P. (1962) *On Adolescence: A Psychoanalytic Interpretation*. New York: Free Press of Glencoe.

Brannen, J., Dodd, K., Oakley, A. and Storey, P. (1994) *Young People, Health and Family Life*. Open University Press: Birmingham.

Brannen, J. and Storey, P. (1996) *Child Health in Social Context*. London: Health Education Authority.

Brooks-Gunn, J. (1989) Pubertal processes and the early adolescent transition. In W. Damon (Ed.) *Child Development Today and Tomorrow*. San Francisco: Jossey-Bass.

Buchanan, C.M., Eccles, J.S. and Becker, J.B. (1992) Are adolescents the victims of raging hormones: evidence for activational effects of hormones on moods and behaviour at adolescence. *Psychological Bulletin*, 111, 62–107.

Clausen, J.A. (1986) *The Life Course: A Sociological Perspective*. Englewood Cliffs, NJ: Prentice-Hall.

Conger, J.J. (1981) Freedom and commitment: families, youth and social change. *American Psychologist*, 36, 1475–1484.

Davis, K. (1940) The sociology of parent–youth conflict. *American Sociological Review*, 5, 523–535.

Dusek, J.B. and Flaherty, J.F. (1981) The development of the self-concept during the adolescent years. *Monograph of the Society for Research in Child Development*, 46, 1–67.

Freud, A. (1966) *The Ego and the Mechanisms of Defence* (Rev. edn). New York: International Universities Press.

Gecas, V. and Seff, M. (1990) Families and adolescents: a review of the 1980s. *Journal of Marriage and the Family*, 52, 941–958.

Hall, G.S. (1904) *Adolescence: Its psychology and its relation to physiology, anthropology, sociology, sex, crime, religion, and education*. New York: D. Appleton.

Hall, S. and Jefferson, T. (Eds) (1976) *Resistance through Rituals*. London: Hutchinson.

Hauser, S.T. and Bowlds, M.K. (1990) Stress, coping and adaptation. In S.S. Feldman and G.R. Elliott (Eds) *At the Threshold: the developing adolescent*. Cambridge, MA: Harvard University Press.

Hawton, K. (1986) *Suicide and Attempted Suicide Among Children and Adolescents*. Newbury Park, CA: Sage.

Hoffman, L.W. and Manis, J.B. (1978) Influences of children on marital interaction and parental satisfaction and dissatisfaction. In R.M. Lerner and G.B. Spaner (Eds) *Child Influences on Marital and Family Interaction: A life-span perspective*. New York: Academic Press.

Holmbeck, G.N. and Hill, J.P. (1988) Storm and stress beliefs about adolescence: prevalence, self-reported antecedents, and effects of an undergraduate course. *Journal of Youth and Adolescence*, 17, 285–306.

Jessor, R. and Jessor, S.L. (1977) *Problem Behavior and Psychosocial Development: A Longitudinal Study of Youth*, San Diego, CA: Academic Press.

Koocher, P.G. (1974) Talking with children about death. *American Journal of Orthopsychiatry*, 44, 404–411.

Montemayor, R. (1983) Parents and adolescents in conflict: all families some of the time and some families all of the time. *Journal of Early Adolescence*, 3, 83–103.

Offer, D. and Boxer, A.M. (1991) Normal adolescent development: empirical research findings. In M. Lewis (Ed.) *Child and Adolescent Psychiatry: a comprehensive textbook*. Baltimore: Williams & Wilkins.

Offer, D. and Schonert-Reichl, K.A. (1992) Debunking the myths of adolescence: findings from recent research. *Journal of the American Academy of Child and Adolescent Psychiatry*, 31, 1003–1014.

Pasley, K. and Gecas, V. (1984) Stresses and satisfaction of the parental role. *Personnel and Guidance Journal*, 2, 400–404.

Piaget, J. (1960) *The Child's Concept of the World*. Patterson, NJ: Littlefield Adams.

Puura, K., Almqvist, F., Tamminen, T., Piha, J., Kumpulainen, K., Rasanen, E., Moilanen, I. and Koivisto, A-M. (1998) Children with symptoms of depression—what do the adults see? *Journal of Child Psychiatry*, 39(4), 577–585.

Rice, F.P. (1975) *The Adolescent: Development, Relationships, and Culture*. Boston: Allyn and Bacon.

Rollins, B.C. and Feldman, H. (1970) Marital satisfaction over the family life cycle. *Journal of Marriage and the Family*, 32, 20–28.

Rutter, M. and Smith, D.J. (Eds) (1995) *Psychological Disorders in Young People. Time Trends and their Causes*. Chichester: Academia Europaea by John Wiley.

Simmons, R.G. and Blyth, D.A. (1987) *Moving into Adolescence: the impact of pubertal change and school context*. Hawthorne, NY: Aldine.

Small, S.A, Cornelius, S. and Eastman, G. (1983) Parenting adolescent children: a period of adult storm and stress? Paper presented at the annual meeting of the American Psychological Association, Anahiem, CA.

Part I

SPECIFIC MENTAL HEALTH PROBLEMS

Chapter 2

Young People and Alcohol Use

Martin Plant

Alcohol has been called, with good reason, 'our favourite drug' (Royal College of Psychiatrists, 1986). Beverage alcohol is legal and widely consumed in most countries. Moreover, alcohol consumption has been a feature of human society for at least seven thousand years (McGovern *et al.*, 1996). Throughout recorded human history there has been concern about aspects of alcohol consumption whenever and wherever this has been widespread. Most people drink in moderation on most occasions, but some do not. Heavy and inappropriate drinking is associated with a toll of adverse consequences. The latter include alcohol dependence ('alcoholism'), accidents, injuries, illnesses, premature mortality, public disorder, crime and a host of social, familial and workplace difficulties. During recent decades, concern has periodically focused on the consumption of alcohol by children, adolescents, teenagers or others variously described as 'young people'. This concern has been fuelled by the belief that at least some young people drink in ways that either are a nuisance or cause harm to the drinker or to other people. Moreover, it has often also been assumed that the 'young' are especially vulnerable to the effects of alcohol due to their inexperience and immaturity. These concerns are part of a much broader interest in 'young people' as being distinctive in terms of their culture, lifestyles and health-related behaviours. Other areas of allied interest include tobacco smoking, illicit drug use and sexual behaviour (Plant and Plant, 1992).

This chapter sets out to examine evidence about the drinking habits and patterns of 'alcohol-related problems' amongst young people. In addition, consideration is given to evidence on the impact of past

Young People and Mental Health. Edited by P. Aggleton, J. Hurry and I. Warwick.

attempts to prevent heavy and harmful drinking or to respond to such drinking when it occurs. Finally, some priorities for future intervention and research are identified. For the purposes of this chapter 'young people' are defined as being below the age of 21. Even so, studies vary greatly in relation to the age of their subjects. Accordingly, the age groups cited in the following review also vary.

ALCOHOL CONSUMPTION BY YOUNG PEOPLE

Alcohol consumption in the UK is not high by international standards. In fact, UK consumption is similar to that in countries such as the Netherlands, the USA and Canada. Consumption levels are much higher in some Mediterranean countries and in Eastern Europe. During recent years UK levels of alcohol consumption have been relatively stable, while those in some Eastern European countries have been rising (Brewers and Licensed Retailers, 1999; Plant, 1997). Surveys of the drinking habits of British youth do not have a long history, however, even though many have been carried out in recent years. Davies and Stacey (1972) carried out a classic and influential study of Scottish teenagers. This indicated that drinking was widely viewed as a symbol of maturity and sociability. A parallel study by Jahoda and Cramond (1972) revealed that even children in the 5–10 age range often had very clear and often quite negative, concepts of alcohol and its consumption by adults. Since these pioneering studies, research into various aspects of youthful drinking has proliferated. Some of this is reviewed in this section. The section which follows, on alcohol-related problems amongst young people, deals with evidence of adverse consequences associated with alcohol consumption by young people.

The 1970s work on children and alcohol by Jahoda and Cramond has been replicated by Fossey (1994). The latter, using a series of game-like activities with children in Birmingham and Edinburgh, reached remarkably similar conclusions to the earlier investigators. In particular, Fossey noted that young children were often able to distinguish bottles of alcoholic and non-alcoholic drinks, and often disapproved of drinking, especially that by women. In contrast to the negative way in which children of primary school age view drinking, it is clear that adolescents and teenagers generally have a quite different perspective. Many studies have indicated that at, or after, adolescence, substantial proportions of people begin to drink with increasing regularity. Most British adolescents aged 11 and above have at least tasted drinks containing beverage alcohol (Plant and Plant, 1992; Goddard 1997a, 1997b). A national survey of UK teenagers aged 15–16 showed that 94% of both girls and boys had consumed alcohol. The highest proportions of abstainers (15%) were amongst young women in Northern Ireland (Miller and Plant, 1996).

The consumption of alcohol is not universal in all parts of the UK. Loretto (1994), for example, found that relatively high proportions of teenagers in Northern Ireland were non-drinkers. A survey of teenagers in the Western Isles of Scotland (ranging from Barra to Lewis) also found that a considerable proportion, 19%, had reportedly never consumed an alcoholic drink (Anderson and Plant, 1996; Anderson *et al.*, 1998). Western Isles teenagers were also remarkably likely to report that if they did drink, they did so heavily. Nearly 40% of males and a third of females indicated having consumed at least 11 units on their last drinking occasion.

A number of studies have lent support to the conclusion that drinking is commonplace amongst adolescents and that the proportions who do drink increase steadily throughout the teenage years (Plant *et al.*, 1985; May, 1992; Goddard, 1997a, 1997b). Given the evidence cited above, this is clearly an oversimplification.

The Trend Is Up

The studies cited above suggest the view that alcohol consumption amongst British teenagers is a normative but not universal behaviour. Goddard (1996, 1997a, 1997b) has compared the results of surveys carried out in 1990, 1992, 1994 and 1996. These showed that amongst 11–15 year olds in England, the mean alcohol consumption of those who reported having drunk in the previous week had risen markedly. This is shown in Table 2.1.

As this table indicates, consumption had risen amongst both girls and boys. The proportions of either gender who were drinking at least once per week also rose between 1990 and 1994. Amongst girls this proportion rose from 10 to 14%, while the corresponding increase amongst boys was from 15 to 19%. Moreover, Goddard also reported that the proportion of boys who usually did not drink alcoholic beverages rose slightly, from 40 to 42% over this period. In contrast, the proportion of girls who usually did not drink fell from 45% to 43%. This is consistent with evidence that alcohol consumption amongst adult women has converged slightly with that of men (Plant, 1997).

Comparable information for Scottish teenagers is shown in Table 2.2. As this indicates, alcohol consumption had also increased over the period 1990–1996. Moreover, mean consumption levels amongst

Table 2.1 Mean alcohol consumption of those aged 11–15 who had drunk in the last seven days (England) (1990–1996)

Alcohol consumption (units)	1990	1992	1994	1996
Girls	4.8	4.7	5.4	7.0
Boys	6.0	7.0	7.4	9.7
Total	5.4	6.0	6.4	8.4

Sources: Goddard (1996: 13; 1997a: 15).

Scottish teenagers were somewhat higher than those of English teenagers. This conclusion is consistent with that of other national survey findings (Plant *et al.*, 1990; Plant and Foster, 1991; Miller and Plant, 1996).

In 1996, Goddard found that 18% of girls and 21% of boys in England aged 11–15 years reported drinking about once a week (Goddard, 1997a). The corresponding proportions amongst their Scottish counterparts aged 12–15 years were 21% and 24% respectively (Goddard, 1997b).

It is apparent that an individual's drinking habits often change at different stages of the life course. Some young people do drink heavily and in a potentially risky way. Some suffer adverse consequences because of this. Nevertheless for many, probably most, such individuals, this is simply a step along a trajectory or 'drinking career'. A common pattern is for relatively heavy alcohol consumption amongst young, single people, to be followed by much lighter consumption later in life, especially following marriage or the assumption of other responsibilities. It is not the case, for example, that teenagers who drink heavily will inevitably remain heavy drinkers or move on to develop chronic drinking problems (Plant *et al.*, 1985; Fillmore, 1988). In spite of this, young people, especially older teenagers and those in their twenties, are at high risk of involvement in periodic heavy drinking and the unwelcome effects that may ensue from this.

Table 2.2　Mean alcohol consumption of those aged 12–15 who had drunk in the last seven days (Scotland) (1990–1996)

Alcohol consumption (units)	1990	1992	1994	1996
Girls	6.0	6.9	6.9	10.0
Boys	10.3	9.1	10.6	11.9
Total	8.4	8.2	8.7	11.1

Sources: Goddard (1997b: 15).

Alcopops

In mid-1995 a new range of drinks were introduced to the UK. These have become colloquially known as 'alcopops' and have triggered a considerable amount of mass media debate, outrage and controversy. These drinks have fruit flavours and are being marketed in bright packaging which some believe has been designed to have particular appeal for young people. They have been marketed under such names as *Hoopers Hooch, Two Dogs, Purple Passion* and *Love Byte* (McKibben, 1996). Public indignation about the introduction of alcopops, growing into what certainly has been at least partly a 'moral panic', has been inflamed by the assumptions that children have been deliberately enticed into early alcohol consumption. This is also assumed to have raised youthful alcohol consumption levels.

At the time of writing, there appears to be little evidence of the extent to which alcopops may have influenced young people's drinking habits. Some initial evidence suggests that these are now popular drinks amongst teenagers and that levels of awareness concerning such new drinks is high. Even so, alcopops, which are quite expensive, are not particularly associated with either heavy drinking or intoxication (Crawford and Allsop, 1996; Raw and McNeill, 1996; Forsyth, 1997). Available evidence suggest that teenagers who are heavier drinkers have a preference for drinks such as vodka and cider (Forsyth, 1997). Goddard (1997a, 1997b) found that alcopops accounted for 17% of the total alcohol consumed by English teenagers in 1996. Beer, lager and cider accounted for 57%. In Scotland, alcopops accounted for 18% of teenage consumption, compared with 23% for spirits and 36% for beer, lager and cider. She concluded that:

> 'The survey therefore provides some support for the suggestion that those who drink alcopops may do so because the taste of alcohol is masked by the addition of fruit or cola, but little for the contention that were it not for the availability of alcopops, many children would not be drinking at all.' (Goddard, 1997b: 11)

Alcopops have been widely criticised because they may blur the boundaries between traditional alcoholic beverages and those that do not contain alcohol. This symbolism may be important. Even so, evidence does not support the view that the marketing of this range of drinks has led more young people to imbibe alcoholic beverages (Plant and Plant, 1997a). It should be noted that media concern has at other times focused on young people's consumption of specific types of drink. Examples include lager, cider and the imbibing, especially in the West of Scotland, of Buckfast tonic wine. At the time of writing it appears that alcopop sales in the UK are falling. If this trend continues, it will be a repetition of the short-lived appeal of alcopops in Australia (T. Stockwell, 1997, personal communication).

ALCOHOL-RELATED PROBLEMS AMONGST YOUNG PEOPLE

As already emphasised, heavy and inappropriate drinking are associated with a range of adverse consequences. This section considers these under the sub-headings of social, health and legal consequences.

Social Consequences

Most of the adverse effects associated with drinking amongst young people are 'acute', due to intoxication or heavy drinking. Youthful heavy drinking is associated with a variety of adverse consequences, mainly of a non-serious nature. An example of this is provided by a survey of UK 15 and 16 year-old school students in 1995 (Miller and Plant, 1996). A substantial majority, 78.5% of girls and 77.3% of boys, reported having at some time been intoxicated. Within the UK, levels of intoxication were lowest amongst girls in Northern Ireland (62.1%). In addition, approximately a quarter of those of either sex reported having been drunk 10 times or more in the past year. This study also offers details of the extent of a range of problems which young people attributed to their own drinking. These are shown in Table 2.3.

As indicated by this table, a substantial proportion of the young people surveyed reported having experienced some problems due to their own drinking. Gender differences, though evident in relation to 'delinquency' or antisocial behaviour (males having higher levels), were generally small in relation to individual, relationship and sexual problems or experiences.

A large-scale international study compared teenage drinking in the UK and in 22 other European countries (Hibell *et al.*, 1997). This study showed that from 1 to 6% of teenagers aged 15–16 reported that they expected to experience negative consequences from their drinking. The highest levels were noted in Croatia and Ireland (6%). When asked about their *actual* experience of alcohol-related problems—individual, sexual, relationship or 'delinquency'—the highest rate was reported by UK respondents. This study showed that British teenagers were more

Table 2.3 Experience of problems attributed to alcohol consumption (percentages)

Type of problem	Boys	Girls
(a) Individual		
Reduced school or work performance	10.1	11.2
Damage to objects or clothing	33.1	32.8
Loss of money or valuables	23.0	25.4
Accident or injury	17.1	16.2
(b) Relationship		
Quarrel or argument	35.5	43.1
Problems in relationship with friends	18.2	23.3
Problems in relationship with parents	17.7	22.0
Problem in relationship with teachers	3.9	3.2
(c) Sexual experiences		
Engaged in unwanted sex	15.5	18.9
Engaged in unprotected sex	13.4	13.4
(d) Delinquency		
Scuffle or fight	28.2	16.3
Victimised by robbery or theft	4.7	1.4
Driving motorcycle/car under influence of alcohol	7.6	1.9
Trouble with police	21.2	12.2

Source: P. Miller (1997), personal communication.

likely than those in most of the other countries studied to report experience of intoxication. Moreover, intoxication appeared to be most commonplace in northern Europe. Only Danish teenagers were more likely than those in the UK to report having consumed alcohol. Only Denmark and Finland reported levels of teenage drunkenness approaching those of their UK counterparts.

Another recent survey, cited earlier, examined teenagers in the Western Isles of Scotland. This showed, as have other studies, that a variety of adverse consequences are acknowledged by teenagers who drink. Such consequences are also more likely to be reported by older teenagers than by younger ones. For example, 25% of 13 year olds in this study reported having at some time been sick due to drinking, while 42% of 15 year olds gave such a response. Other consequences attributed to drinking included trouble with parents and having fights and arguments (Anderson *et al.*, 1995; Anderson and Plant, 1996).

Health Consequences

Most of the ill effects attributable to youthful heavy drinking are due to acute intoxication rather than to chronic heavy drinking (Plant and Plant, 1992). Accordingly, only very small numbers of people below the age of 21 are recorded as being admitted to UK hospitals for diagnoses such as 'alcohol dependence'. In addition, very few young people develop alcohol-related conditions such as liver cirrhosis. Surveys indicate that a substantial minority of teenagers and younger drinkers sometimes experience 'low level' discomfort resulting from heavy sessional intake. Such effects include feeling dizzy, being too ill to attend school or work, falling over, temporary memory loss, hangovers, nausea and headaches (Plant and Plant, 1992; Anderson and Plant, 1996). Many young people sometimes drink to intoxication. For most, this is really part of learning to drink and about the potential effects of alcohol. The majority, fortunately, do not develop serious or long-term problems and regulate their consumption so that they mainly drink in moderation. During recent years, a number of media reports have noted that some UK hospitals are admitting more young people for severe intoxication. These reports are consistent with survey evidence suggesting that youthful heavy drinking has been increasing (Goddard, 1997a, 1997b).

Legal Consequences

It is legal for people in the UK to consume alcohol once they are aged five or older. Even so, it is not generally legal for those below the age of 18 to purchase alcohol or to consume it in licensed premises. The legal situation has been succinctly summarised by Lister Sharp (1994):

'Young people are allowed into bars, at the licensee's discretion, from the age of 14 in England, Wales or Scotland, but 18 in Northern Ireland. Children, including those below the age of 14, may also be allowed into parts of licensed premises where there is sale only or consumption only, but not both.

Throughout the United Kingdom people may both purchase and consume alcohol in bars from the age of 18. In addition, 16–18 year-olds may purchase beer, cider and perry (and wine in Scotland) to drink with a meal in a dining room or separate eating area. Children from the age of 5 are entitled to drink alcohol in places other than bars.' (Lister Sharp, 1994: 558)

It is surprising, in view of the concern often expressed about the 'problem of underage drinking', how little the law in relation to this phenomenon has been enforced. Lister Sharp concluded that, over the period from 1970 to 1990, there was little attempt either to prosecute people for selling alcohol to those under 18 or to prosecute those below this age who had tried to purchase it. She concluded that prosecution statistics gave little clue to the extent to which the laws related to under-age drinking were breached. She did, however, also conclude that there was no evidence to suggest that underage drinking had increased in the UK over the period 1970–1990. In fact, there has been a remarkable decline in the numbers of cautions or convictions related to underage drinking between 1985 and 1995 (Table 2.4).

As Table 2.4 indicates, the total number of cautions and convictions in England and Wales of people below the age of 18 buying liquor fell from 1925 in 1985 to only 351 in 1995. The corresponding numbers for those cautioned or convicted of selling intoxicating liquor to people under 18 fell from 485 to only 269. During the same decade, the annual numbers of those under 21 who were cautioned or found guilty of offences of drunkenness in England and Wales also declined markedly, from 19 951

Table 2.4   Persons found guilty or cautioned for offences involving under age drinking under the Licensing Act 1964 (England and Wales)

Year	Persons under 18 buying liquor	Persons selling intoxicating liquor to persons under 18
1985	1925	485
1986	2324	411
1987	—	—
1988	—	—
1989	2314	1045
1990	1689	727
1991	880	400
1992	627	276
1993	376	235
1994	316	236
1995	351	269

Source: Home Office (1997).

to 9731 (Home Office, 1997). These trends run curiously counter to available evidence indicating that teenage drinking has been increasing.

Convictions for drinking and driving have also declined in recent years (Brewers and Licensed Retailers Association, 1995). The great majority of those who are cautioned or convicted of drunkenness offences are men. In 1995, the latter comprised 91.4% of such offenders in England and Wales. It is, however, notable that while women comprised only 8% of those under the age of 18 who were cautioned or convicted of drunkenness in England and Wales during 1985, they accounted for 11% of such offenders in 1995. Conversely, the proportion of offenders aged 18–21 who were female declined from 14 to 12% over the same period (Home Office, 1997). There is clearly a discrepancy between trends as measured by surveys of self-reported drinking habits and 'official' figures such as those related to recorded crimes. The latter may be strongly influenced by changing enforcement policies. In addition, information about female offenders may reflect gender differences in enforcement.

RISK FACTORS AND HEALTH PROTECTING BEHAVIOURS

Young people who drink heavily are also more likely to smoke tobacco, to use illicit drugs and to engage in other potentially risky behaviours. The latter may include, for example, high risk or unprotected sex and driving without seat belts. Some people appear to be more risk inclined than others (Plant and Plant, 1992; World Health Organization, 1994a). The theory that 'problem behaviours' in youth cluster together has been documented by the classic work of Jessor and Jessor (1977). There is also evidence that young people who have not been raised by two parents are more likely than those who have been, to drink heavily, to use tobacco and illicit drugs and to be aggressive or delinquent (Miller, 1997). This author has also concluded:

'Subjects who lived in families without both parents present were more likely to have psychological symptoms, to have lower levels of social support and, more importantly, to engage in fewer hobbies and constructive leisure time activities and to score more highly on the "sociable delinquent factor".' (Miller, 1997: 128)

It should be emphasised, however, that the existence of such connections does not prove the existence of any simple causal explanation. There may be many reasons why individuals raised in specific circumstances behave in particular ways. Even so, these findings serve to emphasise that social and behavioural problems do often cluster together. In recent years, considerable attention has been paid to whether or not drinking leads people to engage in risky behaviours and, in particular, whether it promotes high risk sex (World Health Organization, 1994a;

Stall and Leigh, 1994). This interest has been stimulated by the widely accepted belief that alcohol consumption may engender 'disinhibition' or the impairment of personal judgement and restraint (Room and Collins, 1983). The evidence that has emerged from enquiries in this field suggest that the alcohol–sex connection is far less clear cut than many commentators had previously supposed. Most studies have confirmed that young people who drink heavily are more likely than lighter drinkers to engage in unprotected sex and other behaviour such as illicit drug use. Even so, it has not been convincingly or repeatedly demonstrated that alcohol consumption on a particular occasion does, in fact, increase a person's chances of having unprotected sex. It should be stressed that alcohol consumption often occurs in situations and contexts also likely to facilitate sexual activity. For many young people, dating commonly involves 'going for a drink'. Many drinking locales, such as bars and clubs, may be sexual meeting places. Moreover, as Plant (1997) has stressed, there are important gender differences in the significance of alcohol consumption in relation to sex. Females are more likely than males to be wary of drinking if it places them at higher risk, or if they fear a loss of control.

The aetiologies of drinking and problem drinking are complex. Many factors may influence whether an individual drinks, and if so, when, what and how much. In many societies alcohol consumption is socially acceptable, popular and an integral part of leisure or conviviality. The extent to which drinking is normative varies considerably between societies and subgroups within society. A host of social and cultural influences relate to drinking customs or to the prevalence of abstaining, often for religious reasons. As noted above, the development of drinking habits is usually strongly influenced by early learning experiences and especially by the example set by parents or other important people in the child's life.

INTERVENTIONS FOR PRIMARY AND SECONDARY PREVENTION

Health promotion and health education are frequently, and very reasonably, viewed as being of great importance in efforts to combat or curb heavy or risky drinking and alcohol-related problems. Sadly, the track record of initiatives in this field in relation to preventing heavy or harmful drinking amongst youth has not been very good (Plant and Plant, 1997b; Plant, 1997). A number of past health promotion initiatives have assumed that the provision of factual information about alcohol will lead to behaviour change. Generally speaking, this does not appear to have worked. In addition, some major recent endeavours have been focused upon the assumption that youthful heavy drinking may reflect a lack of knowledge, social skills or self confidence. These assumptions are also flawed. Most young people drink because of important social and cultural factors, combined with the simple fact that they enjoy drinking.

Some authors have concluded that to reduce the level of alcohol-related problems, it is necessary to reduce national levels of *per capita* alcohol consumption (World Health Organization, 1994b). In fact, there is little sign in most countries of any real or tangible political commitment to such an approach. Alcohol control policies have to be both politically and publicly popular to have any chance of success. Some policies are not necessarily 'exportable' to other contexts. For example, the consumption of alcohol is proscribed for people below the age of 21 in the USA (Hingson *et al.*, 1997). In spite of evidence that this has reduced teenage alcohol consumption, there is little sign that other countries wish to emulate this policy.

The most promising practical approaches to the prevention of alcohol-related problems can be placed under the broad heading of 'harm minimisation'. The latter are designed, not to eliminate drinking *per se*, but to curb the harmful consequences sometimes associated with alcohol consumption. Harm minimisation approaches generally involve the enforcement of some form of controls on the drinking environment. Such strategies have been reviewed in detail elsewhere (Plant *et al.*, 1997). They include the rigorous enforcement of laws related to the sale and consumption of alcohol, and other laws related to public nuisance and alcohol-impaired driving. In addition, the training of bar staff and the use of local bylaws to adjust licensing hours have also produced promising results in some places.

Responses to alcohol problems may be implemented at either national or local level. In either case, alcohol as an issue needs to be raised so that it receives an appropriate degree of attention as a health and social policy issue. The seriousness of alcohol-related problems in many contexts should be acknowledged. Even so, it also needs to be stressed that most drinkers generally consume only moderate quantities of alcohol. Moreover, the young do not have the monopoly of alcohol-related problems. Indeed the overwhelming majority of those with chronic drinking problems or who are alcohol dependent are above the age of 25.

Alcohol control policies need to be shown to be effective to become sustainable. This requires both public and political support. Some policies may work in one context, but be inappropriate or unacceptable in another setting. Care is required to ensure that specific approaches are appropriate for local situations. It should be emphasised that young people's drinking is likely to be strongly influenced by that of their parents and the others with whom they interact. A recent study in the Western Isles of Scotland has shown that, while some parents are not particularly well informed about alcohol-related matters, most believed that parents should play a major role in the alcohol education of their school age children. Clearly, parents and other adults could be harnessed as an important resource for health promotion. They should certainly be included in any attempt at community education in relation to alcohol and other social and health issues (Plant *et al.*, 1998). Many areas of the UK are served by agencies providing help, counselling, treatment and support for people with alcohol-related problems. Even so, many of these agencies mainly deal with older clients. This could be a problem in some cases. It should therefore be a priority for such agencies to consider ways to make themselves available and attractive to younger people with alcohol-related problems.

PRIORITIES FOR INTERVENTION AND RESEARCH

It is surprising how few initiatives, including even major ventures, to prevent or respond to alcohol-related problems have been evaluated properly. Lack of funding is clearly a major limitation. Even so, it would be desirable if, whenever possible, activity could be influenced, if not wholly directed, by available evidence on what has been shown to be effective. There is considerable information to suggest that health promotion may heighten awareness and increase knowledge. Changing behaviours is harder to accomplish and sometimes, as noted above, this may involve negative results. In fact, it appears to be the case that so far no educational method has been identified to reduce youthful alcohol consumption.

As stressed in the preceding section, heavy and inappropriate or harmful drinking, though not uncommon amongst the young, is not only a youthful prerogative. Responses to alcohol problems should therefore not only be aimed at young people. The whole community should be involved in strategies to curb alcohol problems. A number of 'harm minimisation' policy options have recently been identified (Plant *et al.*, 1997). Recent evidence suggests that there is little difference in the effectiveness of some of the major therapeutic approaches for 'problem drinkers' (Project Match Research Group, 1997). A number of treatment options exist. As emphasised by Cameron (1995), these may have great value in assisting people to get through difficult times in their lives without necessarily ceasing to consume alcohol altogether (Peele and Brodsky, 1991).

There have been quite a large number of studies of youthful drinking habits conducted in the UK. Even so, few longitudinal studies have been carried out and there has been a remarkable dearth of properly designed international comparative surveys of youthful drinking and alcohol-related problems. One recent exception, it should be noted, has been provided by the 26-country study by Hibell *et al.* (1997). It would be very helpful if, in future, a higher priority could be given to the evaluation of policies designed to curb heavy and harmful drinking. In addition, both scientific knowledge and public policy would be greatly helped if 'sentinel' studies of youthful drinking and other potentially risky behaviours were carried out at regular intervals. The recent work of Goddard (1996, 1997a, 1997b) has been of great value in charting recent trends amongst British youth.

In conclusion, most young people drink, but mainly in moderation. Alcohol consumption and allied problems have been increasing amongst British youth. In spite of this, the public response to this situation will not be effective if it is based either upon moral panic or upon the misconception that only young people have problems with alcohol.

ACKNOWLEDGEMENTS

The Alcohol & Health Research Centre (A&HRC) is supported by the beverage alcohol industry, charities, research councils, health trusts and government departments. Particular thanks are due to Diageo plc, Allied Domecq plc, the PF Charitable Trust and the North British Distillery Company Ltd. The author is very grateful to Moira Plant and Patrick Miller of the A&HRC, to Eileen Goddard of the Office for National Statistics and to Bruce Ritson of the Alcohol Problems Clinic, Royal Edinburgh Hospital for information and advice.

REFERENCES

Anderson, K. and Plant, M.A. (1996) Abstaining and carousing: Substance use among adolescents in the Western Isles of Scotland. *Drug and Alcohol Dependence*, 41, 189–196.

Anderson, K., Plant, M.A., Baillie, R., Nevison, C., Plant, M. and Ritson, B. (1995) *Alcohol, Tobacco, Illicit Drug Use and Sex Education Amongst Teenagers: A Report to the Western Isles Health Board*. Edinburgh: Alcohol & Health Research Group.

Anderson, K., Plant, M.A. and Plant, M.L. (1998) Associations between drinking, smoking and illicit drug use among adolescents in the Western Isles of Scotland: Implications for harm reduction. *Journal of Substance Misuse*, 13, 13–20.

Brewers and Licensed Retailers Association (1999) *Statistical Handbook*. London: BLRA.

Cameron, D. (1995) *Liberating Solutions to Alcohol Problems: Treating Problem Drinkers Without Saying 'No'*. Northvale, NJ: Jason Aronson.

Crawford, A. and Allsop, D.T. (1996) *Young People and Alcohol in Scotland: A Survey of Brand Preferences of 15–17 Year Olds Conducted in February 1996*. Glasgow: Scottish Council on Alcohol.

Davies, J.B. and Stacey, B. (1972) *Teenagers and Alcohol*. London: HMSO.

Fillmore, K. (1988) *Alcohol Use Across The Life Course: A Critical Review of Seventy Years of International Longitudinal Research*. Toronto: Addiction Research Foundation.

Forsyth, A. (1997) 'The evidence'. Talk presented at Alcopops: New drinks, New dangers? A national conference organised by the Addictions Forum, Leicester, 18 August.

Fossey, E. (1994) *Growing Up With Alcohol*. London: Tavistock/ Routledge.

Goddard, E. (1996) *Teenage Drinking in 1994*. London: HMSO.

Goddard, E. (1997a) *Young Teenagers and Alcohol in 1996. Volume 1. England*. London: Office for National Statistics.

Goddard, E. (1997b) *Young Teenagers and Alcohol in 1996. Volume 2. Scotland*. London: Office for National Statistics.

Hibell, B., Andersson, B., Bjarnason, T., Kokkevi, A., Morgan, M. and Narusk, A. (1997) *The 1995 ESPAD Report: Alcohol and Other Drug Use Among 26 European Countries*. Stockholm: Swedish Council for Information on Alcohol and Other Drugs.

Hingson, R., Berson, J. and Dowley, K. (1997) Interventions to reduce college student drinking and related health and social problems. In M.A. Plant, E. Single and T. Stockwell (Eds) *Alcohol: Minimising the Harm: What Works?*, pp. 143–170. London: Free Association Books.

Home Office (1997) *Aspects of Crime Drunkenness 1995*. London: Home Office.

Jahoda, G. and Cramond, J. (1972) *Children and Alcohol*. London: HMSO.

Jessor, R. and Jessor, S. (1977) *Problem Behavior and Psychosocial Development: A Longitudinal Study of Youth*. New York: Academic Press.

Lister Sharp, D. (1994) Underage drinking in the United Kingdom since 1970: Public policy, the law and adolescent drinking behaviour. *Alcohol and Alcoholism*, 29, 555–563.

Loretto, W. (1994) Youthful drinking in Northern Ireland and Scotland: Preliminary results from a comparative study. *Drugs: Education, Prevention and Policy*, 1, 143–152.

May, C. (1992) A Burning issue? Adolescent alcohol use in Britain 1970–1991. *Alcohol and Alcoholism*, 27, 109–115.

McGovern, P.E., Glucker, D.L. and Exner, L. (1996) Neolithic resinated wine. *Nature*, 381, 480–481.

McKibben, M.A. (1996) *Pop Fiction? The Truth About Alcopops*. London: Alcohol Concern.

Miller, P. (1997) Family structure, personality, drinking, smoking and illicit drug use: a study of UK teenagers. *Drug and Alcohol Dependence*, 45, 121–129.

Miller, P. and Plant, M.A. (1996) Drinking, smoking and illicit drug use among 15 and 16 year olds in the United Kingdom. *British Medical Journal*, 313, 394–397.

Peele, S. and Brodsky, A. (1991) *The Truth About Addiction and Recovery*. New York: Fireside Books.

Plant, M.A. and Foster, J. (1991) Teenagers and alcohol: Results of a Scottish national survey. *Drug and Alcohol Dependence*, 28, 203–210.

Plant, M.A. and Plant, M.L. (1992) *Risktakers: Alcohol, Drugs, Sex and Youth*. London: Tavistock/Routledge.

Plant, M.A. and Plant, M.L. (1997a) Alcopops: New threat or moral panic? Paper presented at 23rd Alcohol Epidemiology Symposium of the Kettil Bruun Society for Social and Epidemiological Research on Alcohol, Reykjavik, Iceland.

Plant, M.A. and Plant, M.L. (1997b) Alcohol education and harm minimisation. In M.A. Plant, E. Single and T. Stockwell (Eds) *Alcohol: Minimising the Harm*, pp. 193–210. London: Free Association Books.

Plant, M.A., Peck, D.F. and Samuel, E. (1985) *Alcohol, Drugs and School Leavers*. London: Tavistock.

Plant, M.A., Plant, M.L., Thornton, C. and Mason, W. (1998) *Parents and Health Education: An Exploratory Study in the Western Isles*. Report for the Western Isles Health Board, Edinburgh, Alcohol & Health Research Centre.

Plant, M.A., Bagnall, G., Foster, J. and Sales, J. (1990) Young people and drinking: Results from an English national survey. *Alcohol and Alcoholism*, 25, 685–690.

Plant, M.A., Single, E. and Stockwell, T. (Eds) (1997) *Alcohol: Minimising the Harm: What Works?* London: Free Association Books.

Plant, M.L. (1997) *Women and Alcohol: Contemporary and Historical Perspectives*. London: Free Association Books.

Project Match Research Group (1997) Matching alcoholism treatments to client heterogeneity: Project Match post treatment drinking outcomes. *Journal of Studies on Alcohol*, 58, 7–29.

Raw, M. and McNeill, A. (1996) *Young People and Alcohol: A Survey of Attitudes and Behaviour Towards New Types of Alcoholic Drinks in England*. London: Health Education Authority.

Room, R. and Collins, G. (Eds) (1983) *Alcohol and Disinhibition: Meaning and Nature of the Link*. Washington, DC, NIAAA Research Monograph 12, US Department of Health and Human Services.

Royal College of Psychiatrists (1986) *Alcohol: Our Favourite Drug*. London: Tavistock.

Stall, R. and Leigh, B. (1994) Understanding the relationship between drug and alcohol use and high risk activity for HIV transmission: Where do we go from here? *Addiction*, 89, 131–134.

World Health Organization (1994a) *Alcohol and HIV/AIDS*. Copenhagen: World Health Organization.

World Health Organization (1994b) *European Alcohol Action Plan*. Copenhagen: World Health Organization.

Chapter 3

Young People and Drugs

John B. Davies

The use of illicit drugs, particularly by young people, continues to cause concern in the media, among politicians, and among a large section of the public in both the UK and the USA. The fear that society itself could be undermined by drugs has been voiced from time to time by politicians of all parties, and the concerns expressed have a long history going back to the 'drugs boom' of the 1960s. There is no doubt that increasing numbers of young people use illicit drugs, and that the numbers encountering problems arising from that use continue to increase steadily. The way in which these problems manifest themselves particularly (but by no means exclusively) in deprived inner-city areas is cause for great concern, where there is a complex interaction between drug use, crime and deprivation; and there is media talk of entire communities being 'in the grip of' heroin. At an individual level, deaths due to use of illicit drugs continue to rise, with Home Office statistics showing a steady increase; numbers of young people have fallen foul of the drug ecstasy, sometimes with fatal results; and there are reports from some major cities that teenage recreational drug use has now embraced heroin. Research currently under way (McKeganey *et al.*, 1998) shows that disturbing numbers of Scottish children down to and including primary school age have some experience of heroin use, and in a recent Scottish incident, heroin was discovered in the school bag of a nine year-old boy. Individual tragedies occur with some regularity and the range of drugs in use and the prevalence of drug use amongst all sections of society, but especially amongst young people, continues to increase.

The official response to this increasingly uncontrolled situation in the UK is basically 'more of the same', that is an approach epitomised by a 'War on Drugs'. The aim is to reduce the prevalence of drug use and

Young People and Mental Health. Edited by P. Aggleton, J. Hurry and I. Warwick.
© 2000 John Wiley & Sons Ltd.

availability of drugs by a variety of measures, and ultimately to remove the drug menace from our midst altogether. The foundation stone for the approach is the Prevention of Drugs Act 1971 and its subsequent modifications, which define the illegal status of different 'drugs'. In practice, the components of drug policy are diverse but involve the attempt to tackle both the supply and the demand sides of the equation. They include police and customs activity, punitive legislation and custodial sentences, and drug education targeted at progressively younger age groups.

There is also an increasing acknowledgement of the role of harm reduction, mainly brought about as a consequence of the perceived necessity for needle exchange in preventing the spread of disease via injecting drug use, and also the dangers of dehydration and exhaustion associated with use of certain amphetamine-based drugs (notably ecstasy); though this approach does not sit easily or logically within the current philosophy. Giving guidelines on the safer use of a substance at the same time as insisting on its illegal status sends out a very discrepant message.

It is argued here that a change is now due, and that creative public and political minds need to give consideration to alternatives previously considered too radical. The basis for this suggestion is that the present situation cannot be taken as an endorsement for the efficacy of the currently favoured approach, and that the history of 'drug prevention' is more a story of failure than of success. The horror stories that unfortunately typify the rhetoric of drug misuse take place within the *existing* framework of illegality, and it is difficult to see how the present approach can continue to be justified given the steadily increasing prevalence of drug use and drug-related harm. A fundamental re-think of drug policy is necessary *in the interests of public health*.

PREVENTION OF WHAT?

The problems arising from the use of illicit substances by young people have given birth to a huge literature. A large part of this literature is made up of prevalence studies; that is, surveys making use of questionnaires and other self-report measures carried out at regular intervals by a variety of different agencies over a long period of time. It appears that major interest amongst politicians, the media and researchers is attracted by strong evidence of increasing prevalence over the last two decades, and counting the problem is assumed in some sense to mean the same as understanding it. However, it can be argued that too great an emphasis on head-counting has resulted in the neglect of studies of the nature and dynamics of drug use. Consequently, the aim of understanding how and why drugs have the wide-ranging effects they do (ranging, for example, from the long-term non-problematic use of cocaine on the one hand (see Harrison and Mugford, 1994) to death apparently as a consequence of taking a single ecstasy tablet) has to some extent been hi-jacked by a seemingly endless stream of head-counting exercises. It seems likely that further prevalence studies will simply duplicate what we already know, albeit in slightly revised form; namely that large numbers of young people in the UK, possibly a majority, have used an illicit drug at some time; that a significant proportion use illicit drugs either regularly or from time to time; and that the problem is becoming more widespread. In such a situation, simply counting heads gives few clues as to how best to tackle the problem. The issue of what to do remains largely unaddressed by the types of data collected from such studies, and the assumption that a head-counting exercise feeds automatically and logically into policy recommendations is not an obvious one.

Meanwhile, the prevalence data of the last twenty years clearly demonstrate an accelerating increase, which at least permits discussion of the question 'What is it that drug prevention prevents?' It certainly has not reduced the prevalence of use.

THE MAIN COMPONENTS OF PRIMARY PREVENTION: THE LAW AND EDUCATION

The increasing prevalence of drug use among all sections of society, but most notably among young people, runs roughly parallel to the increasing amounts of money and human resources devoted to attempts to reduce demand by means of the law (harsher sentencing, increased police activity, customs, drug squads, etc.). Scottish data indicate increasingly severe penalties over a period of years applied particularly for crimes of 'possession with intent to supply' at a time when sentencing tariffs for other serious crimes did not increase (Haw, 1989). Therefore, at the very best we may argue that the acceleration in drug use has been marginally slowed by such measures, and even that would be an act of faith rather than empirically demonstrated fact.

Similarly, and despite substantial improvements and developments in best practice, there is a lack of clear and unambiguous evidence that drug education translates easily into reduced prevalence. For the most part, educational endeavours in this area have been shown to produce increases in knowledge if they achieve anything; evidence for attitude change with respect to drugs is less common; and actual behaviour change has proved the most difficult of all. Certain approaches based on 'life skills' show the most promise, but other approaches based on largely discredited approaches such as fear arousal and 'just say no' still continue to find favour and support, particularly in the media. A recent summary of alcohol-related drug education by Foxcroft et al. (1997, 1998), for example, shows that while some initiatives have an impact on use and/or age of onset, some endeavours are associated with *increased* use in the short and medium term (up to one year; and from one to three years), and there is no shortage of education that appears to have no effect whatsoever. A number of earlier studies have showed similarly disappointing results.

This is clearly an area where it cannot be assumed that anything must necessarily be better than nothing. It is possible to arouse an interest that was not there before, and thus produce 'false positives'. In a less negative vein, however, it nonetheless remains the case that there is a shortage of hard evidence showing that drugs education is capable of living up to the expectations that are held of it. However, the 'life skills' approach seems to offer more hope than some of the more traditional drug-education methods, when offered in an appropriate form and context.

The advantages and disadvantages of this approach have been discussed in Davies and Coggans (1991), and more recently by Hurry and Lloyd (1997: 35–36). In the latter case, evidence was found that a life-skills programme could delay onset of drug use, though the authors are typically guarded about their conclusions. They write, 'The significance of the results reported here is that they demonstrate that a substantial and well delivered drugs education programme in primary school can have an impact on delaying children's subsequent experimentation with drugs as they move into the age group more at risk', and '. . . these findings need to be replicated with larger samples and over a longer study period . . . Without such information we risk spending money on drugs education which fails to produce the desired results.'

Drugs education therefore seems to be making progress, and can claim some successes at the level of providing useful information and possibly delaying the age of onset; realistic goals which may be achieved through this route. Overall, however, there is little reason to suppose that drug education *per se* will be any more successful in actually reducing drug use prevalence at the population level than any of the legal or judicial attempts, or of stemming the steady increase.

The question then arises as to whether it is a reasonable expectation that the UK will be a drug-free (or more realistically, relatively drug-free) place at some time in the future, and that the so-called 'War on Drugs' will have been effectively won. The answer to this question is, of course, largely speculative and a matter of personal opinion; yet the answer 'Yes' seems scarcely credible on the basis of current performance. Despite the best efforts of police, courts, customs, agencies, educators and many others, prevalence continues to increase. On the other hand, if the answer to the above question is 'No', we must face the prospect of learning to live with these substances and with the people who use them on an increasing scale. If this indeed is the prospect, it then becomes necessary to revisit the dangers associated with, and attributed to, illicit drug use and ask whether such a prospect is necessarily catastrophic, or is both manageable and liveable with.

This leads to a consideration of the applicability of harm reduction strategies. To fully embrace harm reduction goals, however, it may be necessary to adopt towards the problem of drug use a set of beliefs and attitudes that lead naturally to policies which will be advantageous to public health in terms of *living with drugs* (see Gossop, 1982, for the first use of this term), while minimising the various harms they do. The prevalence data indicate that we are already 'living with drugs' on some scale, and there is no evidence that this trend is likely to reverse; also, controlling something at the same time as making it illegal is not a logically satisfying juxtaposition. At the present time, there is a mismatch between this reality and a set of attitudes crystallised in the 'War on Drugs' which focus on *stamping drugs out*, a goal which assumes that a 'War on Drugs' is necessary and that it can be won, and that prevention of use (rather than harm) is an achievable goal. This basic mismatch is the main source of the problem encountered by our society with drugs and particularly drug use by young people.

PREVALENCE

A wide variety of data on prevalence of illicit drug use indicates that personal experience with the use of illicit drugs may no longer be considered the province of a deviant minority. Popular theories of drug use as a consequence of abusive or disturbed childhoods, inadequate or disturbed personality, inability to cope, susceptibility to peer pressure, and so forth, while they may have applicability in specific cases, become increasingly implausible as the number of people in a population who are involved in the activity in question increases. While it may be useful for some purposes to conceptualise a small percentage of a given population as having particular problems that uniquely dispose them to illicit drug use, these types of inadequacy or deficiency theories become increasingly inapplicable as prevalence rises and the activity spreads into more statistically normal parts of the population (Davies and Coggans, 1991). Deficiency theories still apply, but to a progressively smaller and smaller proportion of the population. It has even been found in some studies that it is the young users rather than the non-users who show the best psychological adjustment (Shedler and Block, 1990).

While such findings are not typical, and probably depend on the samples used in the studies, it makes little sense to conceptualise roughly one-third of the youthful population as being inadequate or deficient in some respect, simply on the basis of their familiarity with illicit drugs. Consequently, satisfying and pragmatically useful solutions to the drug problem require us to retreat from deficiency theories of drug use as general explanations, and look for something more dynamic and positive about this popular form of activity.

Official indicators such as Home Office records give details of addict notifications and these indicate that the prevalence of drug misuse has moved steadily and sharply upwards over the last three decades. For example, in Scotland between 1975 and 1990 notified addict numbers rose from 58 to 1184. The numbers of persons cautioned and convicted for drug offences also rose from 500 in 1975 to 2626 in 1988 (Home Office, 1990–1991; Scottish Office, 1991 (cited in Plant and Plant, 1992)). Plant and Plant (1992) cite a survey of some 1000 15 and 16 year olds conducted between 1979 and 1980 in the Lothian region. At that time, approximately 10% of this population had some experience with illicit drugs, mainly cannabis or glues and solvents. Plant and Plant report that four years later one-third of this study group had experience of such drugs. In 1991, Coggans *et al.* found that, in a self-report questionnaire study carried out as part of the evaluation of drug education in Scotland, almost 23% of the sample of Scottish teenagers involved had used illicit drugs at some time.

On a broader front, the Government White Paper, *Tackling Drugs Together* (DoH, 1995), gives a picture of drug misuse statistics for England. The paper suggests that in any one year roughly 3 million people (some 6% of the population) take an illegal drug. Fourteen per cent of 14 to 15 year olds report taking an illegal drug; and among young people living in inner-city areas, some 42% of those aged between 16 and 19, and 44% of those aged 20 to 24 have taken illicit drugs at some time. Cannabis is the most frequently cited drug and 24% of young people aged between 16 and 29 report long-term cannabis use according to Keene (1997). With respect to developmental trends, data from Swadi (1988) are frequently cited indicating regular and progressive increases in the prevalence of over-use of solvents or illicit drugs between the ages of 11 and 16. According to Swadi's data, prevalence rises from 13% of the target population at age 11 to 26% at age 16. Swadi also reports higher rates of use by males than females, with the prevalence of weekly or daily use of cannabis being in the region of 9% for males and 7% for females.

Finally, recent data from Scotland show, amongst many other things, an increase in *all* age groups for 'use of any drug in the last 12 months' (National Health Services in Scotland, 1998: 72) compared to the 1993 data, indicating that use of illegal drugs is not just a problem amongst young people. Also, deaths due to use of all illicit drugs for 1996 stand at 267, of which 172 involved people who were previously known or suspected to be dependent (National Health Services in Scotland, 1998: 68). In a separate table in this same report (describing drugs involved in a number of deaths: 1996; p. 69), the largest numbers of fatalities involved the use of (in isolation or in combination) methadone, diazepam, morphine, temazepam and heroin (91, 72, 51, 37, and 31, respectively). Ecstasy was involved on only seven occasions and cocaine on three. It is apparent that prescribed drugs and minor tranquillisers, plus heroin, are far more frequently involved in fatalities than is the rave drug ecstasy, despite the recent prominence given to the latter.

The above figures come from careful research. However, brief consideration of some more homely examples may shed further light on these matters. Data of a perhaps less well-established pedigree came from a Scottish university where the students conducted their own survey of drug use (*Strathclyde Telegraph*, 1994). Notwithstanding certain methodological problems these data, even if approximately true, provide an insight into prevalence rates amongst a group of young people who would normally be regarded as amongst the most bright and intelligent, and to whom we would look for direction and guidance in the future. In the student survey, 68% of male students reported that they 'use drugs'. For females the percentage was 37%. Further questions dealing with the specific drugs taken, and frequency of use, showed that the most common drug used (44%) was cannabis, followed by LSD (22%), speed (amphetamine) (22%) and ecstasy (8%). With respect to frequency of use, only 34% of users reported using occasionally, 29% reported using weekly, and 9% reported using drugs every day. Interestingly, there were major differences in the percentages reported by different faculties. Percentage of use by course showed that arts and social studies were in the lead (46%), followed by business studies (22%), science (18%) and engineering (10%). Law, for reasons unknown, reported only 3%. In answer to the question 'Would you consider yourself addicted?', 5% of the student population responded 'Yes', and 95% responded 'No'.

In summary, a wealth of prevalence data from many sources attests to the fact that the occasional use of illicit drugs is now commonplace amongst young people, and that regular drug use is also common and on the increase.

CONTEXT

The meaning of an utterance is defined by the context within which it occurs (Edwards and Potter, 1992). In a similar kind of way, drug messages are also defined by context, and what appears to be an unacceptable or even an horrific image can become mundane, attractive and even humorous in different contexts. It may well be the case that messages devised by older people, but targeted at young people, miss the mark since the meaning that is assumed to be intrinsic to the message becomes transmuted within a younger, and different, culture. This is the traditional problem with shock/horror or fear arousal approaches to drugs education, which have been shown to be the usual preference amongst those who are not familiar with the drug-using scene (Finnigan, 1988, 1996), and it has been shown to be largely ineffective on drug-using target groups.

During 1996, a student stood for election as President of the Students Union at a Scottish university, employing a poster depicting himself in the same pose (undergoing the 'sweats' associated with heroin withdrawal) and wearing the same type of clothes as the character 'Rents' in the film *Trainspotting*, a character normally assumed to represent the aversive aspects of heroin use. The poster used a similar type of photograph and media presentation as were used to advertise that film. That other students found this particular poster appealing is evidenced by the fact that this candidate won the election. Finally, at the time of writing this chapter, an identical image has again been used at university level to attract students to take part in *University Challenge*, this time showing Jeremy Paxman in the role of 'Rents'. The poster used the original 'Rents' poster with Paxman's head superimposed. It can be surmised that what constitutes a shocking or unattractive image in the minds of some people communicates entirely different meanings when transplanted into a different context.

Whilst it would be unfair to say that the money spent on education, prevention and interdiction has been wasted, we clearly cannot claim that their impact on *prevalence* has been such as to either curb or reduce the extent of drug use amongst young people though they may collectively have a number of other effects, both beneficial and possibly deleterious. Furthermore, it is apparent that messages about the negative aspects of drug use do not fall on fertile ground if the images and messages presented do not reflect the reality as perceived by the target audience. Telling young people the 'facts' will not work if the facts are heavily edited in the pursuit of negative imagery, or are simply wrong. This is the problem with drugs education for young people. Most young users do not die; most do not experience major negative consequences; and many will 'talk endlessly and relentlessly about their (drug) experiences' and assure the listener 'that raving definitely was the best thing since sliced bread' (Sherlock, 1997). Right or wrong, this is the raw material with which the drugs educator increasingly has to deal. And messages about the horrors and dangers from people who have never 'done it' addressed to those who have done it frequently and enjoyed the experience must inevitably appear out-of-touch and propagandist.

ALTERNATIVES TO PREVENTION

If, as argued, prevention is an unachievable goal, what are the alternatives? Perhaps in its place we should be seeking a situation in which, while the prevalence of actual use is higher (it increases year by year anyway), the incidence of drug-related harm is low. In other words, we may have to concede a higher rate of drug use in exchange for a lowered rate of the problems that arise from it; and challenge the assumption that prevalence and harm are necessarily linked by some simple mechanism.[1]

The most obvious route to such a situation would be the abandonment of *drugs prevention* as a goal altogether, and the substitution in its place of a policy aimed at reducing the public health risks *associated with use*, rather than use *per se*. It can be argued that fundamental changes to the law would be helpful in that respect, and that the current illegality of drugs actually adds to the public health risks associated with drugs. The arguments on this topic centre around lack of quality control (which is a major factor in causing drug deaths due to accidental overdose), stimulation of illegal street markets, and the surrounding of what is basically a public health issue with a culture of criminality and gangsterism. Detailed discussion of a number of these issues can be found elsewhere (Coomber, 1998). A further issue concerns the social and legal consequences for young people who are arrested and convicted on a drugs charge, where the legal consequences for the young person concerned may be far more damaging than the likely effects of the drug itself. The amounts of cannabis or ecstasy involved are frequently small.

Concentration on prevention of drug use may also obscure real opportunities for useful and necessary intervention in the drug use cycle. For example, young drug users generally observe that their own use and that of their colleagues seldom leads to addiction or dependence. They will also be aware, however, that there *are* risks to the activity (Sherlock, 1997) and that accidents do sometimes happen. Under a prevention strategy of the type envisaged by a 'War on Drugs' the specific nature of these risks frequently goes unaddressed and unnoticed.

For example, recent work carried out by Sherlock (1997) looks in some detail at ecstasy use amongst young people in the north of England. Her work illustrates how the motives and intentions of young ravers simply collide with any ideology which seeks merely to 'stamp it out'. Meanwhile Sherlock points out important dangers that may well be overlooked by any approach to drug use concentrating purely on prevention of use. Sherlock obtained 25 tablets which were handed in to the Leeds Addiction Unit under an amnesty. These were analysed under a Home Office licence in the Department of Pathological Sciences at Leeds University. The 25 tablets each marketed as ecstasy had a number of names including *Dove, Loveheart, New Yorker, Purple Heart, Rhubarb and Custard, Adam and Eve, California Sunrise, White Burger, Double Diamond, Snowball, White Lightning, Strawberry Milk Shake* and the rather wickedly named *Dead on Arrival* (the name of this latter can only have been selected with the aim of driving parents into paroxysms at the very name of the tablet). Whilst all these tablets were ostensibly ecstasy tablets, the range of substances they contained was surprising and in one instance particularly alarming.

While most of the tablets contained the basic ecstasy ingredient (methylenedioxymethamphetamine: MDMA) to some degree, there was wide variation, ranging from 140 mg per tablet to as low as 2 mg per tablet. This variance makes it impossible to monitor dose on the basis of number of tablets taken, and makes comparison with the doses taken by fellow-ravers a hazardous business. In addition, tablets contained a number of other stimulants including caffeine, amphetamine,

methamphetamine and ephedrine. Some tablets also contained paracetamol. Two tablets of particular concern contained the drug ketamine.
The *Strawberry Milkshake* tablet was found to contain 197 mg of ketamine
per tablet and *White Lightning* was found to contain 186 mg of ketamine.
The doses of ketamine found in these samples are of considerable concern. The effects of ketamine are very different from those that would be
expected of MDMA. The user, according to Sherlock, may feel distressed by the intensity of the experience and by how dissimilar the
effects are to those of ecstasy. It is also apparently the case that the usual
route of administration for ketamine is to snort or inject. Sherlock reported that Jansen (1997) indicates that swallowing ketamine can be a
particularly unpleasant way to ingest the drug as the effects begin to
develop very slowly and the user becomes aware of communication and
coordination difficulties before dissociation occurs. Ketamine taken by
this route will also last for an uncomfortably long time. Ketamine can
also render the user relatively helpless in terms of controlling body
movements.

The problem lurking behind the variations in content between the
different kinds of tablets may even be understated by Sherlock's data,
however. Given that there is little quality control over the production of
these kinds of tablets, it is by no means certain that two tablets of the
same name and apparently from the same source would necessarily
have the same constituents on two different occasions. Consequently,
there may be variation not merely between tablet types but also *within*
tablet types from different batches, since the degree of individual
quality control is unknowable. The mismatch between a strategy based
on 'Just say no' or a 'War on Drugs' which assumes that the majority of a
target audience will not take drugs and will in fact be prepared to 'say
no' contrasts with the perceptions and needs of a group of people who
use drugs, sometimes with some regularity and who are confronted by
an array of substances, all apparently marketed under the same generic
label whose contents vary in terms of MDMA from virtually non-
existent to substantial doses, which may be accompanied in some instances by large doses of a different drug, with effects which are totally
unrelated to the experience the user is seeking. Meanwhile in the wake
of serious tragedies, the too easy equating of death with ecstasy use
completely bypasses the major risks deriving from non-standardised
dose and variable content. It is probably true, therefore, that taking
ecstasy has something in common with Russian roulette; but this derives from lack of any attempt at quality control. Any other drug, prescribed or illicit, might be expected to develop a similar reputation if
dispensed in a similar way.

Different perceptions of the drug use phenomenon lead to the imposi-
tion of a set of drug policies that are frequently mismatched to the needs
of the target population, particularly where the hedonistic and usually
problem-free use of drugs by teenagers is concerned. It should be plain
from prevalence data that drug use is now something that is indulged in

by a substantial and an ever-increasing proportion of the population and that much of this increase is specific to younger people. It should also be clear that while it may be possible to stamp out behaviours that are viewed as deviant in circumstances where this 'deviance' is only displayed by a small percentage of the population, it makes no sense at all to demonise or criminalise an activity which has over the last two decades shown signs of becoming statistically normal. The disproportionate response by those who favour drug wars as a solution to the problems created by drugs and the tunnel vision which the same people show when considering other dangerous activities in which they participate (e.g. drinking, smoking, driving cars, accidents in the home, unsafe sex) is sufficient to alienate a large proportion of the younger population whenever the issue of drugs is mentioned.

Ecstasy deaths in particular probably receive more attention than it is reasonable to expect. Ecstasy deaths in the UK during the period 1997 to 1998 number something in the region of 60. Given the probable number of users of ecstasy, this fatality rate is quite unremarkable compared with deaths due to other legally prescribed pharmaceuticals and other causes. Whilst any avoidable death from any cause is a tragedy for those involved, it is also reasonable to conclude that the amount of energy and outrage expended on drug-related deaths is out of proportion compared to deaths from other causes; most young drug users do not die as a consequence of their habit and most of them do not become addicted. This ought to be good news, but paradoxically any suggestion that illegal drug use is not as dangerous or as relentlessly addicting as we perhaps imagined often meets with resistance. This is probably because of the contrast between this view and the view that drugs such as ecstasy may justifiably be called 'lethal' (from a statistical point of view they are substantially less 'lethal' than cars) and that anyone who dabbles in minor drugs is on an inevitable slippery slope towards addiction and the use of heroin and cocaine. The evidence simply does not support this latter view.

DRUGS FOR FUN

There appear to be certain truths about drug use which it is difficult to discuss openly. For example, it is evident that most young people using drugs do so for fun, rather than because they are addicted or enslaved to some compelling pharmacology (Davies and Coggans, 1991; Best *et al.*, 1995; Sherlock, 1997). Another sensitive topic is the controlled use of drugs usually described as intrinsically and inevitably 'addictive'. Harrison and Mugford (1994) have compiled a set of refereed papers on the phenomenon of controlled cocaine use, and Shewan *et al.* (1998) describe controlled heroin use in a sample of Glasgow heroin users. This also should be good news, in the sense that the problem is seen not to reside solely in substances which compel their own use, but in the interaction of pharmacology, the motives and aims of the user, and the setting in which the drugs are used. The suggestion that addiction requires a combination of *drug*, *set*, and *setting* is clearly illustrated, and suggests the need for an approach to drugs that does not concentrate simply on substances and their banishment, but takes into account people, their aims and goals, and where and how they live their lives.

Arguments about 'controlled use' are not new. In the academic literature on alcohol problems, this particular argument took place a decade and a half ago, and the battle has to some extent, been won. It is now accepted that viewing alcohol problems within an exclusively disease-oriented framework offers neither an adequate description of the phenomenon, nor an adequate framework for treatment (Heather and Robertson, 1981). For a great many people who might at one time have been described as 'alcoholics', a reasonable outcome is a return to controlled drinking rather than the abstinence that hitherto was felt necessary. There is a large literature on this topic. Consequently, it is not coincidental that a return to controlled drinking is now probably the most frequent treatment aim of all alcohol agencies, and that in certain parts of the UK (e.g. Scotland), the term 'alcoholism' with its disease connotations has been removed from all the Scottish councils (they are now called Councils on Alcohol). A similar debate is now emerging in the area of drugs, and the battle promises to be equally bloody.

With specific reference to young people, it is still probably true to say, however, that the heavier and more feared drugs, such as cocaine, heroin and other opiates, are not generally the province of young drug users, although this situation is changing. For example, in the student survey cited earlier, there was no mention whatsoever of cocaine or heroin use. While it is probably overly optimistic to conclude that there is no cocaine or heroin use amongst young people, it is nonetheless true that for the majority of youngsters dabbling in drugs, the menu will be drawn from amongst the 'dance drug' list (mostly amphetamine, ecstasy, LSD and cannabis). Furthermore, it appears that many young people see the world of cocaine and heroin, and particularly of injecting drug use, as being the world of 'junkies'; a world which they see as quite different from their own extraverted world of recreational use and dance drugs. The majority of young people appear to make an important distinction between the heavy drugs of dependence and their own highly context dependent use of drugs as an accompaniment to dances and raves.

There is, in fact, a world of difference between the purposive use of drugs to accompany a specific social activity whose enjoyment is enhanced by their use and the chronic dependent use of drugs as a substitute for any other kind of activity. However, there are recent disturbing reports from Aberdeen and Manchester (personal communications) that this hitherto clear distinction is being eroded, and that heroin use (mostly smoking, but including injection use) is moving into the dance and rave scene, and recent data from McKeganey *et al.* (1998) confirm this impression. It is possible that once again an obsession with prevention, and the demonising of certain drugs, has distracted attention away from certain ecological features of the rave scene which could perhaps have been used to advantage. A prevention orientation tends to exaggerate the powers and dangers of certain substances in the interests of 'putting people off', but this can have unfortunate side-effects on young user-groups. It has been reported to the author by a number of workers in the field that repeated stressing of the dangers of heroin may have produced a desire amongst certain young people to move from 'kids' drugs' to 'real drugs'.

TALKING ABOUT DRUGS: FUNCTIONAL EXPLANATIONS

Much of the information about what drug use is actually like comes from what people who use drugs tell us about their habit. However, just like everyone else, the way drug users explain why they do the things they do varies according to the situation and circumstances. For example, in a formal setting when talking to a drug 'expert', heroin users are more likely to emphasise the addicted, dependent and helpless aspects of drug use; whereas in a bar talking to an informal interviewer familiar with the drug scene, they emphasise the hedonistic and volitional aspects of their use (Davies and Baker, 1987). In a similar way, problem smokers' explanations for smoking were found to vary between 'addicted' and 'volitional' according to their beliefs about what the therapist thought about the extent of their habit (McAllister and Davies, 1992).

The variable and functional nature of how drug users explain their habit has been shown in more detail in a recent study funded by the Scottish Office (Davies, 1997a, 1997b). In a study of drug users based in South Ayrshire, Newcastle upon Tyne, the central belt of Scotland and the Lothians, over 550 drug users were contacted, open ended conversations were carried out with each individual, and these were tape recorded and subsequently transcribed. A principled and replicable form of discourse analysis suggested that there were five kinds of conversations that could be identified amongst these drug users. Of particular relevance are the types of conversations designated Type 1 and Type 3. Type 1 conversations are hedonistic and volitional; that is, people exhibiting this type of discourse indicate that they use drugs on purpose, find the experience highly satisfactory, get a great deal of pleasure from it, and in no way see their drug use as a response to stress or as a type of support for inability to cope. A Type 3 conversation, on the other hand, may best be typified by the epithet 'helpless junkie'. People showing this type of conversation say that they are unable to stop or control the habit, that they experience no pleasure or fun from their drug use, but are merely using it to 'keep straight', and that the reasons for their dependent habit are inextricably woven into a complex and sometimes lengthy pattern of social and developmental causes to which the drug use is seen as a response. These two conversations are clearly distinct and very different.

Furthermore, whilst the Type 3 'addicted' pattern of self-presentation was associated with use of heroin, methadone and 'harder' drugs, and with a history of agency contact and treatment for drug problems, the implications of the Type 1 'hedonistic/purposive' were very different. People employing Type 1 discourse were likely to have a drug diet based on cannabis, ecstasy and LSD (dance drugs); they were less likely to enter treatment, and less likely to describe problems of addiction arising from their drug use. A group of 27 drug users whose talk followed the Type 1 pattern, remained intact and out of agency or treatment contact for the whole duration of the study (about 18 months). On the other hand, a group of 33 users who recounted Type 3 'helpless addict' stories suffered a level of erosion that was little short of catastrophic, with only three remaining out of treatment at the end of the study.

The problem is that when young people do encounter problems with drug use, as happens from time to time, some agencies and some parents may be unhappy with the Type 1 way of describing drug use. Experience suggests that parents and agencies often wish to recast and replace the hedonistic (and helpful) discourse normally associated with drug use with a Type 3 framework. Parents in particular may see some benefit in recasting their offspring's drug use as the consequence of an illness, a conceptual framework which removes responsibility and thereby any implication that the behaviour might have been carried out on purpose. This preference for a particular form of explanation has been shown both with respect to drugs (Davies 1997b) and elsewhere, and is known in the psychological literature as a 'functional attribution' showing a 'self-serving bias'. To put this in more straightforward terms, if Samantha is caught smoking cannabis in the playground, whilst Samantha's perception might be that she was having fun right up to the point where she was caught, Samantha's Mum and Dad may well prefer a framework that suggests that Samantha had no choice in the issue, was compelled to do it by wicked peers and an addictive pharmacology and is now a helpless addict. Consequently she cannot be blamed or held responsible for any of these behaviours.

Unfortunately, it seems likely that an illness framework, particularly for young people, is highly undesirable and counter-productive. Where a habit is seen as volitional and purposive, one might reasonably expect the person to respond to some persuasion and to implement some sensible decisions with respect to their drug use. It also requires of course that they take responsibility for their actions in the first place. By contrast, within an illness framework responsibility is removed.

Unfortunately, so usually is the capacity for any future control. A person defined as a helpless addict within an illness framework is quite likely to construct themselves in the same way as anyone suffering from any other illness. Illnesses are treated by doctors and doctors either produce cures or they fail. Treating one's substance use problems within the same framework and seeing oneself as an addict places all the responsibility for change in the lap of agencies, doctors and other helping professionals and also removes any sense of responsibility should they fail in their endeavours.

A number of groundbreaking papers on the topic of smoking 'addiction' by Eiser illustrate this point, and the principal ones have been described in Davies (1997c). To summarise, smokers who believed that they were 'addicted' were less likely to make an attempt to stop and less likely to succeed if they did. The same, I believe, is likely to be true for other substances. The data from the Scottish Office study cited above show that helpless and addicted modes of self-description go with the 'doggedly determined' use of heroin and opiates, whereas the non-addictive and much more hopeful discourses of Type 1 tend to go with controlled patterns of use. The implication is clear. The almost inevitable link that occurs in our language, such that whenever the word 'drug' is used the word 'addict' follows, has to be broken. Meanwhile the self-definition (attribution) of addiction remains one of the most incapacitating cognitions it is possible to hold (Davies 1997c). The premature labelling of young hedonistic drug users as 'addicts' is one of the more destructive manifestations.

It remains only to say that the attribution of addiction is made functional by the legal and punitive setting within which we as a society have chosen to cast the use of certain substances to change the state of consciousness; and that the addiction attribution reinforces the association between using drugs and being a 'helpless addict' when the habit goes wrong. It is only functional because the current legal framework makes necessary such a form of explanation as an escape from the consequences of describing one's behaviour as deliberate and hedonistic; but in the process, one becomes divorced from the volitional sources of one's own actions. The 'helpless addict' is to a considerable degree a creature of our own creation; and in the opinion of this author it is the least suitable role in which to cast young people when their drug use comes to light or causes problems.

CONCLUSIONS

The main conclusions are implicit in the above arguments. Despite best efforts on a number of fronts, the prevalence of illicit drug use continues to rise, most markedly amongst young people. In seems inconceivable that a future can be envisaged when the use of illicit drugs has been eliminated. Therefore, the future in prospect will require us for better or worse to *live with* drugs. There may be some comfort for those who find such a prospect rather frightening in noting that we shall not be alone in this endeavour. The ESPAD report (Hibbell *et al.*, 1995) compares drug use rates in 26 European countries, and whilst there are differences in base rates, the problem is endemic; general rather than specific.

Living with drugs, whilst being the only option available, is however possible; and it can be done in such a manner that use is controlled and monitored, while the harms that arise from all drug use, both legal and illegal, are reduced as far as possible. In order to deal rationally with this prospect we have to replace current prevailing attitudes to illicit drugs, characterised by arbitrary ethical pronouncements, philosophically untenable theory and an almost pathological lack of creativity, with a set of beliefs and responses that makes this option possible to do with some style and effectiveness. Drug use manifests itself within social and cultural contexts; and to the extent that that is true, we produce our 'drug problem' in the terms that we want it. Basically, we inadvertently design our own drug problem, and we experience it in the terms we have devised. If we devise and design differently, we change the problem.

Meanwhile, however, there are obstacles to progress, and many of these are political. Foxcroft *et al.* (1998) write (p. 9), 'Policy makers often use research and science to legitimate their stance, but this use is often selective and therefore biased, typically serving a political agenda . . .'; also 'It is . . . naive to think that policy based on research and science is objective and value free. Similarly, science is neither objective nor value free. The decision by funding agencies and researchers to support and focus on particular issues is subject to a whole range of political and social influences. Civil servants and scientific experts play a key "gatekeeping" role . . . it is important to understand how gatekeepers mediate the relationship between research and policy . . .'

With respect to young people's drug use, prevailing attitudes stifle progress. As a society we hold these attitudes because, basically, they are the only ones we are allowed to hold. Through a process of impression management, we are induced to elevate the troubling but manageable problem of young people using drugs into a major threat to society, and consequently into a demon that has to be stamped out. And thereby we set ourselves an impossible task, that of winning a war on drugs. In fact young people require something rather less grandiose, and rather more helpful by way of quality control, harm minimisation, and change to the law.

ENDNOTE

1. The idea of such a relationship comes from work by Ledermann (1956) who studied the relationship between mean *per capita*

consumption (m.p.c.c.) of alcohol, and the prevalence of 'alcoholism' in different populations. He observed relationships between m.p.c.c. and problem drinking and postulated that the two were linked mechanistically in such a way that prevalence of problems was predictable from knowledge of m.p.c.c. The mechanistic nature of Ledermann's theory has been challenged by studies of the impact of differing drinking patterns and cultures on rates of problem drinking which suggest that the idea is descriptive but not necessarily predictive.

REFERENCES

Best, D., Mortimer, R., Macmillan, D. and Davies, J.B. (1995) *Fast Forward Peer Research Project: Evaluation Report*. Edinburgh: Report to Fast Forward (Leith); Scottish Office.

Coggans, N., Shewan, D., Henderson, M. and Davies, J.B. (1991) *The National Evaluation of Drug Education in Scotland. Research Monograph 4*. London: Institute for the Study of Drug Dependence.

Coomber, R. (1998) *The Control of Drugs and Drug Users*. Reading: Harwood Academic.

Davies, J.B. (1997a) Conversations with drug users: a functional discourse model. *Addiction Research*, 5(1), 53–70.

Davies, J.B. (1997b) *Drugspeak: the analysis of drug discourse*. Reading: Harwood Academic.

Davies, J.B. (1997c) *The Myth of Addiction: attributional perspectives on the nature of addiction*. Reading: Harwood Academic.

Davies, J.B. and Baker, R. (1987) The impact of self-presentation and interviewer bias effects on self-reported heroin use. *British Journal of Addiction*, 82, 907–912.

Davies, J.B. and Coggans, N. (1991) *The Facts about Adolescent Drug Abuse*. London: Cassell.

DoH (1995) *Tackling Drugs Together* (White Paper), Department of Health.

Edwards, D. and Potter, J. (1992) *Discursive Psychology*. London: Sage.

Finnigan, F. (1988) Stereotyping in addiction: an application of the Fishbein-Ajzen theory to heroin using behaviour. PhD Thesis, University of Strathclyde.

Finnigan, F. (1996) How non-heroin users perceive heroin users and how heroin users perceive themselves. *Addiction Research*, 4(1), 25–32.

Foxcroft, D., Lister-Sharp, D. and Lowe, G. (1997) Alcohol misuse prevention for young people: a systematic review reveals methodological concerns and lack of reliable evidence of effectiveness. *Addiction*, 92(5), 531–537.

Foxcroft, D., Lister-Sharp, D. and Lowe, G. (1998) How can we improve our knowledge base? Lessons from a systematic review of alcohol misuse prevention programmes for youth. *Alcohol Update*, 34, 7–9.

Gossop, M. (1982) *Living with Drugs*, 1st edn. Aldershot: Gower.

Harrison, L. and Mugford, S. (Eds) (1994) Cocaine in the community: international perspectives. *Addiction Research* (special issue) 2, 1.

Haw, S. (1989) *The sentencing of drug offenders in Scottish courts*. Report to SHHD Criminality and Law Research Group. SHHD Library.

Heather, N. and Robertson, I. (1981) *Controlled Drinking*. London: Methuen.

Hibbell, B., Andersson, B., Bjarnason, T., Kokkevi, A., Morgan, M. and Narusk, A. (1995) *The 1995 ESPAD Report: Alcohol and other drug use among students in 26 European countries*. Council of Europe, Stockholm: Modin Tryck A.B.

Hurry, J. and Lloyd, C. (1997) *A follow-up evaluation of project Charlie: a life skills drug education programme for primary schools*. Central Drugs Prevention Unit: Home Office Paper 16.

Jansen, K.L.R. (1997) Adverse psychological effects associated with the use of ecstasy (MDMA) and their treatment. In N. Saunders (Ed.) *Ecstasy Reconsidered*. Exeter: BPC Wheaton.

Keene, J. (1997) *Drug Misuse: Prevention, harm minimisation and treatment*. London: Chapman & Hall.

Ledermann, S. (1956) Alcool-Alcoolisme-Alcoolisation: Données Scientifiques de Caractè Physiologique, Economique et Social. Travaux et Documents, Cahier No. 29, Institut National d'Etudes Demographiques. Presses Universitaire de France.

McAllister, P. and Davies, J.B. (1992) Attributional bias as a function of clinical classification. *Journal of Drug Issues*, 22(1), 139–153.

McKeganey, N. *et al.* (1998) Scottish Office research currently under way. Centre for Drug Misuse Research, University of Glasgow.

National Health Services in Scotland (1998) *Drug Misuse Statistics Scotland*. Information & Statistics Division.

Plant, M. and Plant, M. (1992) *Risk-takers: Alcohol, drugs, sex and youth*. London: Tavistock/Routledge.

Shedler, B. and Block, J. (1990) Adolescent drug use and psychological health: a longitudinal inquiry. *American Psychologist*, 45, 612–630.

Sherlock, K. (1997) Psycho-social determinants of ecstasy use. PhD Thesis, University of Leeds.

Shewan, D., Dalgarno, P., Marshall, A., Lowe, M., Campbell, M., Nicholson, S., Reith, G., Mclafferty, V. and Thomson, K. (1998) Patterns of heroin use among a non-treatment sample in Glasgow (Scotland). *Addiction Research*, 6(3), 215–234.

Strathclyde Telegraph (1994) Student drugs survey, 35, 3.

Swadi, H. (1988) Drug and substance use among 3333 London adolescents. *British Journal of Addiction*, 83, 935–942.

Chapter 4

Emotional Disorders in Young People

John Pearce

What are emotions? How can they be described and measured? Certainly it is not a simple matter. For example, overwhelming feelings of panic may appear out of the blue or great happiness may be dissipated in a moment. High levels of anger are not necessarily stored away in the unconscious as a fixed quantity only to reappear in an altered form later on. It is not an unusual experience for anger to fade away with time so that little or none of it remains. Strong feelings of love may suddenly be switched to hate by what may seem to be a really insignificant event. Thus emotions can appear and disappear, change and metamorphose in the most unexpected ways. Emotions are never totally predictable and they always have the capacity to surprise.

Emotions interact with the two other main aspects of mental functioning, namely thinking and behaviour in a highly complex way. Add to this the influences of the environment, past experiences and the changes that occur with development and it becomes difficult to conceptualise. This chapter will therefore start by focusing on a model that aims to provide a simple and practical understanding of emotional processes.

UNDERSTANDING EMOTIONS

The three main aspects to mental function—feeling, thinking and behaviour—are not separate entities but always interact with each other. For example, fear can often be overcome by simply behaving in a

Young People and Mental Health. Edited by P. Aggleton, J. Hurry and I. Warwick.
© 2000 John Wiley & Sons Ltd.

confident way or thinking positive thoughts. This explains why cognitive behaviour therapy is one of the most successful approaches for treating emotional disorders. Emotions may occur alone in a simple form such as anxiety or anger, or they may be mixed and much more complicated as in jealousy or grief which contain elements of anxiety and anger as well as sadness.

Parents recognise marked differences between the way their children react emotionally. Even within the same family there can be quite marked variations. Nevertheless, it is usually possible to link a particular emotional reaction style to another member of the family and there is some evidence for a genetic component in the way in which emotions are expressed (Robinson et al., 1992). These differences can be recognised from early infancy onwards. The combination of intense emotional reactions, being slow to adapt to change and general unpredictability have been recognised as a combination of characteristics that make some children unusually difficult to manage (Chess and Thomas, 1991). Such children are significantly more likely to have temper tantrums of high intensity and frequency. Babies who have stable emotions and cope well with change are likely to be easy to bring up, although there is a tendency for temperamental characteristics to fluctuate during the process of child development due to variable genetic influences (Plomin, 1983).

It is the negative emotions such as misery, anger and anxiety that tend to concern us more than positive emotions such as joy, excitement and contentment. This is quite understandable because it is very rare for positive emotions to become a problem or to develop into a disorder. This chapter will mainly focus on the negative emotions because they are the ones that indicate when something is wrong and where something needs to be altered or improved. Fortunately, we normally experience many more positive than negative emotions so there is something seriously wrong if this is not the case.

EMOTIONAL DEVELOPMENT

Observing the process of emotional development in young children can help to explain how emotions function and interact with each other. A baby's cry at birth is a non-specific expression of distress or discomfort, and the reason for the crying is usually unclear, although parents have been shown to be able to distinguish between the cry of hunger and of pain in babies (Zeskind et al., 1985). However, it is a common experience for many parents that it is quite difficult to distinguish one cry from another, even in older infants. While it may be difficult to work out the significance of a baby crying, the baby's emotions do elicit caring and protective responses in others. This important function of emotions in eliciting empathic responses continues throughout life (Stotland, 1969).

A significant step in emotional development occurs when a baby first smiles and the emotional bond between parent and child is greatly strengthened. At this early stage the smiling has much more significance for the parent than for the child. It motivates parents to work hard at building up a relationship and to be even more responsive to their child's emotional reactions. During the first few months, babies develop the full range of facial expression associated with emotions such as sadness, anger, disgust, fear and contempt (Izard et al., 1980). However, it should not be assumed that these represent the fully developed inner experience of these emotions. It is not until around the age of six to eight months that babies show a very specific emotional expression such as clinging behaviour and reassurance seeking that confirms the child's inner experience of separation anxiety, and that signals the development of an emotional attachment to the parent. Thus, separation anxiety is developmentally the first specific emotion and it serves as a reminder of the fundamental link between emotions and relationships.

The next stage in the development of emotions occurs around the age of 18 months to three years, when toddlers develop temper tantrums. At this stage, it is clear that the child is not just angry in a general and unfocused way but that the anger is definitely directed against a specific person. As in the case of separation anxiety, the environmental trigger will make the angry nature of the emotional response quite clear. Nobody who has witnessed a temper tantrum will have any doubt that the child is angry whereas a screaming baby could equally well be in pain or simply bored and hungry.

It is not until around about the age of seven or eight years that children gain the capacity to experience feelings of depression (Harrington, 1993). There is no doubt that younger children experience sadness and may feel miserable, but these are non-specific emotional responses to distress. This generalised distressed response is present from an early age and only gradually develops into a specific depressive reaction. The key elements of a depressive emotional response are thoughts of hopelessness and worthlessness. These two cognitions require a level of maturity and self-awareness that does not usually crystallise until around the age of seven or eight. The concept of time is required in order for a child to feel hopeless about the future and this does not develop fully until around the age of seven years. The concept of death requires an understanding of 'forever' as well as an awareness of the uniqueness of the individual self that cannot be changed or replaced. Children below the age of seven are gradually developing an understanding of death but it is not until after this age that—in the West anyway—it becomes reasonably well established. Fortunately, suicidal behaviour is rare in young children, but around the age of eight years clear suicidal impulses do occasionally occur (Hawton, 1986).

This developmental model of emotional responses can also be used to explain the relationship between stress and emotions. The first specific emotion to be experienced at low levels of stress is anxiety. As the stress

Anxiety is the first emotion to be felt by the child when experiencing stress

increases the anxiety may develop into anger but it is only at very high levels of stress that a depressive reaction will develop. This explains why anxiety is the most frequently experienced emotion and why all other emotional reactions contain an element of anxiety.

Naturally there is considerable individual variation in the way emotions are experienced. Some children are much more emotionally vulnerable than others and have high levels of arousal even when resting and are slow to habituate to repeated stressful stimuli. Such children are much more likely to experience anxiety and to have a lower threshold for anger and depressive feelings. Other children who have been exposed to repeated adverse life events can easily develop a negative view of themselves and of the world and will therefore be more vulnerable to depressive thoughts and feelings.

A further factor in the way emotions are experienced may be the effect of hormonal changes during adolescence. This probably has the effect of heightening the experience of all emotions and therefore increasing the frequency of feelings of anxiety, anger and depression (Rutter, 1980). The precise reason for this is not known but it is reasonable to assume that the sex hormones sensitise neurotransmitter systems in the brain. It is interesting to note that emotional problems occur with rather similar frequencies in boys and girls up to adolescence but after that stage emotional problems are more common in females (Shepherd *et al.*, 1971).

Perhaps the most striking issue that arises from the developmental model of emotional expression is the apparent lack of recognition given to anger and its disorders. Nevertheless, it is reasonable to assume that conduct problems are very closely related to anger which is often characterised by aggressive behaviours. Although the focus of this chapter is on anxiety and depression in young people it is important to remember that in terms of the developmental model (Figure 4.1) anger may often form a link between anxiety and depression.

SOME DEFINITIONS

Anxiety is the feeling of uneasiness or tension caused by the anticipation of a feared situation. The word anxious is closely related to the Latin verb *angere*, which means to torment or to strangle. It is also the origin for the word anger, which is another example of the link between anxiety and anger. If someone is described as anxious or as suffering from anxiety it may mean that this is an entirely normal and expected response to the anticipation of fear. It may also describe a person who is generally rather sensitive, has high levels of arousal and a low threshold for experiencing anxiety. The former is a description of an emotional state and the latter is a description of an emotional trait. Anxiety can also be used as a description of a pathological state where the emotional reaction is out of proportion to what would normally be expected to the

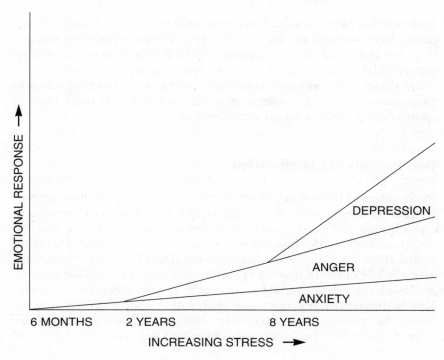

Figure 4.1

extent that it can be considered a disorder of anxiety. The word depression is also used in these different ways to describe a normal emotional reaction, an emotional response style or a disorder of mental function.

The Difference Between a Disorder and an Illness

It is important to be able to distinguish between normal mood states and pathological states or disorders. A disorder occurs where the emotional state is of such severity and/or duration that it interferes with everyday life and is out of proportion to what would normally be expected in the circumstances taking into account the young person's family background, culture and stage of development. An emotional disorder is an extension of normality and occurs at a particular point on a continuum of distress where it is so severe as to cause disability. An illness, on the other hand, is where the symptoms are qualitatively different from normality. For example, someone suffering from a depressive illness might experience paranoid delusions or hallucinations that would be quite outside the range of normal experience. The difference between 'normal' and pathological depression is determined partly by the extent of the disability and partly by how 'out of proportion' it is in relation to the apparent causes. For example, a child brought up in an abusive and dysfunctional family might develop suicidal depression in later adolescence. The traumatic events from the past do not explain the suicidal state, but they may be contributing factors. It is wise never to assume that suicidal behaviour is a 'normal' reaction, however stressful the event. Clearly, the notion of 'disability' and being 'out of proportion to the apparent causes' is a matter of judgement and little more than an approach to simplify a highly complex area.

Two Systems of Classification

The problem of definition is compounded by the fact that there are two systems of classification: the World Health Organisation International Classification of Diseases, now in its tenth version (ICD 10), and the American Psychiatric Association *Diagnostic and Statistical Manual of Mental Disorders*, now in its fourth version (DSM IV). Each version has been slightly different from the previous one and although the systems of classifications are gradually approaching each other there are still notable differences. It is fair to say that neither system is entirely satisfactory. Nevertheless the systems of classification do serve as a structure around which disorders can be conceptualised and research carried out.

ANXIETY STATES

It is important to remember that anxiety is an essential emotion that serves to protect us from danger. People function at their best when they have a reasonable level of anxiety and arousal. Young people who experience low levels of anxiety due to their temperamental make-up or their developmental immaturity often engage in dangerous activities. Risk-taking behaviour generally increases during adolescence and it is perhaps fortunate that this coincides with a time when there is an increased awareness and experience of mood problems, possibly due to the hormonal changes during puberty (Angold and Rutter, 1992).

Epidemiology

In addition to generalised anxiety, a number of different anxiety states have been identified. These include separation anxiety, avoidant disorder, overanxious disorder, simple phobia, school phobia, social anxiety, panic disorder and sometimes obsessional compulsive disorder. While it would seem to be evident that there are different forms of anxiety, there is only a moderate level of agreement about the different sub-categories. It is therefore difficult to get an agreed prevalence rate for anxiety in young people. Werry (1991) reported that individual symptoms of anxiety occur in up to

36% of adolescents. He also noted that adolescents were more concerned about social issues than younger children, whose main worry was about future events. Anxiety disorders generally become increasingly frequent as adolescence approaches (Graham, 1979). Boys and girls report similar levels of anxiety symptoms until adolescence, when boys report less anxiety than girls and the main worries of adolescence are academic failure, social embarrassment, death and wars.

Another problem in determining the prevalence rate of anxiety states is that it all depends on precisely where the line is drawn between normal and pathological. For example, Kashani and Orvaschel (1988) noted that 17.3% of adolescents experienced significant anxiety but this rate was reduced to half that level when using the criteria of significant handicap in everyday function. However, most studies seem to agree that anxiety disorders of one sort or another occur in at least 5% of young people and it is unlikely that clinically significant anxiety occurs in more than 10% of this group. Less serious anxiety symptoms are much more common, occurring in at least 30% of the adolescent population at any one time.

Co-morbidity

Because anxiety is the most commonly experienced emotion, it is not surprising that anxiety is often found to be associated with other clinical disorders. At least 30% of young people already suffering from one type of anxiety state have another associated anxiety disorder at the same time and high levels of depression have also been found to be associated with anxiety (Anderson *et al.*, 1987). Bernstein (1991) reported the coexistence of depression and anxiety in 50% of school refusers and this group tended to have more severe disorder. Anxiety has also been reported to coexist with attention deficit and hyperactivity disorder (ADHD) in some 25% of cases and much the same findings have been reported for conduct disorder (Anderson *et al.*, 1987).

Another type of association links anxiety with substance abuse. The hypothesis is that young people find that they are able to treat the uncomfortable symptoms of anxiety with substances such as alcohol, marihuana or opiates, which may lead to later dependency (Cambor and Millman, 1996). This association is difficult to prove because young people who regularly use or misuse substances tend to suffer from a wide range of psychopathology.

The Associated Features of Anxiety

Children who experience severe anxiety are more likely to come from families with an increased frequency of anxiety problems. This is particularly so if there is a family history of maternal depression (Moreau *et al.*, 1989), which once again highlights the important relationship between anxiety and depression. Socio-cultural factors also play a part in influencing anxiety states (Fonesca *et al.*, 1994). For example, Dutch children score higher for anxiety and Portuguese score lower than most children, and young people from dysfunctional families are more likely to express fears of violence compared with those from higher social status families, who are more likely to express fears of accidents. This suggests that anxiety symptoms are strongly influenced by the real as well as perceived dangers that young people are exposed to. Sleep and appetite problems are commonly associated with extreme anxiety. It is likely that both are the result of the secondary effects of high arousal levels associated with anxiety. These changes in sleep and eating patterns are non-specific because they are also associated with depression and indeed with any form of stress including excitement. The physical symptoms of high states of arousal form an important component of anxiety states and are outlined in Table 4.1.

Anxiety may present initially with physical rather than psychological symptoms. However, it should be possible to make a diagnosis of an anxiety state on the basis of the pattern of symptoms. It is important to remember that anxiety states can occur in young people who appear entirely normal and for the most part behave normally. A good example of this is a specific phobia where the behaviour is quite normal provided the feared situation is avoided. Even in generalised anxiety states the distress may be experienced in a very personal way and not demonstrated to the outside world, and it is easy to see why anxiety is classified as an internalising disorder. However, externalising disorders, such as conduct disorder, may be associated with high levels of arousal and anxiety. In this case, the anxiety may have the effect of reducing

Table 4.1 The physical symptoms of anxiety

Affected system	Resulting symptoms
Rapid heartbeat	Palpitations
Rapid breathing	Shortness of breath
Muscle tension	Aches and pains
Changes in gastrointestinal function	Nausea/diarrhoea
Changes in eye muscle tone	Blurred vision
Changes in cerebral function	Poor concentration
Changes in the genito-urinary system	Frequency of micturition
Changes in the balance between the sympathetic and the para sympathetic system	Dry mouth and increased sweating

offending behaviour or at least making the young person more responsive to appropriate punishment (Walker *et al.*, 1991).

Specific Forms of Anxiety

The difficulty in separating the various forms of anxiety has already been alluded to above. The shared characteristics include a high level of physiological arousal that is sufficient to cause physical and/or emotional discomfort. In addition, there is a perception of danger and threat that may be either real or imagined. The symptoms tend to vary in strength to quite a marked degree over time and depending on the situation. All anxiety states have an 'infectious' quality. In other words, it is difficult to be with someone who is in an anxious state without also feeling anxious oneself. This can be an aid to recognising anxiety in others even if they try to hide their feelings of anxiety.

Phobias

A phobia is an overwhelming sense of fear that is out of proportion to the situation, is beyond control or reason and leads to avoidance of feared stimulus. It is also maladaptive and will reoccur whenever the person is in the feared situation. Simple phobias that relate to fear of animals, heights or the dark often have an onset in early childhood. More complex phobias that involve social situations commonly start in adolescence. Epidemiological surveys have generally come up with a frequency of between 2% and 3% prevalence rate for specific phobias in the general population of young people, with an increased frequency in females compared with males (Anderson *et al.*, 1987).

Genetic studies involving identical and non-identical twins have shown that there is a significant genetic component in the aetiology of phobias (Kendler *et al.*, 1992). However, specific phobias are also quite strongly influenced by environmental factors such as direct exposure to the feared situation or witnessing other people experiencing a phobic reaction.

It is paradoxical that even someone with a very severe phobia may live a perfectly normal life and be entirely symptom free provided they avoid the feared situation. This is not too difficult to achieve with a fear of snakes or claustrophobia, but much more difficult with agoraphobia or social phobia where avoidance reactions can seriously impinge upon a person's everyday life.

The assessment of a phobic state requires an analysis of both the subjective experience that the phobia causes and the objective effects that the phobia has on the person's everyday life. A useful strategy is to keep a daily diary that records both the subjective feelings of discomfort and the avoidant responses. It is also helpful to obtain a direct observation of how a young person reacts when experiencing the phobia.

School Refusal

School refusal is a good example of a complex phobic reaction where very careful assessment is required in order to understand the process by which the phobia developed. For example, the phobia might be a very normal and understandable reaction to genuine fear of bullying or academic failure. On the other hand, the phobic response may occur against a background of separation anxiety or depression. Occasionally school phobia may simply be presented as an excuse for not attending school.

It is important to distinguish school refusal from truancy. A simple distinction is that the whereabouts of the school refusing child is always known whereas this is usually not the case for the truant. Young people with school refusal tend to come from relatively stable home backgrounds and to be socially conforming with at least average academic achievement. Truancy on the other hand is usually part of the pattern of antisocial behaviour and academic failure. Symptoms associated with school refusal are often absent during weekends and school holidays but start to cause problems shortly before a return to school is due.

Separation Anxiety

Separation anxiety occurs as part of normal development and is most obvious between the age of one to three years. Separation anxiety may become a problem if it persists into later childhood. The typical child with separation anxiety will find any separation from the parent difficult and this will be particularly noticeable when being left at school or with strangers. As children enter adolescence, the prevalence rate of separation anxiety disorder reduces steadily and occurs in less than 1% of teenagers (Kashani and Orvaschel, 1998).

Overanxious Disorder

The different forms of anxiety commonly occur in association with a generalised anxiety state, sometimes called overanxious disorder. This is the most common form of anxiety disorder and occurs in approximately 7% of teenagers (Kashani and Orvaschel, 1988). An important finding in relation to generalised anxiety in teenagers is the close link with depressive disorder. Strauss et al. (1988) reported that 47% of adolescents with generalised anxiety also suffered from a major depressive disorder. Further evidence of a strong link between anxiety and depression is the finding that mothers with a depressive disorder are more likely to have children with generalised anxiety (Weissman et al., 1992).

Social Phobia

Social phobia characteristically occurs with greatest frequency during adolescence, which is in any case a time of acute self-consciousness. Although shyness is very common during adolescence, true social phobia with typical avoidance reactions that are disabling occurs in about 1% of young people (McGee *et al.*, 1990). An extreme form of social phobia is elective mutism where children will only speak to people who they know well and trust. As with any other anxiety state, there is a strong tendency for social phobia to run in families, with both a genetic and a learned element.

Post Traumatic Stress Disorder (PTSD)

Post traumatic stress disorder has been closely linked with anxiety states. At the same time it is often described as a normal reaction to an abnormal situation and there is continuing debate as to just how abnormal this reaction is to events that by definition are exceptionally threatening or catastrophic and outside normal experience. Key features include:

- Persistently re-experiencing the traumatic event
- Avoiding stimuli associated with the trauma
- A numbing of general responsiveness
- Evidence of increased arousal and anxiety

It may continue directly on from the event or have a delayed onset. Many young people with PTSD have associated symptoms of depression and anxiety. Although PTSD is a clearly recognisable form of emotional response, it is probably best to see it as a separate condition similar to bereavement reactions rather than to consider it a form of anxiety. Both bereavement reactions and PTSD are highly complex emotional states, involving mixed emotions and marked changes in cognition and behaviour that are directly related to an exceptionally distressing event. However, both reactions may become abnormal if they persist for longer than three months or so and continue to interfere with a person's everyday life.

Obsessional Compulsive Disorder (OCD)

Obsessional compulsive disorder (OCD) is a condition that is closely linked with anxiety but like PTSD is best considered as a separate entity. Obsessions are repeated thoughts or impulses that are intrusive and unwanted. Compulsions are the repetitive behaviours that are performed in response to the obsession and have to be carried out in a stereotyped way. Often, the obsessional thought will involve a fear or anxiety about a perceived threat. Anxiety and tension are reduced by following a particular ritual, but the benefit does not last long, so the whole process has to be repeated again and again. There is increasing evidence that OCD is very closely related to abnormal brain function. Family studies show that there is little overlap between anxiety states and OCD.

The prevalence rate of OCD in adolescents is approximately 1% (Flament et al., 1988). OCD tends to occur in episodes with relatively symptom-free periods of respite in between, which is unlike most anxiety states. Also, OCD responds remarkably well to medication that inhibits serotonin re-uptake in the brain and this contrasts with anxiety states where medication only plays a very limited role.

Panic Disorder

Panic disorder is another example of a condition which although closely linked with anxiety is probably best considered as a separate entity. It was not formally recognised as a disorder until the 1980s and very little research has been carried out on the condition in young people. The key feature of panic disorder is that overwhelming feelings of intense fear and discomfort occur spontaneously and suddenly without any obvious explanation. The attacks are accompanied by very high states of physiological arousal and fear of dying or losing control. The peak age of onset is during adolescence, although adults with panic disorder often describe feelings of panic starting in earlier childhood. Lifetime prevalence of panic disorder has been reported as being around 1.5% (Robins et al., 1984). The spontaneous nature of panic disorder differentiates it from the feelings of panic associated with phobias and anxiety which are triggered by specific events or situations.

The tendency for panic disorder to start during adolescence and the relative responsiveness to treatment with anti-depressants suggest that altered neuro-chemical sensitivity is a major part of the problem. It is interesting to note that panic can be induced in people who already have panic disorder by relatively low doses of caffeine. Panic can be induced in quite normal individuals as a result of substance abuse, especially the abuse of amphetamine-related compounds, and as a result of drug or alcohol withdrawal. Certain types of epilepsy can also cause panic and symptoms of panic can occur in association with asthma, heart disorders and various metabolic disorders.

Risk and Protective Factors

There are some risk factors such as female gender and genetic loading that are fixed. In spite of this, most young people with these risk factors do not suffer from anxiety states. Perhaps the most important risk factor is anxiety itself, the reason being that anxiety so easily leads to even more anxiety. This is because anxiety is highly 'infectious' and more easily picked up than any other emotion. Thus, having an anxious parent, teacher or family doctor can make all the difference to how young people manage their feelings of anxiety. It is a common experience that anxious young people tend to provoke protective responses in others, especially their parents. But the desire to protect children from the discomfort of anxiety and to provide them with high levels of security may actually increase feelings of anxiety. For example, checking to see if a burglar is hiding behind the curtains in order to reassure a young person would almost invariably increase anxiety.

Any stimulant drug is likely to increase the risk of developing an anxiety state but there is considerable individual variation. Withdrawal from sedative drugs such as alcohol, opiates and barbiturates usually results in a compensatory phase of increased arousal which in turn increases the risk of anxiety.

Young people who have not been exposed to anxiety provoking situations in a carefully managed and graduated way are at increased risk for developing anxiety states. Learning to cope with anxiety is particularly important for young people who have high levels of arousal as part of their temperamental make-up. This is because a high arousal when at rest is usually associated with slow habituation to anxiety provoking stimuli.

Protection against anxiety is not merely achieved by removing risk factors. Young people can be given positive protection from anxiety by learning to recognise and understand their emotions. Anxiety provoking situations that are identified at an early stage and dealt with appropriately will make them significantly less likely to cause problems in the future. Managing anxiety provoking situations in this way will normally lead to an increase in self-confidence. It is important to remember that self-confidence only increases as a result of action and achievement. It does not increase by simply talking or thinking about the feared situation—repeating 'I can do it' to oneself makes no difference to confidence levels until you actually have done it!

Anxiety Management

Perhaps the most important aspect of treatment for anxiety is to remember how 'contagious' anxiety is. It is therefore important to identify who is actually generating the anxiety because this may not be originating from the young person. It is particularly important to identify this in families where anxiety can cycle between family members and eventually spiral out of control. With this is mind, it is clearly important to try and remain calm and confident, carefully monitoring one's own anxiety levels. If someone is found to be contributing to the general atmosphere of anxiety and tension then steps should be taken to protect the young person from this influence.

The key for all treatment is that the fear or anxiety has to be faced up to. Avoidance reactions will only make matters worse. There are two main ways of facing up to fear.

The In At The Deep End Approach

Here, the fear is tackled immediately and head on. The school phobic child is made to return to school. The child who is anxious in the dark is put in a darkened room. The young person with dog phobia is given a dog to look after, and so on. The principle is very similar to learning to swim by jumping in at the deep end. The 'in at the deep end approach' can be successful in reducing levels of anxiety but there can be significant risks attached. Anxiety can actually be increased if the person is not successful in learning a coping strategy. This rapid approach to treatment can only be justified if there is full agreement on the part of the young person and if there is general agreement that what is being expected of the young person is not unreasonable. For example, it is not acceptable to force a school phobic teenager back to the school where he is being bullied. This type of intervention needs to be very carefully and confidently managed.

The Gradual Approach

This method of treating anxiety is sometimes called 'desensitisation' and it involves carefully graduated exposure to the feared situation. The key to success is to make sure that the young person never experiences a level of anxiety that cannot be managed quite easily. Intervention usually starts by agreeing a hierarchy of anxiety provoking situations. At the top of the list for somebody with spider phobia would be something like having a large hairy spider crawl over the face. And at the other end of the hierarchy there might be a picture of a tiny and rather friendly spider looked at from across the other side of the room. The management plan would aim to assist the young person in progressing gradually to the top of the hierarchy by working their way up the hierarchy, only moving on when that particular stage has been successfully achieved. The problem with this approach is that it requires high levels of motivation and perseverance. There is also plenty of scope for anxiety levels to build up quickly at any stage if the rate of progression is too fast or the person is having a bad day.

Other Ways of Working

There are several variations on these two main approaches. For example, the exposure can sometimes be carried out in the imagination. Younger children are particularly good at doing this but some imaginative teenagers can also be helped in this way. Relaxation can assist in the management of anxiety since it is extremely difficult if not impossible to be anxious without being tense at the same time. There are marked individual differences in how well and in what way people are best able to relax. So it is important to adjust the relaxation technique to suit the person.

Psychotherapy or counselling is often recommended for the alleviation of anxiety states either on an individual basis or in the form of group therapy. There is little evidence that any of these approaches are effective unless they are aimed at helping the young person to face up to the fears by setting appropriate targets of achievement. Simply knowing that other people have similar experiences or understanding the origins of the anxiety according to a particular theory might make a person feel better about being anxious but it will not change the anxiety itself unless it is followed by action.

The drug treatment of anxiety states has been rather disappointing due mainly to side effects and the fact that symptoms tend to return immediately the medication is stopped (Klein and Last, 1989). On the other hand, drugs can be used as an adjunct to help a young person face up to a feared situation. Drugs should only be prescribed for young people with anxiety disorders by doctors who are both trained and experienced in their use. They should never be the first line response and should always be used in conjunction with a support treatment aimed at helping the young person to achieve the ultimate goal of facing their fears. Obsessional compulsive disorder and panic disorder are different from anxiety states in many ways as has been outlined above. They are both more likely to respond to treatment with a combination of cognitive and behavioural approaches and drugs that inhibit the reuptake of serotonin.

Self medication with alcohol, cannabis and other illegal substances is not uncommon amongst young people with anxiety states. The risk of getting into drug-related problems is likely to be higher than normal because the immediate relief of anxiety symptoms may drive the young person to repeatedly take more drugs (Cambor and Millman, 1996).

What Happens to Anxious Young People?

There have been few detailed studies of the long-term outcome for anxiety in childhood and adolescence. However, by combining cross-sectional and longitudinal data and looking at retrospective studies in adults, it is clear that anxiety states tend to persist over long periods and follow a relapsing and remitting course. This means that each episode of anxiety disorder is likely to improve spontaneously, but may appear again later on. This underlines the importance of teaching young people to recognise their feelings of anxiety and to manage them in an appropriate way at the earliest possible stage. Very few people suffer from lifelong disabling anxiety disorder and where they do this is usually complicated by a range of other factors such as significant personality problems.

Where anxiety is linked with depression, the outlook is more closely associated with the depressive disorder than with the anxiety. On the other hand, if anxiety occurs with attention deficit disorder or conduct disorder, the outlook for these two conditions appears to be rather less serious than where anxiety is absent.

DEPRESSIVE DISORDERS

There has been debate as to whether depression in young people manifests itself in a different way from depression in adults. So far, the evidence suggests that there is not much difference although the younger the child the more diffuse the symptoms are. As in adults, the negative cognitions of hopelessness and worthlessness are central features of depression. Other important factors include loss of enjoyment, loss of energy, loss of sleep and loss of weight. Anger in the form of irritability and short temper together with anxiety symptoms are important associated features of depression, as are suicidal thoughts (Pearce, 1978).

Depression can occur as a dimensional disorder along a continuum from mild to very severe or it can occur as separate discrete categories of depression. On the one hand, there is a depressive syndrome also called major depressive disorder or dysthymia, the symptoms of which can occur quite normally in the general population. On the other hand, there is depressive illness, also called bipolar disorder, characterised by extremely rapid changes of mood or psychotic symptoms such as delusions or hallucinations which do not occur normally in the general population.

The Epidemiology of Depression

A review of the epidemiology of depression by Poznanski and Mokros (1994) concluded that significant depression in young people had a prevalence rate of between 2% and 6% depending on the diagnostic criteria. The frequency of depressive disorders increases markedly during adolescence and the increase is greater in girls than in boys. Bipolar disorder or manic depressive psychosis is much more rare and has an estimated lifetime prevalence of approximately 1%. The onset occurs in adolescence in less than 30% of cases (Strober et al., 1988). There is some evidence that there has been a general increase in the rate of depression amongst young people over the last thirty or forty years and this has been paralleled by an increase in adolescent suicide (Poznanski and Mokros, 1994).

Very high levels of co-morbidity are found in association with a diagnosis of depression so that it would be quite unusual to come across a young person with depressive disorder who did not have other significant problems. Kashani *et al.* (1987) found the following associated conditions in young people diagnosed as depressed:

- 75% Anxiety disorder
- 50% Oppositional disorder
- 33% Conduct disorder
- 25% Substance abuse

Different Types of Depression

Dysthymia (Depressive Neurosis)

Dysthymia is a mild and chronic form of depression where the condition almost becomes a style of life. Pessimism and low self-esteem are important features and there may be other associated depressive symptoms. It is unclear how useful this concept is and what the significance is for the person who suffers from it. What does seem to be clear is that it is not unusual for a more acute depressive disorder to occur in the context of long-standing dysthymia (Kovacs *et al.*, 1984).

Depressive Syndrome

This term is used to describe the characteristic cluster of symptoms that occur together with depression. It avoids the issue as to whether or not the depression is a disorder, an illness or merely a normal response to adversity and it does not necessarily imply any degree of handicap or disability. It is a useful distinction between a simple lowering of mood occurring in isolation and a clinically more significant condition where the low mood has 'picked up' more symptoms. Although Zeitlin (1986) found that there was no link between an adult diagnosis of depression and an earlier diagnosis of depression in childhood, there was continuity of a group of symptoms that were characteristic of the depressive syndrome from childhood to adulthood.

Major Depressive Disorder

This is the main diagnostic category for depression used in the *Diagnostic and Statistical Manual of Mental Disorders* of the American Psychiatric Association. At least five of nine characteristic symptoms have to be present for at least two weeks and represent a change from a person's usual functioning. The symptoms must include either depressed or irritable mood or loss of interest and pleasure and there should be functional impairment. These criteria make it quite easy to diagnose depression without the key features of depressed mood together with feelings of worthlessness and hopelessness. It is not surprising that epidemiological studies from the USA have identified relatively high rates of depression, and have found it possible to diagnose major depressive disorder in children as young as two and a half years. Nevertheless, the concept of major depressive disorder is a useful one in that it emphasises the point that it is a significant problem which should not be ignored.

Bipolar Depression (Psychotic Depression)

Bipolar depression is characterised by episodes of typical but severe depressive disorder alternating with mania or hypomania. It is a disabling condition that is often associated with psychotic symptoms. One of the most striking features of bipolar disorder in adolescence is the marked change from previously normal behaviour. Often the symptoms are quite extreme and occasionally bizarre. The diagnosis should be considered in any case where there is a regular pattern of marked mood changes and difficult behaviour or where there is a family history of psychiatric treatment for depression.

Depressive Conduct Disorder

This term is sometimes used to described those children where depression and conduct disorder seem to have equal importance. Certainly it is not unusual to come across young people who have low self-esteem and a feeling of failure who seem to gain satisfaction from deliberately engaging in antisocial behaviour.

Cyclothymia

This is chronic disturbance of mood where there are swings up as well as down. The condition is rather more severe than the normal mood swings of adolescence but not severe enough to cause much disability.

Anaclitic Depression and the Depressive Position

Although both these terms include the word depression, neither condition is actually related to depressive disorder. The word anaclitic means dependency and anaclitic depression was used to describe the reactions of infants who were separated from their parents in a nursery (Spitz and Wolf, 1946). The depressive position was a term used by Melanie Klein to describe the stage in infancy when a baby realises that she or he cannot control the world all the time or possess their mother totally

(Klein, 1949). Both are interesting ideas but have nothing to do with depression in young people.

Grief

The symptoms of grief and depression are very similar and easily confused. Grief that persists and becomes pathological may in time develop into depression. The key difference between the two emotional states is that in grief, although there may be feelings of self-blame and guilt, feelings of worthlessness do not occur. Suicidal thoughts, if present, are more closely related to joining the deceased rather than to get away from oneself and life in general.

Suicidal Thoughts and Behaviour

There is a close link between suicide and depression, but there are many other causes for suicidal attempts. Many suicide attempts in young people are motivated more by avoidance of feared situations or anger directed at a particular person following an argument. A common theme for suicide attempts is an overwhelming feeling of despair and being over-powered by strong emotions. Nevertheless, more than 25% of young people have suicidal thoughts and the risk of suicidal behaviour must be taken seriously (Pearce, 1978).

Risk and Preventive Factors

It would be very unlikely for a young person to develop a depressive disorder if he or she has high self-esteem and has not suffered any major adverse life events or had any significant losses, unless there is a high genetic loading for depressive illness. Most cases of depression in young people are strongly related to easily identifiable adverse life events, especially those involving loss, abuse and rejection (Reynolds and Johnston, 1994). This may take the form of a single event or a series of apparently minor adverse events that compound each other over time. It is important to remember that some adversities are much less obvious than others. For example, bullying, abuse and marital disharmony are often kept secret. Academic or personal failure may not seem significant to others but to the individual might feel as though it is disastrous. Almost all drugs of abuse can cause depression although coexisting adverse life events and low self-esteem are often associated with substance abuse.

A risk factor that is often forgotten about is depression itself. Depressive disorder leads to isolation, giving up previous activities and generally adopting a lifestyle where there are likely to be few positive and rewarding experiences. This is not to say that living a life of pleasure will protect against depression, but high self-esteem and a good level of self-confidence will.

The Neurobiology of Depression in Young People

There is a vast body of research that links brain structure and function with various emotions. Little of this research has been done on
young people, but there is no reason to think that the findings would
be very different. Numerous abnormalities of the neuro-transmitter
system have been found but the significance of these is not well
understood. What seems to be most important is not the actual levels
or type of neuro-transmitter but rather the balance between the
various neuro-transmitters at the different sites where they act
(Emslie *et al.*, 1994). Neuro-endocrine abnormalities have been regularly reported showing alterations in the secretion of cortisol growth
hormone and thyroid hormones (Casat and Powell, 1988). Again,
there is uncertainty about the significance of these changes and
whether or not they are specific to depression or whether they are
non-specific reactions to stress.

Sleep disturbances are a consistent finding in depression, mostly in
the form of problems with waking. There are reports of a shortened time
before the onset of the first rapid eye movement (REM) sleep and an
increased amount of REM activity (Emslie *et al.*, 1994). This seems to be
more marked in children with more severe depression who are suicidal
or who have required inpatient treatment.

Interventions to Alleviate Depression

The mainstay of treatment is to try and remove the cause of the depression if at all possible. In many cases the adverse events or losses will be
irreversible. Nevertheless, it is essential to make sure that any remaining
issues concerning the past events are resolved as quickly as possible
(Stark, 1990); for example, contact problems after a divorce, unresolved
grief following a significant loss or relationship difficulties following a
major argument. These difficulties need to be tackled with a down to
earth, problem solving approach using the method described by Stark
(1990). This involves three stages of cognitive restructuring at which the
following questions are asked:

1. What is the evidence for the child's pessimistic and depressive
    thoughts?
2. What alternative, more positive ways of looking at the past events
    are there?
3. How could the future be better than the depressed child expects?

It is helpful to know that the natural history of a depressive episode in
young people is for it to resolve spontaneously (Harrington, 1993). This
usually happens within six months to a year even without treatment,

unless there is some adverse influence actively keeping the person depressed or if the depression has become self perpetuating as described above.

The primary problem in depression is the abnormal thinking processes that lead young people to view the world, themselves and the future in a very pessimistic and negative way. It is therefore quite appropriate that cognitive therapy is currently the preferred treatment option. This involves helping young people to identify the abnormal depressive thinking patterns and to actively learn to replace these with more appropriate and positive thoughts.

Anti-depressant drugs are commonly used for adult depressive disorder, where their efficacy has been well established. This is not the case for young people, where there is much less research and what research there is has limited scientific credibility in most cases. At the present time there is no evidence that anti-depressant medication is effective in treating depression in young people. Equally there is no evidence that it is ineffective and most clinicians conclude that anti-depressant medication has a place in the treatment for certain individuals where other first line treatment has failed. In view of the lack of proved efficacy of anti-depressants, and the general complexity of treatment resistant cases, prescribing should be left to those who have special training and experience of this condition.

Family therapy may be indicated where there is a dysfunctional family system. It is not unusual that the young person's depression is a factor in causing or maintaining the family problems. Most parents find it extremely difficult to provide an appropriate level of sympathetic support and understanding for their irritable, withdrawn and depressed teenager. Sometimes it is helpful to explain to parents that their child is ill and needs to be treated in much the same way as one would treat somebody with pneumonia or chickenpox. While the young person is ill parents need to provide support and sympathy and make allowances for bad behaviour. They need to provide extra time and attention and deal with the depressed young person in an optimistic way without forcing them to do anything more than they can cope with.

The increased risk of attempted suicide must always be kept in mind. Low self-esteem and feelings of hopelessness accompanied by expressions of suicidal ideas must always be taken seriously. Simple measures to restrict access to the methods for suicide together with increased supervision and monitoring are appropriate ways of showing care and appreciation for how the suicidal person feels. If there is reason to believe that there is imminent risk of suicidal behaviour a detailed risk assessment should be made by a suitably trained professional.

Finally, it is important to help young people to learn from the experience of being depressed so that in the future they will be able to identify the type of stresses that they find difficulty coping with. The young person needs to find a way to reduce stress rather than let it build up to the point where he or she can no longer cope.

Outcome of Depressive Disorder

The normal expectation is for depression to resolve spontaneously in less than a year. There is however a tendency for depression to reoccur; for example, Kovacs *et al.* (1984) reported a 70% relapse rate within five years. Zeitlin (1986) reported the continuity of depressive symptoms from childhood to adulthood and Harrington *et al.* (1990) has shown that depression has a strong tendency to continue into adult life and to be associated with a generally poor outlook when compared to young people who have non-depressive psychiatric disorders.

One of the problems with depression in young people is that it occurs at a time when rapid changes are taking place and important decisions have to be made. Academic progress is critical at this stage and any time lost can be difficult to make up. This, together with the relatively poor outlook for depression in young people, confirms the need for active intervention at an early stage.

CONCLUSIONS

Anxiety and depression are common symptoms and have a complex interaction with each other. An understanding of the development of emotional responses helps to explain the nature of this relationship. Youth and adolescence are times when emotions run high, which makes it especially important to be able to distinguish between a normal and a pathological emotional state. The latter is identified by characteristic patterns of symptoms which interfere with everyday life. One of the developmental tasks for young people is to set a direction for their adult life. Any emotional problem during this time may interfere with this process and have serious consequences. This chapter outlines the epidemiology of the various disorders of anxiety and depression and how they might best be understood and managed so that young people are able to make the most of their future.

REFERENCES

Anderson, J.C., Williams, S.M., McGee, R. and Silva, P. (1987) DSM-III disorders in pre-adolescent children: Prevalence in a large sample from the general population. *Archives of General Psychiatry*, 44, 69–76.

Angold, A. and Rutter, M. (1992) Effects of age and pubertal status on depression in a large clinical sample. *Development and Psychopathology*, 4, 5–28.

Bernstein, G.A. (1991) Comorbidity and severity of anxiety and depressive disorders in a clinic sample. *Journal of the American Academy of Child and Adolescent Psychiatry*, 30, 519–532.

Cambor, R.L. and Millman, R.B. (1996) Alcohol and drug abuse in adolescence. In M. Lewis (Ed.) *Child and Adolescent Psychiatry: a Comprehensive Textbook*, pp. 69, 736–752. Baltimore: Williams & Wilkins.

Casat, C. and Powell, K. (1988) Utility of the dexamethazone suppression test in children and adolescents with major depressive disorder. *Journal of Clinical Psychiatry*, 49, 390–393.

Chess, S. and Thomas, A. (1991) Temperament. In M. Lewis (Ed.) *Child and Adolescent Psychiatry. A Comprehensive Textbook*, pp. 145–159. Baltimore: Williams & Wilkins.

Emslie, G.J., Weinberg, W.A., Kennard, B.D. and Kowatch, R.A. (1994) Neurobiological aspects of depression in children and adolescents. In W.M. Reynolds and H.F. Johnston (Eds) *Handbook of Depression in Children and Adolescents*, pp. 143–165. New York: Plenum Press.

Flament, M., Whitaker, A., Rapoport, J., Davies, C., Kalikow, K., Sceery, W. and Shaffer, D. (1988) Obsessive compulsive disorder in adolescence: an epidemiological study. *Journal of the American Academy of Child and Adolescent Psychiatry*, 27, 764–771.

Fonesca, A.C., Yule, W. and Erol, N. (1994) Cross-cultural issues. In T.H. Ollendick, N.J. King and W. Yule (Eds) *International Handbook of Phobic and Anxiety Disorders in Children and Adolescents*. New York: Plenum Press.

Graham, P. (1979) Epidemiological studies. In H.C. Quay and J.S. Werry (Eds) *Psychopathological Disorders of Childhood*, 2nd edn, pp. 185–209. New York: John Wiley.

Harrington, R. (1993) *Depressive Disorder in Childhood*. Chichester: John Wiley.

Harrington, R.C., Fudge, H., Rutter, M., Pickles, A. and Hill, J. (1990) Adult outcomes of childhood and adolescent depression: I. Psychiatric status. *Archives of General Psychiatry*, 47, 465–473.

Hawton, K. (1986) *Suicide and Attempted Suicide Among Children and Adolescents*. Beverly Hills, CA: Sage Publications.

Izard, C.E., Huebner, R. and Risser, D. (1980) The young infant's ability to produce discrete expressions. *Developmental Psychology*, 16, 132–140.

Kashani, J.H. and Orvaschel, H. (1988) Anxiety disorders in mid-adolescence: A community sample. *American Journal of Psychiatry*, 145, 960–964.

Kashani, J.H., Carlson, G.A. and Beck, N.C. (1987) Depression, depressive symptoms and depressed mood among a community sample of adolescents. *American Journal of Psychiatry*, 144, 931–934.

Kendler, K.S., Neal, M.C., Kessler, R.C., Heath, A.C. and Eaves, L.J. (1992) The genetic epidemiology of phobias in women. *Archives of General Psychiatry*, 49, 273–281.

Klein, M. (1949) *The Psychoanalysis of Children*. London: Hogarth.

Klein, R.G. and Last, C.G. (1989) *Anxiety Disorders in Children*. New York: Sage.

Kovacs, M., Feinberg, T.L., Crouse-Novak, M.A., Paulauskas, S.L. and Finkelstein, R. (1984) Depressive disorders in childhood. I. A longitudinal prospective study of characteristics and recovery. *Archives of General Psychiatry*, 41, 229–237.

McGee, R., Feehan, M., Williams, S., Partridge, F., Silva, P.A. and Kelly, J. (1990) DSM-III disorders in a large sample of adolescents. *Journal of the American Academy of Child and Adolescent Psychiatry*, 29, 611–619.

Moreau, D.L., Weissman, M. and Warner, V. (1989) Panic disorder in children at high risk for depression. *American Journal of Psychiatry*, 146, 1059–1060.

Pearce, J.B. (1978) The recognition of depressive disorder in children. *Journal of the Royal Society of Medicine*, 71, 494–500.

Plomin, R. (1983) Developmental behavioural genetics. *Child Development*, 54, 253–259.

Poznanski, E.O. and Mokros, H.B. (1994) Phenomenology and epidemiology of mood disorders in children and adolescents. In W.M. Reynolds and H.F. Johnston (Eds) *Handbook of Depression in Children and Adolescents*, pp. 19–39. New York: Plenum Press.

Reynolds, W.M. and Johnston, H.F. (1994) The nature and study of depression in children and adolescents. In W.M. Reynolds and H.F. Johnston (Eds) *Handbook of Depression in Children and Adolescents*, pp. 3–17. New York: Plenum Press.

Robins, L.N., Helzer, J.E., Weissman, M.M., Orvaschel, H., Greunberg, E., Burk, J.D. and Regier, D.A. (1984) Lifetime prevalence of specific psychiatric disorders in three sites. *Archives of General Psychiatry*, 41, 949–958.

Robinson, J.A., Kagan, J., Reznick, J.S. and Corley, R. (1992) The heritability of inhibited and uninhibited behaviour: a twin study. *Developmental Psychology*, 28, 1030–1037.

Rutter, M. (1980) Emotional development. In: M. Rutter (Ed.) *Foundations of Developmental Psychiatry*. London: Heineman.

Shepherd, M., Oppenheim, B. and Mitchell, S. (1971) *Childhood Behaviour and Mental Health*. London: University of London Press.

Spitz, R.A. and Wolf, K.M. (1946) Anaclitic depression: an inquiry into the genesis of psychiatric conditions in early childhood. *Psychoanalytic Study of the Child*, 2, 313–342.

Stark, K.D. (1990) *Childhood Depression: School Based Intervention*. New York: Guilford.

Stotland, E. (1969) Exploratory investigations of empathy. *Advances in Experimental Social Psychology*, 4, 271–314.

Strauss, C.C., Lease, C.A., Last, C.G. and Francis, G. (1988) Developmental differences between children and adolescents with overanxious disorder. *Journal of Abnormal Child Psychology*, 16, 433–443.

Strober, M., Morrell, W., Burroughs, J., Lampert, C., Danforth, H. and Freeman, R (1988) A family study of bipolar I disorder in adolescence: Early onset of symptoms linked to increased familial loading and lithium resistance. *Journal of Affective Disorders*, 15, 255–268.

Walker, J.L., Lahey, B.B., Russo, M.F., Christ, M.A.G., McBurnett, K., Loeber, R., Stouthamer-Loeber, M. and Green, S.M. (1991) Anxiety, inhibition and conduct disorder in children: I. Relation to social impairment. *Journal of the American Academy of Child and Adolescent Psychiatry*, 30, 187–191.

Weissman, M.M., Fendrich, M., Warner, V. and Wickramaratne, P. (1992) Incidence of psychiatric disorder in offspring at high and low risk for depression. *Journal of the American Academy of Child and Adolescent Psychiatry*, 31, 640–648.

Werry, J.S. (1991) Overanxious disorder: a review of its taxonomic properties. *Journal of the American Academy of Child and Adolescent Psychiatry*, 30, 533–544.

Zeitlin, H. (1986) *The Natural History of Psychiatric Disorder in Children. Maudsley Monograph 29.* Oxford: Oxford University Press.

Zeskind, P.S., Sale, J. and Mais, M.L. (1985) Adult perceptions of pain and hunger cries: a synchrony of arousal. *Child Development*, 56, 549–554.

Chapter 5

Eating Disorders

Andreas Karwautz and Janet Treasure

Eating disorders in young people are commonly seen in two variants: anorexia nervosa and bulimia nervosa. Anorexia nervosa is often defined as a refusal to maintain body weight over a minimal norm leading to a body weight of 15% below that expected for age, gender and height. It is associated with an intense fear of gaining weight or becoming fat, a disturbance in the experience of one's own body, and (in the case of women) the absence of three consecutive menstrual cycles (American Psychiatric Association, 1994). Two subtypes of this disorder are commonly seen: one in which weight loss is caused by dieting alone, and one (comprising about 50% of cases) in which the person uses binge eating, vomiting, laxatives, or diuretics as well.

Bulimia nervosa, the second major eating disorder, is defined by binge eating or the excessive intake of food in a brief period of time, with a sense that the eating is out of control. It is associated with a fear of becoming fat, counterbalanced by inappropriate compensatory behaviour. This may include purging, i.e. vomiting, the use of laxatives and diuretics. Alternatively, it may be accompanied by non-purging behaviour, i.e. fasting, excessive exercise, and with a preoccupation with body shape and weight.

In infants, children and younger adolescents several other eating and feeding disorders/problems can occur (Tables 5.1 and 5.2) (Christie *et al.*, 1998).

Additionally, there has been recent talk of a new diagnostic category called binge eating disorder. This disorder differs from bulimia nervosa by a lack of compensatory behaviour. Obesity, which is not generally regarded as a mental disorder, will not be further discussed here. No consistent psychological abnormalities have so far been found in obese people.

Young People and Mental Health. Edited by P. Aggleton, J. Hurry and I. Warwick.
© 2000 John Wiley & Sons Ltd.

Table 5.1   Other eating problems (American Psychiatric Association, 1994)

Pica: the deliberate ingestion of non-nutritive substances, such as hair or wallpaper, is inappropriate to the developmental level and must not be part of a culturally sanctioned practice.

Rumination disorder: including repeated regurgitation and rechewing of food and does not occur exclusively during the course of anorexia nervosa or bulimia nervosa.

Feeding disorder of infancy or early childhood: a persistent failure to eat adequately with significant failure to gain weight or loss of weight before the age of six.

Table 5.2   Other feeding and eating syndromes in children (Christie *et al.*, 1998)

Food avoidance emotional disorder: an emotional disorder in underweight children (partial anorexic symptoms) presenting with inadequate food intake combined with mood disturbance.

Food refusal: characterized by refusal of meals in certain situations or with certain people.

Pervasive refusal syndrome: characterized by refusal to eat, to drink, to walk, to speak and to care for oneself, sometimes seen as symptoms of a post-traumatic stress disorder caused by sexual or physical abuse.

Selective eating: including eating only a very restricted spectrum of food (only two or three different kinds of food), which sometimes causes social difficulties.

Because early intervention is important to avoid an eating disorder developing a chronic course, it is crucial to identify the signs and symptoms of eating disorders early. Some of the possible early warning signs that may be apparent when working closely with young people are listed in Table 5.3.

PREVALENCE AND INCIDENCE OF EATING DISORDERS

Anorexia nervosa is one of the top three chronic conditions affecting young people in their teenage years. While its incidence in the general population is 8 per 100 000, approximately 1% of teenage girls experience this problem. Anorexia nervosa most usually has its onset in the mid-teenage years but it can start as early as age eight. Between 90 and 96% of those affected are young women. It has a large impact in terms of physical and psychological morbidity and psychosocial impairment.

The prevalence of bulimia nervosa is 1–3% in adolescence. A threefold increase in detection was reported between 1988 and 1993. Its onset typically occurs during the late teens and early adult years. Children under the age of 14, however, have been identified and it has been

Table 5.3 Possible early signs of an eating disorder

That teachers may observe:
(1) A child (before puberty) is not gaining weight in a way appropriate for her age compared with the rest of the class.
(2) A child is not gaining in height relative to the rest of the class.
(3) A child or young person is losing weight. She may disguise her thinness by wearing large baggy clothes.
(4) A child who is sensitive to the cold, has a blue nose and hands and a peaky appearance.
(5) A child who wears numerous layers of clothes to fight off the cold.
(6) A child who skips school meals or eats only fruits and vegetables.
(7) A child who may have become preoccupied with studying and exercising.
(8) A child who may have become socially withdrawn and sad.
(9) A child who appears excessively conscientious and very eager to please other people.

That parents or other carers may observe:
(1) She may find ways to avoid having meals with the rest of the family; she may prepare her own food; she may say that she has already eaten or will eat later; she may cook for the family but not eat herself.
(2) She may eat (large amounts of) vegetables and fruits and avoid food containing carbohydrates and fats.
(3) She may eat very slowly, cut the food into tiny pieces and push it around the plate.
(4) She may have become very active, going out for long walks, runs, frequently using the gym to have influence on her body shape.
(5) She may have started to drink large amounts of coffee and diet drinks.
(6) Her mood will have altered: more tearful, irritable, worried, impatient.
(7) She might have stopped going out with friends or stopped participating in family events.
(8) She might eat in binges. Large amounts of food will disappear from the fridge and from the stores at home. Maybe she hoards food in her room.
(9) She may vomit after eating. Therefore, she may use the bathroom many times a day and at night. There may be an odour of vomiting.
(10) She may use laxatives.

suggested that the occurrence of bulimia nervosa in these young people is increasing (Fombonne, 1998).

No accurate incidence and prevalence data is available on other eating disorders affecting young people, but they seem to be rare.

RISK FACTORS

When it comes to explaining why some young people develop anorexia nervosa we need to take into account the clinical and epidemiological pattern of this disorder, such as the age of onset, and the sex ratio. The relative stability in the incidence of anorexia nervosa over time and across cultures suggests either that environmental explanations will need to be very general, or that individual factors may be more pertinent. In contrast, the rapid rise in bulimia nervosa could be explained by some general environmental aetiological factors. The contemporary emphasis on dieting appears to be a prime candidate. However, this cannot explain individual susceptibility, which is more likely to be explained by specific environmental factors and/or individual vulnerability.

Current opinion suggests that both anorexia nervosa and bulimia nervosa are best explained by multidimensional or biopsychosocial models (Garfinkel and Garner, 1982; Johnson and Connors, 1987; Halmi, 1995; Connors, 1996; Smolak and Levine, 1996; Treasure, 1998). Often these models do not distinguish between predisposing and maintaining factors. While both disorders may be preceded by dieting, dieting is a common behaviour in adolescence and early adult age in most Western countries, and certainly not every woman who diets develops an eating disorder. Possible additional risk factors include *biological vulnerability* such as that caused by genetic traits such as a susceptibility to dysregulation of the neurotransmitter systems that regulate eating behaviour. *Psychological vulnerability* caused by predisposing personality traits, difficulties in the management of affect, developmental experiences, family conflicts, intrapsychic conflicts may also have an important role to play (Rastam and Gillberg, 1991; Schmidt *et al.*, 1993a, 1993b, 1997; Steiner *et al.*, 1995; Shisslak *et al.*, 1998; Steiner and Lock, 1998).

To understand who is at risk of developing an eating disorder, risk factor models have been created. It seems that several *unspecific* risk factors enhance vulnerability to developing psychiatric disorders in general. Risk factors for these psychological disturbances include temperamental factors, a problematic family environment characterized by a preponderance of negative interactions such as blaming and over-control, a lack of parental support, a lack of empathy and nurturance, and stressful life events such as sexual abuse or other traumatic events.

More specific factors need to be present for a young person to develop an eating disorder. Specific risk factors for body dissatisfaction include having a higher body weight than average, being teased about their weight or size, having parents who themselves dieted, and the presence of strong cultural norms governing weight and shape.

A combination of risk factors of both kinds is thought to lead to an eating disorder (Connors, 1996; Fairburn *et al.*, 1997, 1999). Low self-esteem, insecurity in relationships, and difficulties in managing feelings, combined with body dissatisfaction, may lead to marked dieting behaviour, anorexia nervosa and bulimia nervosa.

A Genetic Component?

Genetic research on eating disorders has involved family studies, twin studies, studies of chromosomal abnormalities and molecular genetic studies (reviewed in Strober, 1991; Woodside, 1993; Hebebrand and Remschmidt, 1995; Treasure and Holland, 1995; Lilenfeld and Kaye,

1998; Sullivan *et al.*, 1998). We now know that eating disorders tend to cluster in families and that the female relatives of people with anorexia nervosa and bulimia nervosa have a ten-fold greater risk of developing an eating disorder than those who are not genetically related to them. Furthermore, there is some evidence from molecular genetic studies that certain genes may play a role in the development of anorexia nervosa and bulimia nervosa (Gorwood *et al.*, 1998; Collier *et al.*, 1999).

Which General Factors are Linked to Eating Disorders?

As stated earlier, women are at a much higher risk for anorexia nervosa and bulimia nervosa than men. Individuals in their mid teens are at highest risk for anorexia nervosa, and those in their late teens and early twenties are especially vulnerable to bulimia. Homosexual men seem to have a greater risk for eating disorders than heterosexual men. There seems to be no strong correlation between social class and the development of anorexia nervosa and bulimia nervosa. Educational achievement is reportedly high among people with anorexia nervosa, but the intelligence of those affected is usually average. Bodily dissatisfaction and dieting, greater perceived pressure to be thin, the internalization of a thin body-ideal, body dissatisfaction, and dieting predict the onset of later bulimic behaviour (Stice and Agras, 1998).

Are There Special Traits that can be Noticed Early in Children and Young People?

No clear pattern of problems around birth can be found in people who later develop eating disorders. In early childhood, digestive problems and 'picky eating' have, however, been found to predate anorectic behaviour (Marchi and Cohen, 1990; Rastam, 1992). In some studies, fighting during mealtimes has been shown to predict later bulimic behaviour (e.g. Marchi and Cohen, 1990). Furthermore, young people with late onset anorexia nervosa have reported suffering more often from stomach aches and severe gastrointestinal problems in childhood (Rastam, 1992).

It may be shocking to realize that nearly half of children aged ten and above express a desire to be thinner than they are. More than a third have tried some form of weight loss (Hill, 1993; Killen *et al.*, 1994). Negative feelings about the body increase the risk of developing eating problems (Killen *et al.*, 1996). Dieting increases the risk of developing bulimia nervosa eight-fold (Patton *et al.*, 1990). Eating problems also appear to be associated with puberty and allied developmental changes (Attie and Brooks-Gunn, 1989; Crisp, 1995; review in Smolak and Levine, 1996).

What Does the Family Contribute to the Development of Eating Disorders?

Eating disorders are particularly common in the immediate relatives of people with anorexia nervosa. In the course of the last few years, numerous studies on the effects of family interaction on eating disorders have been carried out (reviewed in Eisler, 1995). No marked differences have been found between families with and without an anorexic child. It is therefore unlikely that families cause anorexia nervosa in any direct sense. On the other hand, families do have an important impact on either maintaining or interrupting the eating disorder.

Bulimia nervosa, in contrast, is associated with overt adversity in childhood. Often there has been poor family functioning, including physical abuse, sexual abuse and intense arguments (Schmidt et al., 1993a; Fairburn et al., 1997). High levels of family disturbance (linked to, for example, low levels of paternal care) seem to be associated with the greater severity and chronicity of bulimia nervosa (Fairburn et al., 1997).

Negative Life Events as Triggers for the Development of Anorexia Nervosa and Bulimia Nervosa

It has been recognized for centuries that psychosocial difficulties are important triggers to illness and indeed these are now incorporated into some of the recent proposed definitions of eating disorders (Russell, 1995; Szmukler and Patton, 1995). Difficulties in early childhood appear to be of greater importance for the onset of bulimia nervosa than for anorexia nervosa. These difficulties commonly involve interpersonal problems such as teasing and bullying at school or negative life events concerning parents. Sexually upsetting events may be of particular relevance to the onset of anorexia nervosa, but only occur in 20% of cases (Schmidt et al., 1997). In particular, the individual meaning of events and how the person is able to cope with them is the most important aspect. A more general effect may be triggered by a life event that engenders a conflict of loyalties, or an ethical dilemma.

In themselves, stressful life events are common experiences and cannot explain the specific development of an eating disorder. One explanation of this specificity derives from the meaning of an event that is significant; loss events are associated with depression; threat events with anxiety, and so on (Brown, 1993). The events associated primarily with anorexia nervosa raise the possibility that the condition may be linked to emotions of disgust and shame. Alternatively, the response to the event may be an important component in shaping the outcome. Young people with anorexia nervosa and bulimia nervosa tend to display more helpless coping responses—those with anorexia nervosa use avoidance strategies, and those with bulimia nervosa ruminate on their problem (Troop and Treasure, 1997b). It is uncertain whether these varieties of coping styles arise as consequences of the meaning of the event, as the result of developmental experiences, or are linked to temperamental predisposition (Troop and Treasure, 1997a, 1997b).

The Role of Sexually Abusive and Physically Harmful Experiences

This very important topic has been extensively discussed in recent articles by Fallon and Wonderlich (1997) and Wonderlich et al. (1997) as well as in a book (Schwartz and Cohn, 1996). While repeated sexual abuse and physical abuse has been reported by people with bulimia, there is no evidence that rates of abuse are higher in bulimia nervosa than in other psychiatric disorders. Childhood trauma is, however, more strongly associated with bulimia than with anorexia nervosa.

The Role of Personality Traits

Many different personality traits are associated with eating disorders but it is difficult to distinguish traits that predispose to the illness from those which are a consequence of the disorder (Sohlberg and Strober, 1994). Overall, a diagnosis of personality disorder is very common in young people with anorexia nervosa (approximately 67%), in particular obsessive compulsive personality disorder (35%) (Rastam, 1992). Obsessive-compulsive traits and especially perfectionism and the need for symmetry and exactness have been shown also to persist after long-term recovery, suggesting that these traits could be indicators of vulnerability (Srinivasagan et al., 1995). In bulimia nervosa, histrionic and borderline personality disorders occur in about a third of cases (Wonderlich et al., 1990).

Children with low self-esteem are at higher risk of developing an eating disorder in adolescence. The risk has been reported to be eight times higher than in those with high self-esteem (Button et al., 1996).

The Role of Social Support

The perceived adequacy of the available social support is thought to influence vulnerability for mental disorders in general. Some studies have shown that young people with anorexia nervosa and bulimia nervosa have deficits in their social network in terms of poor levels of social adjustment, difficulties in interpersonal relationships and a lack of social support (Herzog et al., 1987; Striegel-Moore et al., 1993; Tiller et al., 1997). Patients with bulimia nervosa often report having received less help from a core tie at the time of suffering an acute life event (Troop *et al.*, 1998).

Comorbidity

It has been estimated that nearly 90% of people with anorexia nervosa suffer at the same time from other psychiatric disorders at the same time as the eating disorder (Rastam, 1992). The most common disorders are major depression and dysthymia, social phobia and obsessive-compulsive disorder. Bulimia nervosa is often associated with depressive disorders and personality disorders. Also, alcohol and drug abuse as well as deliberate self-harm are present for a considerable number of sufferers.

EFFECTIVE INTERVENTIONS

Young people with anorexia nervosa can be notoriously ambivalent about treatment and often switch from being apparently motivated to refusing any change of their behaviour. Therefore, it is difficult to offer effective support and it is very easy to get into fights and battles over food and weight (Ward *et al.*, 1996). To work patiently with this ambivalence to change is therefore important, and this applies even to the first steps of intervention. Difficulties in bringing about change should be openly acknowledged, and the techniques of motivational interviewing (Treasure and Ward, 1997) can be very important at this stage.

The Role of the School

After a teacher or other professional working with young people has recognized someone as possibly suffering from an eating disorder, what should be done? And what role can the school have in primary and secondary prevention? Wherever possible, one teacher should take a key role. In the case of overt anorexia nervosa, the teacher's concerns should be discussed with the parents. Together, they can assess possible problems in different areas: eating behaviour at home and in the school, school work and possible perfectionism doing homework, and difficulties in the young person's interaction patterns with family members and peers (Table 5.4).

In the case of severe anorexia nervosa, the young person should not be encouraged to exercise at school because that may pose a risk to health. She or he should be supported in having snacks and meals on a regular basis. If possible, eating should take place normally with other pupils. The help of a friend may be of use if agreed to by the individual,

Table 5.4   Dangers and consequences of eating disorders

(1) Dangers and consequences of starvation

Medical dangers and consequences
Sensitivity to cold caused by poor circulation
Slow pulse, low blood pressure
Sleeping disturbances
Weak bladder function
Excessive hair growth
Thin bones, sometimes leading to fractures
Loss of menstrual periods
Bloating when eating even small amounts of food
Slow gut function with constipation
Anaemia
Failure of liver function sometimes causing swelling of ankles and legs
High blood cholesterol
Peripheral neuropathy and reduced muscle tissue causing weakness and fatigue
Low glucose
Failure of kidney function
Decreased fertility rate in recovered anorexic patients
Atrophy of the brain
In children growth may be delayed

Psychosocial dangers and consequences
Low mood and depression
Preoccupation with food
Strong urges to overeat can occur
Poor concentration and the need to work more for good results compared to the
    time before the illness
Social isolation: Interest and ability to form relationships is lowered and
    friendships are lost
Low interest in sexuality and reduction of sexual fantasies

(2) Consequences of excessive exercising

Dangerously low sugar levels with hypoglycaemic coma and death
Stress fractures when bones are osteoporotic
Muscles and joints damaged

(3) Consequences of vomiting, the use of laxatives and diuretics

When vomiting is severe and frequent, dental problems arise (erosion of the
    enamel on the teeth)
Water and salt imbalance causing disturbed function of heart, kidney and brain
    (fits)
The glands in the face and on the neck can swell up
Bleeding of the stomach
Laxatives and diuretics can lead to serious water and salt imbalance
Laxatives damage the bowel resulting in severe constipation and reduced function
Diuretics can cause dehydration and salt imbalance and damage the function of
    the kidneys and the circulation

(4) Dangers of taking diet pills

Diet pills taken to excess cause overactivity and excitability of body and mind
    leading to agitation and overactiveness

since this may provide encouragement. Homework should be restricted by setting a time limit for study. During examinations the pupil's working ability could benefit from a hot drink and a snack.

There are no such special recommendations for teachers concerning bulimia nervosa. Bulimic behaviour is usually carried out in secret, and may not be recognized directly, although the emotional and social repercussions may be obvious. The young person concerned should be offered the opportunity to talk about things in confidence. Parents should only be involved with the consent of the individual.

Interventions in the Community

Depending on the age, the severity, and the chronicity of the eating disorder the therapeutic approach should be matched to the patient's needs using models of stepped care (Tiller *et al.*, 1993, 1997; Treasure, 1998). The younger the patient, the more involved the family will need to be in treatment, especially for anorexia nervosa. Older patients with anorexia nervosa who developed their problem at an early age can also be helped if their families are involved.

STEPS OF INTENSITY OF TREATMENT FOR EATING DISORDER

- *Mild symptoms and short history:* psychoeducation from self-treatment books, videos or from general practitioners or other professionals.
- *Moderate severity or no change with step 1:* guided treatment using cognitive behavioural therapy manuals as adjuncts to care.
- *No change with step 2 or severe symptoms:* specialized therapy, e.g. cognitive behavioural therapy, cognitive analytical therapy or interpersonal therapy possibly supplemented with antidepressant therapy.
- *No change with step 3.* Day patient or inpatient treatment.

Early and mild cases of anorexia nervosa and bulimia nervosa can be treated in the community. General practitioners, community psychiatric nurses, or school counsellors trained in the management of these disorders can provide effective care, offering a collaborative therapeutic relationship, education about the consequences of the disorder and nutrition, and regular weight monitoring (for anorexia nervosa). The key person should also try to engage the family or other carers in the treatment. There are several carers' support groups run by specialist centres or the Eating Disorder Association (EDA). Families often need support if they are to care effectively for an eating disordered younger member. To read supportive literature could also be recommended (e.g.

Section II of Treasure, 1997: 33–81). Young people with anorexia nervosa and bulimia nervosa should be encouraged to attend self-help groups (a list for the UK is available from the EDA), which can be especially helpful in the early stages of the illness.

Education can be given in form of a seminar or a self-help manual (Treasure *et al.*, 1996; Thiels *et al.*, 1998). Encouraging self-help is helpful in particular in the early stages of the illness. Autobiographical books of young people who have recovered and videotapes about the illness and its consequences and treatment modalities can aid this approach.

Treatment by More Specialized Facilities

If the young person with either anorexia nervosa or bulimia nervosa fails to respond to the above interventions, more specific treatment may be required. Several forms of psychotherapeutic (and medical treatment) are available. In the case of anorexia nervosa, a second step might be to involve the family more directly, perhaps through family education or family counselling. This work can be done by social workers and members of the community psychiatric team. Both parents should be encouraged to work on the problem together as a team.

If such an approach proves unsuccessful, young people with anorexia nervosa can be offered treatment in day facilities. This usually involves several supervised meals and a higher level of support. If the individual's physical or mental condition is dangerous, and out- or day-patient treatment has failed to produce change, then inpatient treatment may be required (Treasure *et al.*, 1995). Ideally, this should be provided in a specialized unit by a multidisciplinary team involving nurses, psychiatrists, a family therapist, a social worker, an occupational therapist and a dietician. Additionally, a dance therapist, and a body-oriented therapist (body-work, relaxation training) can be involved. Treatment consists of a judicious mixture of staff control over eating while at the same time encouraging autonomy and growth.

If the young person has bulimia nervosa, cognitive behavioural therapy (CBT)—administered in groups or individually—may be the treatment of choice. This can be provided by nurses or other health care professionals (clinical psychologists, general psychiatrists) after some basic training. As a next step, antidepressive medication can be added. Fluoxetine (60 mg/day) has been found to be effective in reducing the severity of bulimic symptoms.

As it has been recognized that CBT does not help a proportion of those affected, usually those with comorbid personality disorders, patients with not enough improvement may need access to a more specialist service. This could provide cognitive analytical therapy (CAT) or interpersonal therapy (IPT) on an out-patient basis. Some young people with bulimia require brief periods of hospitalization at times of crisis, or for the treatment of comorbid depression and alcohol abuse.

PRIMARY PREVENTION

Various efforts have been made to develop prevention programmes for eating disturbances and eating disorders. Usually they have been designed for children at secondary school and college. In the last few years, controlled studies of some of these have been published (e.g. Killen *et al.*, 1993; Killen, 1996; Shisslak *et al.*, 1996; Smolak *et al.*, 1998). Indeed a whole book has been written about this issue (Vandereycken and Noordenbos, 1998). It appears that prevention programmes are able to increase the knowledge about healthy eating, nutrition, body composition and dieting. Changes in eating disorders attitudes are, however, less marked. The least successful aspect of these programmes has been their influence over eating patterns, weight reduction, exercise, and dieting.

Future programmes may need to be more developmentally appropriate and focused on more general risk factors. They may need to include, for example, components to help young people cope with physical, social and emotional changes during puberty; being teased by peers about shape and appearance; dating, sexuality, and the sudden changes in mood characteristic of this stage of development. An example of a possible prevention programme is given in Table 5.5 (Killen, 1996). A series of developmentally appropriate prevention strategies as proposed by Shisslak *et al.* (1996) are also outlined (Table 5.6).

CONCLUSIONS

Eating disorders rank high amongst the common chronic conditions of childhood. Anorexia nervosa is most easily detected, while bulimia nervosa is more covert. Anorexia nervosa occurs early in the teenage years and it usually persists for over five years. Bulimia nervosa has its maximal incidence later. There appears to be no improvement in the course of anorexia nervosa; indeed it may have worsened. Possibly a third of people with anorexia fail ever to recover and the majority of these die

Table 5.5 Stanford eating disorder symptoms prevention programme (Killen, 1996)

1. Weight gain is a normal and necessary part of pubertal growth in females.
2. Excessive caloric restriction is not an effective long-term weight control strategy.
3. Caloric restriction may actually potentiate weight gain and lead to difficulties with weight regulation.
4. Young people can learn to counteract cultural pressures promoting dieting and a thin body ideal.
5. Young people can be trained to adopt more healthy nutrition practices and physical activity regimes.

Table 5.6 Developmentally appropriate prevention strategies (after Shisslak *et al.,* 1996)

Early adolescence
　　Information regarding the bodily changes of puberty
　　Information about emotional arousal, relationships, problems with parents
　　Information about the need to become more and more independent
　　Enhance and deal with acceptance by the peer group
　　Coping with teasing about shape and appearance
　　Regulate emotions by relaxation techniques
　　Education about unhealthy ways to cope with emotions (drugs, alcohol)
　　Teaching problem-solving and time-management skills, and goal setting
　　Teaching healthy food and exercise plans

Middle adolescence (additional topics)
　　Dealing with connections of affects with food consumption
　　Discussion of personal values, self-worth, and achievement
　　Discussion of the role of women in the media
　　Enhancing problem-solving skills
　　Explore the abstract issue of body image and its relation to self-esteem

Late adolescence (additional topics)
　　Validation of needs for emotional connectedness
　　Encouraging the establishment of new social networks
　　Gender role in society
　　Finding other ways than academic achievement to maintain self-esteem

prematurely. Approximately 50% of people with bulimia nervosa respond relatively quickly to treatment but relapses and remissions can mark the overall course. Only a small proportion of individuals continues to have the problem after ten years.

People with anorexia nervosa are at best ambivalent about help to change and at worst totally resistant. This can lead to an unusual relationship between the women with anorexia nervosa and their potential helpers. Strong care-giving emotions are aroused because of the life-threatening nature of the illness, and yet the sufferer repulses these drives.

People with bulimia nervosa differ in that they may be ashamed about asking for help to stop their binges, but they have no ambivalence about this aspect of their problem. On the other hand, they may be more reluctant to give up their methods of weight control. The management of bulimia nervosa has been well researched and treatment can follow evidence-based practices. In contrast, the management of anorexia nervosa remains based largely upon clinical pragmatism.

REFERENCES

American Psychiatric Association (1994) *Diagnostic and Statistical Manual of Mental Disorders*, 4th edn. Washington, DC: American Psychiatric Association.

Attie, I. and Brooks-Gunn, J. (1989) Development of eating problems in adolescent girls: a longitudinal study. *Developmental Psychology*, 25, 70–79.

Brown, G.W. (1993) Life events and affective disorder: replications and limitations. *Psychosomatic Medicine*, 55, 248–259.

Button, E.J., Sonuga-Barke, E.J.S., Davies, J. and Thompson, M. (1996) A prospective study of self-esteem in the prediction of eating problems in adolescent schoolgirls: questionnaire findings. *British Journal of Clinical Psychology*, 35, 193–203.

Christie, D., Bryant-Waugh, R., Lask, B. and Gordon, I. (1998) Neurobiological aspects of early onset eating disorders. In H. Hoek, J. Treasure and M. Katzman (Eds) *Neurobiology in the Treatment of Eating Disorders*. Chichester: Wiley.

Collier, D.A., Sham, P.C., Arranz, M.J., Hu, X. and Treasure, J. (1999) Understanding the genetic predisposition to anorexia nervosa. *European Eating Disorders Review*, 7, 96–102.

Connors, M.E. (1996) Developmental vulnerabilities for eating disorders. In L. Smolak, M.P. Levine and R. Striegel-Moore (Eds) *The Developmental Psychopathology of Eating Disorders. Implications for Research, Prevention, and Treatment*. Mahwah, NJ: Lawrence Erlbaum.

Crisp, A. (1995) *Anorexia Nervosa: Let Me Be*. Hove: Lawrence Erlbaum.

Eisler, I. (1995) Family models of eating disorders. In G. Szmukler, J. Treasure and C. Dare (Eds) *Handbook of Eating Disorders. Theory, Treatment and Research*. Chichester: Wiley.

Fairburn, C.G., Welch, S.L., Doll, H.A., Davies, B.A. and O'Connor M.E. (1997) Risk factors for bulimia nervosa: a community-based case-control study. *Archive of General Psychiatry*, 54, 509–517.

Fairburn, C.G., Cooper, Z., Doll, H.A. and Welch, S.L. (1999) Risk factors for anorexia nervosa. Three integrated case–control comparisons. *Arch. Gen. Psychiatry*, 56, 468–476.

Fallon, P. and Wonderlich, S.A. (1997) Sexual abuse and other forms of trauma. In D.M. Garner and P.E. Garfinkel (Eds) *Handbook of Treatment for Eating Disorders*. New York, London: Guilford Press.

Fombonne, E. (1998) Increased rates of psychosocial disorders in youth. *European Archives of Psychiatry Clinical Neuroscience*, 248, 14–21.

Garfinkel, P. and Garner, D. (1982) *Anorexia Nervosa: A Multidimensional Approach*. New York: Bruner/Mazel.

Gorwood, P., Bouvard, M., Mouren-Simeoni, M.C., Kipman, A. and Ades, J. Genetics and anorexia nervosa: a review of candidate genes. *Psychiatric Genetics*, 8, 7–12.

Halmi, K.A. (1995) Current concepts and definitions. In G. Szmukler, C. Dare and J. Treasure (Eds) *Handbook of Eating Disorders. Theory, Treatment and Research*. Chichester: Wiley.

Hebebrand, J. and Remschmidt, H. (1995) Anorexia nervosa viewed as an extreme weight condition: genetic implications. *Human Genetics*, 95, 1–11.

Herzog, D.B., Keller, M.B., Lavori, P.W. and Ott, I.L. (1987) Social impairment in bulimia. *International Journal of Eating Disorders*, 6, 741–747.

Hill, A. (1993) Preadolescent dieting: Implications for eating disorders. *International Review of Psychiatry*, 5, 87–100.

Johnson, C. and Connors, M.E. (1987) *The Etiology and Treatment of Bulimia Nervosa: a Biopsychosocial Perspective*. New York: Basic Books.

Killen, J.D. (1996) Development and evaluation of a school-based eating disorder symptoms prevention program. In L. Smolak, M.P. Levine and R. Striegel-Moore (Eds) *The Developmental Psychopathology of Eating Disorders. Implications for Research, Prevention, and Treatment*. Mahwah, NJ: Lawrence Erlbaum.

Killen, J.D., Taylor, C.B., Hammer, L.D., Litt, I., Wilson, D.M., Rich, T., Hayward, C., Simmonds, B., Kraemer, H. and Varady, A. (1993) An attempt to modify unhealthy eating attitudes and weight regulation practices of young adolescent girls. *International Journal of Eating Disorders*, 13, 369–384.

Killen, J.D., Taylor, C.B., Hayward, C., Wilson, D.M., Haydel, K.F., Hammer, L.D., Simmonds, B., Robinson, T.N., Litt, I., Vardy, A. and Kraemer, H. (1994) Pursuit of thinness and onset of eating disorder symptoms in a community sample of adolescent girls: A three year prospective analysis. *International Journal of Eating Disorders*, 16, 227–238.

Killen, J.D., Taylor, C.B., Hayward, C., Haydel, K.F., Wilson, D.M., Hammer, L.D., Kraemer, H., Blair-Greiner, A. and Strachowski, D. (1996) Weight concerns influence the development of eating disorders. A four year prospective study. *Journal of Consulting Clinical Psychology*, 64, 936–940.

Lilenfeld, L.R. and Kaye, W.H. (1998) Genetic studies of anorexia and bulimia nervosa. In H.W. Hoek, J.Treasure and M. Katzman (Eds) *The Integration of Neurobiology in the Treatment of Eating Disorders*. New York: Wiley.

Marchi, M. and Cohen, P. (1990) Early childhood eating behaviors and adolescent eating disorders. *Journal of the American Academy of Child and Adolescent Psychiatry*, 29, 1, 112–117.

Patton, C.G., Johnson-Sabine, E., Wood, K., Mann, A.H. and Wakeling, A. (1990) Abnormal eating attitudes in London schoolgirls—a prospective epidemiological study: outcome at twelve month follow-up. *Psychological Medicine*, 20, 383–394.

Rastam, M. and Gillberg, C. (1991) The family background in anorexia nervosa: a population-based study. *Journal of the American Academy of Child and Adolescent Psychiatry*, 30, 283–289.

Rastam, M. (1992) Anorexia nervosa in 51 Swedish adolescents: premorbid problems and comorbidity. *Journal of the American Academy of Child and Adolescent Psychiatry*, 31, 819–829.

Rastam, M., Gillberg, I.C. and Gillberg, C. (1995) Anorexia nervosa 6 years after onset: Part II. comorbid psychiatric problems. *Comparative Psychiatry*, 36, 70–76.

Russell, G.F.M. (1995) Anorexia nervosa through time. In G. Szmukler, C.G. Dare and J. Treasure (Eds) *Handbook of Eating Disorders. Theory, Treatment and Research*. Chichester: Wiley.

Schmidt, U., Tiller, J. and Treasure, J. (1993a) Psychosocial factors in the origin of bulimia nervosa. *International Review of Psychiatry*, 5, 51–60.

Schmidt, U., Tiller, J. and Treasure, J. (1993b) Setting the scene for eating disorders: childhood care, classification and course of illness. *Psychological Medicine*, 23, 663–672.

Schmidt, U., Tiller, J., Blanchard, M., Andrews, B. and Treasure, J.L. (1997) Is there a specific trauma precipitating anorexia nervosa? *Psychological Medicine*, 27, 523–530.

Schwartz, M.F. and Cohn, L. (Eds) (1996) *Sexual Abuse and Eating Disorders*. New York: Brunner/Mazel.

Shisslak, C.M., Crago, M., Estaes, L.S. and Gray, N. (1996) Content and method of developmentally appropriate prevention programs. In L. Smolak, M.P. Levine and R. Striegel-Moore (Eds) *The Developmental Psychopathology of Eating Disorders. Implications for Research, Prevention, and Treatment*. Mahwah, NJ: Lawrence Erlbaum.

Shisslak, C.M., Crago, M., McKnight, K.M., Estes, L.S., Gray, N. and Parnaby, O.G. (1998) Potential risk factors associated with weight control behaviors in elementary and middle school girls. *Journal of Psychosomatic Research*, 44, 301–313.

Smolak, L. and Levine, M.P. (1996) Adolescent transitions and the development of eating problems. In L. Smolak, M.P. Levine and R. Striegel-Moore (Eds) *The Developmental Psychopathology of Eating Disorders. Implications for Research, Prevention, and Treatment*. Mahwah, NJ: Lawrence Erlbaum.

Smolak, L., Levine, M.P. and Schermer, F. (1998) A controlled evaluation of an elementary school primary prevention program for eating disorders. *Journal of Psychosomatic Research*, 44, 339–353.

Sohlberg, S. and Strober, M. (1994) Personality in Anorexia Nervosa: An update and a theoretical integration. *Acta Psychiatrica Scandinavica*, 89 (Suppl. 378), 1–15.

Srinivasagan, N.M., Plotnicov, K.H., Greeno, C. *et al.* (1995) Persistent perfectionism, symmetry and exactness in anorexia nervosa after long term recovery. *American Journal of Psychiatry*, 152, 1630–1634.

Steiner, H. and Lock, J. (1998) Anorexia nervosa and bulimia nervosa in children and adolescents: A review of the past 10 years. *Journal of the American Academy of Child and Adolescent Psychiatry*, 37, 352–359.

Steiner, H., Sanders, M. and Ryst, E. (1995) Precursors and risk factors of juvenile eating disorders. In H.C. Steinhausen (Ed.) *Eating Disorders in Adolescence*. Berlin/New York: de Gruyter.

Stice, A. and Agras, W.S. (1998) Predicting onset and cessation of bulimic behaviors during adolescence: A longitudinal grouping analysis. *Behaviour Therapy*, 29, 257–276.

Striegel-Moore, R.H., Silberstein, L.R. and Rodin, J. (1993) The social self in bulimia nervosa: Public self consciousness, social anxiety and perceived fraudulence. *Journal of Abnormal Psychology*, 102, 297–303.

Strober, M. (1991) Family genetic studies of eating disorders. *Journal of Clinical Psychiatry*, 52 (Suppl. 10), 9–12.

Sullivan, P.F., Bulik, C.M. and Kendler, K.S. (1998) Genetic epidemiology of binging and vomiting. *British Journal of Psychiatry*, 173, 75–79.

Szmukler, G. and Patton, G. (1995) Sociocultural models of eating disorders. In G. Szmukler, C. Dare and J. Treasure (Eds) *Handbook of Eating Disorders. Theory, Treatment and Research*. Chichester: Wiley.

Thiels, C., Schmidt, U., Treasure, J., Garthe, R. and Troop, N. (1998) Guided self-change for bulimia nervosa incorporating use of a self-care manual. *American Journal of Psychiatry*, 155, 947–953.

Tiller, J., Schmidt, U. and Treasure, J. (1993) Treatment of bulimia nervosa. *Int. Review of Psychiatry*, 5, 75–86.

Tiller, J., Sloane, G., Schmidt, U., Troop, N., Power, M. and Treasure, J. (1997) Social support in patients with anorexia nervosa and bulimia nervosa. *International Journal of Eating Disorders*, 21, 31–38.

Treasure, J. (1997) Anorexia nervosa and bulimia nervosa. In A. Stein and G. Wilkinson (Eds) *General Adult Psychiatry*, Vol. 2. London: Royal College of Psychiatrists.

Treasure, J. and Ward, A. (1997) A practical guide to the use of motivational interviewing in anorexia nervosa. *European Eating Disorders Review*, 5, 102–114.

Treasure, J. and Holland, A. (1995) Genetic factors in eating disorders. In G. Szmukler, C. Dare and J. Treasure (Eds) *Handbook of Eating Disorders: Theory, Treatment and Research*. Wiley/Sons, pp. 65–81.

Treasure, J., Todd, G. and Szmukler, G. (1995) The inpatient treatment of anorexia nervosa. In G. Szmukler, C. Dare and J. Treasure (Eds) *Handbook of Eating Disorders. Theory, Treatment and Research*. Chichester: Wiley.

Treasure, J., Schmidt, U., Troop, N., Tiller, J., Todd, G. and Turnbull, S. (1996) A randomized controlled trial of sequential treatment for bulimia nervosa incorporating a self-care manual. *British Journal of Psychiatry*, 168, 94–98.

Troop, N. and Treasure, J.L. (1997a) Setting the scene for eating disorders, II. Childhood helplessness and mastery. *Psychological Medicine*, 27, 531–538.

Troop, N. and Treasure, J. (1997b) Psychosocial factors in the onset of eating disorders: responses to life-events and difficulties. *British Journal of Medical Psychology*, 70, 373–385.

Troop, N.A., Holbrey, A. and Treasure, J.L. (1998) Stress, coping and crisis support in eating disorders. *International Journal of Eating Disorders*, 24, 157–166.

Vandereycken, W. and Noordenbos, G. (1998) (Eds) *The Prevention of Eating Disorders*. New York: New York University Press.

Ward, A., Troop, N., Todd, G. and Treasure, J. (1996) To change or not to change. How is the question? *British Medical Journal*, 69, 139–146.

Welch, S.L., Doll, H.A. and Fairburn, C.G. (1997) Life events and the onset of bulimia nervosa: A controlled study. *Psychological Medicine*, 27, 515–522.

Wonderlich, S.S., Swift, W.J., Slotnick, H.B. and Goodman, S. (1990). DSM-III-R personality disorders in eating-disorder subtypes. *International Journal of Eating Disorders*, 9, 607–616.

Wonderlich, S.A., Brewerton, T.D., Jocic, Z., Dansky, B.S. and Abbott, D.W. (1997) Relationship of childhood sexual abuse and eating disorders. *Journal of the American Academy of Child and Adolescent Psychiatry*, 36, 1107–1115.

Woodside, D.B. (1993) Genetic contributions to eating disorders. In A.S. Kaplan and P.E. Garfinfiel (Eds) *Medical Issues and the Eating Disorders. The Face*. New York: Brunner/Mazel, pp. 193–212.

Chapter 6

Serious Antisocial Behaviour

Sue Bailey

The existence of antisocial behaviour in young people and adults highlights the key dilemma of where and how to set the boundary between normal and pathological, between health and illness. It is important not only to establish the prevalence of antisocial behaviour but also key stages of antisocial careers, age of onset, the probability of persistence after onset, the duration of antisocial behaviour and the age at which such behaviour ceases.

Definitions of antisocial behaviour have arisen largely out of the adult literature, with the cluster of antisocial symptoms being classified differently in different countries. In adults, the flamboyant/dramatic group of personality disorders includes those which have the most impact on society, and includes antisocial (dissocial), impulsive, borderline, histrionic and narcissistic disorders. One of these is invariably present in severe personality disorder, together with one or more disorders from other groups (Royal College of Psychiatrists, 1999).

Diagnostic classification in childhood centres around conduct disorder and oppositional defiant disorder. Conduct disorder is used to denote a syndrome of core symptoms characterised by the persistent failure to control behaviour appropriately within socially defined rules. It contains within it three main components: defiance of the will of someone in authority, aggressiveness, and antisocial behaviour that violates other people's rights, property or person. It should be stressed that these traits can be and are seen as part of normal development.

Conduct disorder is a function of the child, the environment and the context in which the person is operating. Altering any of these can effect

Young People and Mental Health. Edited by P. Aggleton, J. Hurry and I. Warwick.
© 2000 John Wiley & Sons Ltd.

the presentation of conduct disorder. Whether such interventions should be medical, social, moral or legalistic, is open to question. Conduct disorder is often persistent, and has a heavy cost for society, and treatment interventions with long-term evaluated outcomes are only just emerging in the UK. Professional opinion about assertive health interventions in this area is diverse. Goodman (1997) argues that children and adolescents with conduct disorder are naughty, awkward, disruptive, aggressive and antisocial. These are important problems needing social, educational and moral solutions, and a distinctive health component is only able to be identified in a minority of cases. Kazdin (1997), in contrast, has described serious antisocial behaviour as a chronic long-lasting disease that requires continuous monitoring and intervention over the life course.

YOUNG PEOPLE WITH SERIOUS ANTISOCIAL BEHAVIOUR

At any one time there are approximately 7500 young people aged under 21 in the 28 male young offender institutions, and approximately 2500 under 18 year-old boys and girls in what is now being referred to as the Secure (Juvenile) Estate provision (Table 6.1).

In the community at any one time it is likely that there are between 2500 and 5000 young people, who present with a similar level of risk, need and antisocial behaviour. The majority of these are provided for by Youth Justice Services and the Probation Service.

Research evidence is accumulating to show that the rate of mental health disorder is high in young offenders, particularly persistent offenders and those that are convicted. Gunn et al. (1991) found that a diagnosis of primary mental disorder can be made in a third of young men aged between 16 and 18 years who have been sentenced by a court. The prevalence of mental disorder in male remand prisoners aged 21 years and over was found to be 26% (excluding substance misuse) (Birmingham et al., 1996). A third of those supervised by a large probation service had a history of deliberate self-harm (Wessley et al., 1996). The

Table 6.1 Approximate bed numbers 1999—under 21's

1.	Secure care units (local authority provision)	500
2.	Youth treatment centre	40
3.	Under 18 year olds in young offender institutions	1800 (300 aged 15 or 16)
4.	Secure training centres	200
5.	Secure psychiatric adolescent beds, NHS and independent sector	70

prevalence of mental health problems is increased amongst young offenders before, during and following incarceration. The most obvious and serious example of this is demonstrated by the high rates of suicide or attempted suicide amongst young offenders (Liebling, 1991).

In the only UK psychiatric screening of 10 to 17 year olds attending a city centre Youth Court, high levels of both psychiatric and physical morbidity, including learning difficulties, mood disorder, epilepsy, frequent use of alcohol and illicit drugs and frank mental illness, were found (Dolan *et al.*, 1999). In the specialist secure care provision of the Youth Treatment Service, reported mental health problems that justified specialist clinical assessment have been found in 50% of the population (Bhatti *et al.*, 1996).

Kurtz *et al.* (1998) confirmed the view of practitioners in the field that the mental health needs of young people who display high levels of antisocial behaviour, who are psychologically disturbed and who present a danger to themselves and others, and offend are not well recognised or widely understood, and their needs are not safely met.

Violence

Grave acts of violence carried out by young people are one of the most important problems facing both European countries and the USA, not least because of the costs, economically, socially and emotionally. That said, the rate of grave offences committed by children and young people in Britain, particularly juvenile homicide, has not risen to any significant extent between 1980 and 1995 (McNally, 1995). Nevertheless, fear of violent crime at the hands of young people is an important and debilitating problem (Shepherd and Farrington, 1993).

Common disorders that may result in displays of violent, aggressive, sadistic or destructive behaviour inevitably involve serious malfunction of individuals in their social setting. To understand how this arises, there is a need to understand the interplay between processes of individual development and social conditions. Violent offenders commit offences of many types and nearly all chronic offenders have committed a violent offence. Important preventative strategies include understanding of early predictors, availability of early family support and pre-school education.

From Aggression to Violence

Violence is particularly subject to rhetoric, which is born largely out of factual ignorance and understandable fear. Sadistic violent acts carried out by young people often bring with them a surfeit of public and media interest which at times becomes voyeuristic in nature. It is important to recognise that violence occurs in the context of a social system and in the context of individual differences. The development of violent behaviour often involves a loss of sense of personal identifiability and uniqueness, a loss of sense of personal value. The young person engages in actions without concern for future consequences or past commitments.

The onset of boys' aggression is often in the pre-school period. Throughout childhood and into adolescence, increasing numbers of boys experience the onset of aggression (Hacipasalo and Tremblay, 1994). More serious violence tends to increase with age, especially during adolescence. Loeber and Hay (1994) argue that prevalence rates of aggression and violence from pre-school age to young adulthood actually represent diverse groups of youth that can be broken down into four broad groups.

The first of these groups consists of young people who desist from aggression; the second, young people whose aggression is stable and continues at the same level. The third group comprises young people who escalate in the severity of their aggression and make the transition to violence; and the fourth, young people who experience the onset of aggression stability. The pivotal studies of Olweus (1988), replicated in many subsequent longitudinal studies based on different forms of aggression, show that the average correlation between early aggression in childhood or adolescence and later aggression is as high as the stability of intelligence over time.

Sexually Inappropriate Behaviour

Sexual offending in young people constitutes a substantial health and social problem. It represents an important mental health issue, first because abusers often come from disadvantaged backgrounds with a history of victimisation; and second, because victims of abuse suffer high rates of psychiatric disorder. Child mental health services are increasingly being asked to assess and provide treatment not only for victims but also for perpetrators.

The majority of young abusers are male with a history of neglect, physical and/or sexual abuse, below average ability, and high rates of behavioural and psychological problems. In a series of 121 male juvenile sex offenders (the majority of whom had committed rape), many had a previous record of similar or less serious offences, but multi-agency, and indeed previous psychiatric assessment had not explored the presence or evolution of rape fantasies (Dolan *et al.*, 1996). The authors stressed the need in psychiatric interviews to enquire into the presence of rape fantasies and other concurrent violent behaviours, in addition to the paraphilias.

Vizard *et al.* (1996) have highlighted the need to balance the assumptions of the Children Act 1989, 'taking into account the wishes and feelings of the child', with the need to challenge this assumption when the young person may have 'wishes and feelings' directed towards abusing others. A model is suggested that places emphasis on a multidisciplinary team to establish a full interagency systemic context around each referred case of a young sexual abuser, following the child protection procedure and sensitive to the need for early preventative input.

The majority of adult sexual abusers of children started their abuse in their own adolescence, and yet there is as yet no diagnostic category for paedophilia for those under the age of 16. The authors suggest the creation of a new disorder, sexual arousal disorder of childhood, to help identify this vulnerable group who can in turn place vulnerable others at risk. There is currently a lack of epidemiological evidence concerning sexual conduct disorders in young people in the UK. Prospective studies using good baseline data should inform the planning of treatment programmes that should be tailored to young people and not just be taken from existing adult programmes.

Young Arsonists

Firesetting and arson are devastating behaviours impacting on the victim and wider society. There is a paucity of literature that facilitates a consistent view regarding the emergence, maintenance, or promotion of firesetting behaviour. Fineman (1980) stressed the interaction between personal and familial factors in predisposing the young person to the behaviour. Ureeland and Levin (1980) have suggested that it is the culmination of difficulty/fear of direct expression of aggression, and Patterson (1982) argues that firesetting occurs at the end of a continuum of antisocial behaviours. However, the major authors in the field, Kolko and Kazdin (1992), highlight the key features of attraction to fire, heightened arousal, impulsivity and limited social competence.

Above and beyond the global assessment, child mental health services would need to consider the domains of development, social and/or family problems, educational history, personal and/or family history, health history and offence history. The specific domains to be explored are: the history of fireplay; the history of hoax telephone calls; the nature of the behaviour—fires set alone or with peers, or a combination of these; where fires are set—open/green space, occupied/unoccupied dwelling; previous threats/targets; the type of fire—single, multiple seats of fire; ritualistic; motivation—anger resolution, boredom, rejection, cry for help, thrill seeking, fire fighting, crime concealment, no motivation, curiosity and peer pressure.

As with serious property offending, young arsonists are not a homogeneous group, demonstrating a wide range of familial, developmental, social, interpersonal, clinical and 'legal' needs. Thus no one standard treatment approach will be appropriate for all individuals (Repo and Virkkunen, 1997).

THE ORIGINS OF SERIOUS ANTISOCIAL BEHAVIOUR

Much remains to be learnt about personality development during adolescence, and how different factors and influences interact over time to establish the trajectory for serious antisocial behaviour in later life (Bailey, 1992). Theorists have described adolescent personality development from the perspectives of psychosexual development, ego development and defensive operations, identity formation, cognitive development, object relations, and latterly, psychology of self. The developmental tasks of adolescence are often said to be centred on autonomy and connection with others, rebellion and development of independence, development of identity and distinction from and continuity with childhood. We need to know how to define normal functioning and development before we can safely intervene with those who have been designated 'abnormal'.

Surveys of the general population show that 90% of boys admit to acts that could have led to appearance in court; however, most are minor in their nature. Antisocial behaviour is heterogeneous and for many still a normal phenomenon, a deliberate principled act of protest of transient adolescent onset and course. Those with early onset are at far higher risk in the adult life course for development of antisocial personality disorder and importantly also for affective disturbance.

Although more is known about criminal careers and chronic juvenile offending than antisocial careers *per se*, the research literature reveals that there are three major risk areas in children and young people with persistent antisocial behaviour: child centred, family centred and contextual which have an interactive effect on antisocial behaviour, providing support for a proposed cumulative protection model of prevention of both antisocial behaviour and offending.

Child Centred and Family Factors

A range of factors have been associated with serious antisocial behaviour, including child centred factors such as genetic vulnerability, perinatal risk, male gender, cognitive impairment, school underachievement, and hyperactivity or inattention temperament. Influential family factors include criminality in parents and siblings, family discord and lack of supervision. Also important are a lack of affective feeling, abuse, scapegoating, rejection and neglect. Influential contextual factors include drug and alcohol abuse, unemployment, crime opportunity and peer group interaction. Important perpetrating factors include continued substance abuse and unemployment. However, significant turning points include the establishment and maintenance of a harmonious stable relationship, and the continuing potential for growth and developmental change in the individual. In the space available, it is not possible to consider all of these variables. Attention will therefore be focused only on some of the more significant.

Genetic Factors

There is an accumulated body of evidence about the contribution of genetic factors to individual differences in antisocial behaviour in general (Rutter, 1996). Genetic risk may operate through an effect on hyperactivity or inattention, impulsivity and physiological reactivity rather than aggression. The effect could lie in neuropsychological or cognitive function (Moffitt, 1993). Genetic factors may operate through interaction with known environmental risks, parental attitude, role models and lack of supervision. Whatever the nature and extent of the contribution of genetic factors they are most likely to be particularly important in antisocial behaviour associated with early onset pervasive hyperactivity.

Attentional Difficulties

The onset of attention problems (as described in attention deficit and hyperactivity disorder, ADHD) occurs during the pre-school period, the time when aggression manifests itself in some children. Longitudinal studies show that children with attention problems exhibit increased levels of aggression in childhood, adolescence and adulthood, but evidence that early attention problems without concurrent aggression are related to later aggression is debated.

However, a major cluster of individual risk factors is emerging and includes hyperactivity, impulsivity, attention problems, clumsiness, daring or risk taking, and other elements of ADHD. These factors are often closely linked to childhood conduct disorder. Lynam (1996) has argued that children who had both hyperactivity–impulsivity–attention deficit and conduct problems were at risk of serious adult antisocial behaviour and personality disorder.

Cognitive Functioning

Children who display antisocial behaviour often have accompanying academic problems. Boys' aggression scores are negatively correlated to cognitive ability (Sharp *et al.*, 1995). Conduct problems in girls are, in contrast, associated positively with intelligence (Sonuga-Barke *et al.*, 1994). Maguin and Loeber (1996) in a recent meta-analysis demonstrated that it is low intelligence and attentional problems rather than educational performance that predicts later delinquency. Maughan *et al.* (1996)

followed poor and normal readers through adolescence and into early adulthood. Reading disabled boys showed high rates of inattentiveness in middle childhood. Increased risk of juvenile offending among this specific group has been linked to poor school attendance rather than reading difficulties *per se*. Reading problems were associated with some increase in disruptive behaviour of girls in their teens.

Post Traumatic Stress Disorder (PTSD)

There is evolving evidence in the field of PTSD (Pynoos and Nader, 1993) that children suffering the after effects of traumatic stress can manifest this in later violence, this violent behaviour sometimes mirroring the traumatic experience the young person has endured as a previous victim (Dodge *et al.*, 1990). Perry (1994), studying the neurological sequelae of childhood trauma and their links to PTSD in children, suggests that severe trauma during childhood can have a devastating effect on all functions of the developing brain—emotional, cognitive, behavioural and physiological.

Family Functioning

Insecure attachment relationships in infancy predict later behavioural problems in boys. These relationships show themselves in aggressive non-compliance. During pre-school years insecure girls may be either aggressive or especially compliant (Greenberg *et al.*, 1992). Insecure attachment is sometimes associated with maternal depression, which promotes externalising problems (De Mulder and Radke-Yarrow, 1991) and an aggressive stance.

The predominant factors within families that contribute to longer term aggressiveness and risk of violence are in child rearing and parenting styles (Farrington, 1996). Against the background of 'multiple deprivation' three clusters of key factors emerge. In the first cluster is the presence of criminal parents and of siblings with behavioural problems. In the second cluster, the day to day behaviour of primary caregivers is characterised by parental conflict, inconsistent supervision, and physical and emotional neglect, factors associated with the risk of delinquency. Some parents provide little direct reinforcement of prosocial behaviours, reinforcing instead coercive behaviours. Thus the child learns that their own aversive behaviour serves to stop unwanted intrusions by parents (Patterson and Capaldi, 1991). Further, young people who assault others have been shown to have lower rates of positive communication with their families, and may have aggressive relationships with their peers (Perry, Perry and Kennedy, 1992). The third cluster of family factors linked with later violence in the child includes cruel authoritarian discipline, physical control, and, in particular, the shaming and emotional degradation of the child.

Antisocial parents tend to have antisocial children (Farrington, 1996). However, it is unclear how far there is a specific transmission of types of antisocial behaviour as opposed to general transmission of antisocial tendencies. Nor is it clear how far this transmission is attributable to genetic as opposed to environmental factors.

Peer Influences

Children who have frequent disagreements with peers (Shantz and Hartup, 1992) do not make friends. Very aggressive children are rejected by their peers, a process that can start in the early school years (Pope et al., 1989). Aggressive children who are rejected show more diverse and severe conduct problems (Bierman et al., 1993). Moreover, peer rejection promotes association with antisocial peers; dyadic relationships are then formed that provide the focus for peer diverted aggression. Victims often lack social skills and can be aggressive themselves. Repeatedly victimised young people are more likely to become aggressors as well (Hotaling et al., 1989). Aggressive young people may make alliances, bullying others, which results in the emergence of aggressive peer groups and gangs where the individual's rate of violence usually increases (Thornberry et al., 1993). These groups may prove attractive to other previously non-aggressive young people, adding to the group of late onset aggressive adolescents.

Substance Abuse

Alcohol consumption can act as a short-term potent facilitator to aggression, and may specifically apply to individuals with prior high levels of aggressive behaviour and violent acts (Lang, 1993). After the onset of drug dealing, acceleration of the young person's rate of violent acts has been described (Blumstein, 1995). Most adolescents and adults who use illicit drugs do not commit predatory crimes. However, predatory offenders who persistently and frequently use large amounts of multiple types of drugs commit crimes, including violent acts, at significantly higher rates and over longer periods than do less drug involved offenders (Chaiken and Chaiken, 1990).

PROTECTIVE FACTORS

Protective factors can be defined in several different ways. One definition is that protective factors are merely the opposite end of the scale from risk factors. The Ontario Child Health Study (Rowe-Grant *et al.*, 1989) revealed three major protective factors for conduct disorder: getting on well with others, good academic performance and participation in organised activities. Another possible definition of a protective factor is a variable that interacts with a risk factor to minimise the risk factor's effects (Rutter, 1985).

Jessor's (1991) problem behaviour theory describes intra-individual covariation among adolescent problem behaviours such that they cluster to form a risk behaviour syndrome. The patterning of these behaviours reflects a young person's way of being in the world. The environment in which young people live provides socially organised opportunities to learn risk behaviours together, and normative expectations that these behaviours be performed together. Resiliency is associated with a sense of hope or purpose that negative odds can be overcome.

Hoge *et al.* (1996) from a study of Canadian youth serious offences showed that risk variables reflecting family relationship and parenting problems were associated with heightened rates of re-offending and lower overall adjustment. The presence of protective factors relating to positive response to autonomy and effective use of leisure time was associated with more positive outcomes with control for the risk factors. There was no evidence of interaction between risk and protective factors; the latter operated similarly at low and high levels of risk.

Werner and Smith (1982) studied children in Hawaii who possessed four or more risk factors for delinquency before age two, but who nevertheless did not develop behavioural difficulties during childhood or adolescence. Major protective factors included being first born, being active and affectionate infants, being in a small-size family and receiving a large amount of attention from caretakers. Studies to date reinforce the need always to focus on areas of strength and not only on the presence of risk factors, however poor the prognosis for trajectory into adult antisocial behaviour.

Gender

Most juvenile crime is committed by boys, and there remains a large difference between the number of boys held in both Secure Care local authority units and Young Offender Institutions, and the number of girls of a similar age. Understanding both the changing trend for violent behaviour in girls and the protective factors which still operate for girls should help inform preventative measures for both boys and girls. The link between childhood abuse and adult substance abuse and violent behaviour is emerging for women but not as yet for men. Substance misuse and drug dependency feature as a considerable problem for adult women in prison (Mohan *et al.*, 1997). Widom and White (1997) suggest that male control groups may be complicated by undisclosed childhood abuse, obscuring a link for males. It may be that currently girls are more able to disclose abuse than boys. Girls who engage in violent behaviour therefore present as a useful study group in trying to understand the pathway from experiences in childhood to adult serious antisocial behaviour.

In the UK, there is a paucity of literature relating to adolescent girls who offend and who have mental health problems. In a study of 100 consecutive referrals of girls aged 11 to 17 to an Adolescent Forensic Mental Health Service, referrers correctly documented violent and aggressive behaviour in only 54% of cases (Jasper *et al.*, 1998). Over 70% had been the subject of abuse (emotional, sexual, or physical), and the majority had been multiply abused. Half of the violent girls had misused substances, more of the abused group had been violent to objects (50%) or set fires (20%). A high number of deliberately self-harming girls misused substances (50%) and had been sexually abused (54%).

PREVENTION AND INTERVENTION

There are four major types of prevention that relate to reduction of serious antisocial behaviour and juvenile offending (Tonry and Farrington, 1995). First, there is criminal justice prevention, which consists of deterrence, incapacitation and rehabilitation strategies operated by law enforcement and criminal justice agencies. The second type is situational prevention, which is designed to reduce the opportunities for antisocial behaviour and to increase the risk and difficulty of committing antisocial acts. Third, community preventions are interventions designed to change the social conditions and social institutions that influence antisocial behaviour in communities.

The fourth type of prevention is developmental prevention, which consists of interventions designed to inhibit the development of antisocial behaviour in individuals by targeting risk and protective factors that influence human development. Successful early preventive interventions for juvenile offending and related antisocial behaviour depend on the efficacy of parent education and pre-school programmes that enable young children to understand more readily the consequences of their behaviour for self and peers, critically helping them to make safe choices and reach safe autonomy in adolescence.

Lipsey (1995), in a review of outcome studies of education and psychotherapeutic intervention, and Kazdin (1997), in a major review of the effectiveness of psychotherapy in reducing problem behaviour in young people, suggest the importance of three strategies. The primary strategy is population-based preventive intervention; the secondary strategy consists of interventions focused on high risk groups, and the tertiary strategy consists of treatment centred programmes.

Early Prevention

Problems in pregnancy and infancy can be alleviated by home visiting programmes designed to help mothers (Olds *et al.*, 1986). Not only does this lead to teenage mothers having heavier babies and fewer pre-term deliveries, but also post-natal home visits have been shown to be associated with a decrease in recorded child physical abuse and neglect in the first two years of life. The last result is important because of the finding that being physically abused or neglected as a child is predictive of later violent antisocial behaviour (Widom, 1989).

One of the most successful prevention programmes has been the Perry pre-school project. Targeted at disadvantaged African-American children, the children, who were aged three to four, attended a daily prescribed programme backed up by weekly home visits. Seven other 'headstart' projects followed (Schweinhart *et al.*, 1993). Gains in intellectual benefits have been short lived, but at follow-up with some children now in their late twenties who had experienced the programmes, it was found that their school failure had decreased, antisocial behaviour had decreased, and they were more likely to be employed.

Childhood Intervention

Whatever the treatment model, safe interventions have to be based on assessment that has established a global picture of the child or young person including health needs and risk assessment. This should include the situations in which the behaviour occurs, specific triggers, and quantification of the behaviour. Cognitive and emotional assessment has to examine perceptions, thoughts and feelings associated with the behaviour. Interventions have to be applied with continuous monitoring and evaluation of treatment outcomes on all aspects of the young person's life.

Psychological Interventions

Social skills training enhances abilities in positive social interaction. Behaviourally based approaches include instruction, modelling, role-playing, coaching and feedback for children and young people who have previously dealt with new social encounters through antisocial behaviour (Goldstein, 1986; Goldstein *et al.*, 1994).

Self instructional training is designed to modify the things children say to themselves and change the autonomic cognitive events that play a regulatory role in everyday behaviour. Interventions containing cognitive elements have better outcomes than ones which do not (Izzo and Ross, 1990). In social problem-solving, an attempt is made to foster interpersonal problem-solving skills in order to lead to conflict avoidance and hence reduce the risk of aggressive antisocial behaviour (Kazdin, 1995). Anger control training is a widely used form of cognitive behavioural work, combining self instructional methods with relaxation training and a model of stress inoculation. Encouraging results have been reported with aggressive adolescent inpatients with severe behaviour disorders (Fendler and Eiton, 1986).

Increasingly, combined multimodel treatment programmes have been employed. The most complex approach to reduction of violent behaviour in young people is Aggression Replacement Training (ART), formulated to meet the growing problem of juvenile gang violence in the USA (Goldstein et al., 1994). ART brings together social skills training, self instructional and/or anger control training, and moral reasoning enhancement, and is carried out in community and institutional settings.

The most recent intensive home based intensive treatment, multisystemic therapy (MST) is showing good long term outcomes with high risk antisocial adolescents (Henggeler, 1999).

Family Based Interventions

The possibility of training parents in improved child management skills emerged in the 1970s, the most extensive work in this area being undertaken in Oregon (Bank et al., 1991). This work highlighted three key mechanisms by which some parents maintained undesirable behaviour in their children. First, undesirable behaviour may be positively reinforced by a response of angry or irritable attention. Second, desirable behaviour may be extinguished by a lack of attention, and did not enable the child to obtain what they wanted. Third, negative reinforcement (e.g. the removal of an unpleasant stimulus, negative here referring to the absence of something acting as a reinforcer) is likely to continue the behaviours. In the case of a noisy child, the adult's escalating coercion is rewarded by the child eventually being quiet (the removal of the child's noise). Sessions take place 'live' in the presence of the child, and techniques are repeatedly practised so that the parent actually experiences handling the child differently.

Webster-Stratton and Herbert (1994) have developed a model of group treatment enabling parents to receive tuition in parenting techniques at the same time. Parent training is most likely to succeed where the essential nature of play is explored, parents and children are praised, role play is used, and the parents' own childhood is explored. Components that can be added to parent training therapy include home visits, encouraging telephone calls, systemic family therapy, e.g. incorporating attachment theory into a principally structural model (Byng-Hall, 1995).

School and Community Prevention

Liaison with school is essential; teachers may become an important part of therapy, incorporating components of the child's treatment in the classroom. Training for teachers may well benefit other children in the class (Gray *et al.*, 1994). In some cases where change between parent and child has not proved possible, recommendations may be made about schooling within a therapeutic environment available in schools for children with emotional and behavioural disturbance (Department of Education, 1994). Any intervention should be preceded by thorough assessment to detect comorbid conditions. Child mental health clinics are now developing parent training throughout the UK (Smith, 1996).

The influence of peers and community becomes increasingly important for young people. Intervention strategies geared towards peer influence resistance strategies, classroom management, anti-bullying initiatives in school (see Chapter 12) and the utilisation of multiple component programmes across home and school are likely to have more impact.

Hawkins *et al.* (1991) carried out important school based prevention programmes in Seattle that combined parent training, teacher training and skills training. Evaluation, 18 months later, found that boys who received the programmes were significantly less aggressive than controls, and girls, although no less aggressive, were less depressed. At age ten, these children were less likely to have initiated delinquency and alcohol use.

Community Based Approaches

Communities that Care (Hawkins and Catalano, 1992) is a risk focused prevention programme tailored to the needs of each community, and targets four main behaviours that are damaging to the lives of young people and the communities where they live. These are youth crime, drug abuse, school-age pregnancy and sexually transmitted diseases, and school failure. Key leaders in the community, the mayor, school heads, the police chief and business leaders are brought together to agree on goals of a programme for their particular city, town, district or public housing estate. The key leaders set up a community board that is accountable to them and has representatives from the four jurisdictions of health education, care and justice, together with parents, youth groups, church, business and media. The Board carry out a risk assessment, and develop a prevention plan from a menu of strategies tapping into professional help and assistance including child mental health teams. Communities that Care is now established in the UK, modelled on the US programmes and on other preventive public health campaigns in the UK (Communities that Care (UK), 1997).

Some Problems

One of the problems concerning the evaluation of existing prevention programmes derives from the fact that outcomes tend to be related to delinquency and adult crime more than antisocial behaviour *per se*. Moreover, many prevention and intervention programmes are still largely geared towards men, and use techniques that are primarily risk focused rather than those that take an holistic approach addressing quality of life, needs assessment and meeting current need (Kroll *et al.*, 1999).

CONCLUSIONS

The improved allocation of young people with serious antisocial behaviour to treatments that are likely to work is a continuing challenge. New models of treatment delivery have to face the difficulties of retaining cases in treatment, the problems of comorbidity, the relative paucity of long-term follow-up evidence, and difficulties of interpreting the clinical significance of change in the individual.

In order both to understand individual developmental processes and to identify the mechanisms that account for change in the frequency of disorders in the community at large, it is necessary to bring together different kinds of causal explanations. Cicchetti and Newcombe (1997) challenge researchers and clinicians to examine the implicit and explicit assumptions that guide their work and to devise constructive solutions to these potential impediments. Developmental psychopathology may enable us to understand better the processes of adaption and maladaption, as well as the best means of preventing or ameliorating mental health problems.

Key to the reduction of serious antisocial behaviour in young people is appropriate multiagency, strategically co-ordinated mental health care for young people at the stages of prevention, early intervention and ongoing specialist interventions that can be offered through adolescence with safe transfer into adult mental health care to support young people and their families within the community.

Meanwhile debate no doubt will persist as to whether genetic rather than cultural factors are the key determinants in the evolution, pattern and act of serious antisocial behaviour. Whatever the balance, it is increasingly recognised that local communities have a pivotal role to play in helping young people to make pro-social choices.

There will have to be acceptance at a national level that programmes aimed at prevention and early intervention may take a minimum of ten years to demonstrate direct results. Denying mental health and social services benefits to children and adolescents today to save money will only ensure that the future prison population will grow. Above all, there needs to be a recognition of the importance of the power of any one individual adult to influence the life of any young person. Adults who, as children and high-risk adolescents, were exposed to many of the risk factors for serious antisocial behaviour, but proved to be resilient, frequently acknowledge the importance of an adult who, however briefly, communicated intentionally or inadvertently that they believed in that young person, and cared for him or her (Bailey, 1999; Bullock and Little, 1999).

REFERENCES

Bailey, S. (1992) Personality development in adolescence. *Journal of Forensic Psychiatry*, 4(3), 413–419.

Bailey, S. (1996) Adolescents who murder. *Journal of Adolescence*, 19, 19–39.

Bailey, S. (1999) The interface between mental health, criminal justice and forensic mental health services for children and adolescents. *Current Opinion in Psychiatry*, 12, 425–432.

Bank, L., Marlow, J.H., Reed, J.B., Patterson, G.R. and Weinvolt, M.R. (1991) Comparative evaluation of parent training interventions for families of chronic delinquents. *Journal of Abnormal Child Psychology*, 19, 15–23.

Beirman, K.L., Smoot, D.L. and Aumiller, K. (1993) Characteristics of aggressive rejectively aggressive (non rejected) and rejected (non aggressive) boys. *Child Development*, 64, 139–151.

Bhatti, V., Vostanis, P., Lengua, C., Rothery, D. and Cope, R. (1996) *Establishment of Need for the Development of a Child and Adolescent Forensic Service in Birmingham*. Birmingham, South Birmingham Mental Health Trust.

Birmingham, L., Mason, D. and Grubin, D. (1996) Prevalence of mental disorder in remand prisoners: consecutive case study. *British Medical Journal*, 313, 1521–1524.

Blumstein, A. (1995) Young people and why the deadly nexus? *National Institute of Justice Journal*, 229, 2–9.

Boswell, G. (1995) Violent victims. *The Prevalence of Abuse and Loss in the Lives of Section 53 Offenders*. London: The Prince's Trust.

Bullock, R. and Little, M. (1999) The interface between social and health services for children and adolescent persons. *Current Opinion in Psychiatry*, 12, 421–424.

Byng Hall, J. (1995) *Rewriting Family Scripts*. New York: Guildford.

Chaiken, J.M. and Chaiken, M.R. (1990) *Drugs and Predatory Crime: Crime and Justice—A Review of Research 13*. Chicago, IL: University of Chicago Press.

Cicchetti, D. and Newcombe, B. (1997) Special Issue. Conceptual and scientific underpinnings of research in developmental psychopathology. *Developmental Psychopathology*, 9, 189–472.

Communities that Care (UK) (1997) *A New Kind of Prevention Programme. A Guide—1997*. London: Rowntree.

De Mulder, E.K. and Radke-Yarrow, M. (1991) Attachment and affectively ill and well mothers. Concurrent behavioural correlates. *Developmental Psychopathology*, 3, 277–292.

Department of Education (1994) *Special Educational Needs. A Guide for Parents*. London: HMSO.

Dodge, K.A., Bates, J.E. and Petit, G.S. (1990) Mechanisms in the cycle of violence. *Science*, 250, 1678–1683.

Dolan, M., Holloway, J., Bailey, S. and Kroll, L. (1996) The psychosocial characteristics of juvenile sex offenders. *Medical Science Law*, 36, 343–352.

Dolan, M., Holloway, J., Bailey, S. and Smith, C. (1999) Mental health status of juvenile offenders. A survey of young offenders appearing before the juvenile courts. *Journal of Adolescence*, 22, 137–144.

Farrington, D. (1996) *Understanding and Preventing Youth Crime*. York: Joseph Rowntree Foundation.

Fendler, E.L. and Eiton, R.B. (1986) *Adolescent Anger Control: Cognitive Behavioural Techniques*. Elmsford, NY: Pergamon Press.

Fineman, K.R. (1980) Firesetting in childhood and adolescence. *Psychiatric Clinics of North America*, 3, 483–500.

Goldstein, A.P. (1986) Psychological skills training and the aggressive adolescent. In S.J. Aplet and A.P. Goldstein (Eds) *Youth Violence: Program and Prospects*. New York: Pergamon Press.

Goldstein, A.P., Glick, B., Cartnan, W. and Blancero, D.A. (1994) *The Prosocial Gang. Implementing Aggression Replacement Training*. Thousand Oaks, CA: Sage.

Goodman, R. (1997) Child and Adolescent Mental Health Services: Reasoned Advice to Commissioners and Providers: Maudsley Discussion Paper No 4.

Gray, P., Miller, A. and Noakes, J. (1994) *Challenging Behaviour in Schools*. London: Routledge.

Greenberg, M., Speltz, M.L., Deklyen, M. and Endrigg, M. (1992) Attachment security in pre-schoolers with and without externalising behaviour problems. A replication. *Developmental Psychopathology*, 3, 413–430.

Gunn, J., Maden, A. and Swinton, M. (1991) Treatment needs of prisoners with psychiatric disorders. *British Medical Journal*, 303, 338–341.

Hacipasalo, J. and Tremblay, R.E. (1994) Physically aggressive boys from age 6 to 12. Family background, parenting behaviour and prediction of delinquency. *Journal of Consulting Clinical Psychology*, 62, 1044–1052.

Hawkins, J.D., VonCleve, F. and Catalan, R. (1991) Reducing early childhood aggression: results of a primary prevention programme. *Journal of the American Academy of Child and Adolescent Psychiatry*, 30, 208–217.

Hawkins, J.D. and Catalano, R.F. (1992) *Communities that Care*. San Francisco: Jossey-Bass.

Henggeler, S.W. (1999) Multisystemic therapy: an overview of clinical procedures, outcomes and policy implications. *Psychol. Psychiatry Rev.*, 4, 2–9.

Hoge, R.D., Andrews, D.A. and Leschied, A.W. (1996) An investigation of risk and protective factors in a sample of youthful offenders. *Journal of Child Psychology and Psychiatry*, 37, 419–424.

Hotaling, G.T., Straus, M.A. and Lincoln, A.J. (1989) Intrafamily violence and crime and violence outside the family. In L. Onlin and M. Tunn (Eds) *Family Violence*. Chicago, IL: University of Chicago Press.

Izzo, R.L. and Ross, R.R. (1990) Meta-analysis of rehabilitation programmes for juvenile delinquents. *Criminal Justice and Behaviour*, 17, 134–142.

Jasper, A., Smith, C. and Bailey, S. (1998) 100 Girls in Care Referred to an Adolescent Forensic Service. *Journal of Adolescence*, 21, 555–568.

Jessor, R. (1991) Risk behaviour in adolescence: a psychosocial framework for understanding and action. *Journal of Adolescent Health*, 12, 597–605.

Kazdin, A.E. (1995) *Conduct Disorders in Childhood and Adolescence*, 2nd edn. London: Sage.

Kazdin, A.E. (1997) Practitioner review, psychological treatments for conduct disorder in children. *Journal of Child Psychology and Psychiatry*, 38(2), 161–178.

Kolko, D.J. and Kazdin, A.E. (1992) The emergence and re-occurrence of child firesetting. A one year prospective study. *Journal of Abnormal Child Psychology*, 201, 17–37.

Kroll, L., Woodham, A., Rothwell, J., Bailey, S., Tobias, C., Harrington, R. and Marsham, M. (1999) Reliability of the Salford Needs Assessment Schedule for Adolescents. *Psychological Medicine*, 29, 891–902.

Kurtz, Z., Thomes, R. and Bailey, S. (1997) *A Study of the Demand and Needs for Forensic Child and Adolescent Mental Health Services in England and Wales*. London: Report to the Department of Health.

Kurtz, Z., Thomes, R. and Bailey, S. *et al.* (1998) Children in the Criminal Justice and Secure Care Systems: How their mental health needs are met. *Journal of Adolescence*, 21, 543–553.

Lang, R. (1993) Alcohol related violence: psychological perspective. In S. Martin (Ed.) *Alcohol and Interpersonal Violence. Fostering Interdisciplinary Perspectives. NIAA Research monogram No. 24.* Washington, DC: Department of Health and Human Science.

Liebling, A. (1991) Suicide and Self Injury amongst Young Offenders in Custody. Cambridge University Dissertation.

Lipsey, M. (1995) What do we learn from 400 research studies on the effectiveness of treatment with juvenile delinquents? In J. McGuire (Ed.) *What Works: Reducing Reoffending Guidelines from Research and Practice*. Chichester: Wiley.

Loeber, R. (1990) Development and risk factors of juvenile antisocial behaviour and delinquency. *Clin. Psychol. Rev.*, 10, 1–41.

Loeber, R. and Hay, D.F. (1994) Developmental approaches to aggression and conduct problems. In M. Rutter and D. Hay (Eds) *Development Through Life: A Handbook for Clinicians*. Oxford: Blackwell Scientific.

Lynam, D. (1996) Early identification of chronic offenders: who is the fledgling psychopath? *Psychological Bulletin*, 120, 209–234.

Maguin, E. and Loeber, R. (1996) Academic performance and delinquency. In M. Tonry and N. Moms (Eds) *Crime and Justice*. Chicago, IL: Chicago University Press.

Maughan, B., Pickles, A., Hagell, A., Rutter, M. and Yule, W. (1996) Reading problems and antisocial behaviour. Developmental trends in co-morbidity. *Child Psychology Psychiatry*, 37, 405–418.

McCann, J., James, A., Wilson, S. and Dunn, G. (1996) Prevalence of psychiatric disorders in young people in the care system. *British Medical Journal*, 313, 1529–1530.

McNally, R.B. (1995) Homicidal youth in England and Wales 1982–1992. Profile and policy. *Psychology, Crime and the Law*, 1, 333–342.

Moffitt, T.E. (1993) The neuropsychology of conduct disorder. *Developmental Psychopathology*, 5, 135–151.

Mohan, D., Scully, P., Collins, C. and Smith, C. (1997) Psychiatric disorder in an Irish female prison. *Criminal Behaviour and Mental Health*, 7, 229–235.

Olds, D.L., Henderson, C.R., Chamberlain, R. and Tatelbaum, R. (1996) Preventing child abuse and neglect. A randomised trial of nurse home visitation. *Paediatrics*, 78, 65–78.

Olweus, D.C. (1988) Environment and biological factors in the development of aggressive behaviour. In W. Blukkuisen and S.A. Medrick (Eds) *Explaining Criminal Behaviour*. Leiden, The Netherlands: E.J.Britt.

Patterson, G.R. (1982) *Coercive Family Process*. Eugene, OR: Castalia.

Patterson, G.R. and Capaldi, D.M. (1991) Antisocial parents: unskilled and unavailable. In P.A. Cowan and E.M. Hemington (Eds) *Family Transitions*, 218.

Perry, B.D. (1994) Neurological sequence of childhood trauma: PTSD in children. In M. Murray (Ed) *Post Traumatic Stress Disorder. Emergency Concepts*. American Psychiatric Press: Washington DC.

Perry, D.G., Perry L.C. and Kennedy, E. (1992) Conflict and the development of antisocial behaviour. In C.U. Shante and W.W. Hartup (Eds) *Conflict in Child and Adolescent Development*. New York: Cambridge University Press, pp. 301–329.

Pope, A.W., Bierman, K.L. and Mumma, G.H. (1989) Relations between hyperactive and aggressive behaviours and peer relations at three elementary grade levels. *Journal of Abnormal Child Psychology*, 17, 253–267.

Pynoos, R.S. and Nader, K. (1993) Issues in the treatment of post traumatic stress in children and adolescents. In J.P. Wilson and B. Raphael (Eds) *International Handbook of Traumatic Stress Syndromes*. New York: Plenum Press.

Repo, E. and Virkunnen, M. (1997) Young arsonists, history of conduct disorder, psychiatric diagnosis, and criminal recidivism. *Journal of Forensic Psychiatry*, 8(2), 311–320.

Rowe-Grant, N., Thomas, B.H., Offard, D.R. and Boyle, M.H. (1989) Risk protective factors and the prevalence of behavioural and emotional characters in children and adolescents. *Journal of the American Academy of Childhood Adolescent Psychiatry*, 28, 262–268.

Royal College of Psychiatrists (1999) Council Report CR.71. Offenders with Personality Disorder 1–13. London: Gaskell.

Rutter, M. (1985) Resilience in the face of adversity: protective factors and resistance to psychiatric disorder. *British Journal of Psychiatry*, 147, 598–611.

Rutter, M. (Ed.) (1996) *Genetics of Criminal and Antisocial Behaviour (Ciba Foundation Symposium 1994)*. Chichester: Wiley.

Schweinhart, L.J., Barnes, H.O. and Weikart, D.P. (1993) *Significant Benefits*. Ypsilank, MI: High/Scope.

Shantz, C.U. and Hartup, W.W. (1992) *Conflict in Child and Adolescent Development*. Cambridge: Cambridge University Press.

Sharp, D., Hay, D.F., Pawlby, S., Schumucher, G., Allen, H. and Kuma, R. (1995) The impact of postnatal depression on boys' intellectual development. *Journal of Child Psychology and Psychiatry*, 36, 1315–1336.

Shepherd, J.P. and Farrington, D.P. (1993) Assault as a public health problem. *Journal of the Royal Society of Medicine*, 6, 89–92.

Smith, C. (1996) *Developing Parenting Programmes*. York and London: Joseph Rowntree Foundation and the National Children's Bureau.

Sonuga-Barke, E.J.S., Lamparelli, M., Stevenson, J., Thompson, M. and Henry, A. (1994) Behavioural problems and pre-school intellectual attainment. The association of hyperactivity and conduct problems. *Journal of Child Psychology and Psychiatry*, 35, 949–960.

Thornberry, T.P., Krohn, M.D. and Lizotte, A. (1993) The role of juvenile gangs in facilitating delinquent behaviour. *Journal of Research in Crime Delinquency*, 30, 55–87.

Tonry, M. and Farrington, D.P. (1995) Strategic approaches to crime prevention. In M. Tonry and D.P. Farrington (Eds) *Building a Safer Society: Strategic Approaches to Crime Prevention*. Chicago: University of Chicago Press.

Tyrer, P. and Stein, G. (1993) *Personality Disorder Reviewed*. London: Royal College of Psychiatrists, Gaskell.

Ureeland, R.G. and Levin, B.M. (1980) Psychosocial Aspects of Firesetting. In Carter, D. (Ed) *Fire and Human Behavior*, New York, Wiley Press.

Vizard, E., Wynick, S., Hawkes, C., Woods, J. and Jenkins, J. (1996) Juvenile sexual offenders. Assessment issues. *British Journal of Psychiatry*, 168, 259–262.

Webster-Stratton, H.M. and Herbert, M. (1994) *Troubled Families— Problem Children*. Chichester: Wiley.

Werner, E.E. and Smith, R.S. (1982) *Vulnerable but Invincible: A Longitudinal Study of Resilient Children and Youth*. New York: McGraw-Hill.

Wessely, S., Akhurst, A., Brown, L. and Moss, L. (1996) Deliberate self harm and the probation services: an overlooked public health problem? *Journal of Public Health Medicine*, 18(2), 129–132.

Widom, C.S. (1989) The cycle of violence. *Science*, 244, 160–166.

Widom, C.S. and White, H.R. (1997) Problem behaviours in abused and neglected children grown up: prevalence and co-occurrence of substance abuse, crime and violence. *Criminal Behaviour and Mental Health*, 7, 287–310.

Chapter 7

Youth Suicide and Deliberate Self-harm

Michael Kerfoot

The study of suicide and attempted suicide in children and adolescents has, until relatively recently, lagged far behind the study of these acts in adults. The 1980s have, however, seen an increased research interest in this area, particularly in the USA and Europe. Suicidal behaviour in children and adolescents constitutes an important problem for both health and welfare services (Harrington and Dyer, 1993). In the UK, suicide is now the second most common cause of death among young people aged 15–24 years (OPCS, 1990), and similar trends have been observed in the USA. This trend has been reflected in the growing volume of research on adolescent suicide and attempted suicide. Referrals to hospital because of deliberate self-harm remain at a high level in this age group (Hawton and Fagg, 1992), and child mental health teams spend a great deal of time in the assessment and aftercare of overdose cases which, in some districts, account for up to 20% of referrals to these teams (Kerfoot, 1988).

THE PROBLEM OF DEFINITION

The definition of suicidal behaviours, and particularly those which lead to death, is neither straightforward nor easy. In general, suicidal behaviour is made up of two separate phenomena but with a marked degree of overlap between them. In one group can be included those individuals who intentionally kill themselves (suicide), or who harm

Young People and Mental Health. Edited by P. Aggleton, J. Hurry and I. Warwick.
© 2000 John Wiley & Sons Ltd.

themselves with the clear intention of ending their lives, but who unexpectedly survive (attempted suicide). In the other group are those who intentionally harm themselves but in the reasonably secure belief that death will not result from their action. This kind of behaviour is often referred to as 'parasuicide' because it appears to imitate suicidal behaviour, but without clear suicidal intent. It is also referred to as 'deliberate self-harm'. Within either of these groups the assessment of suicidal intent may present little difficulty, but between these two groups will fall a number of individuals in whom suicidal motivation will be hard to assess. The individual may present mixed, unclear or shifting ideas when asked about intent so that it becomes difficult for the professional to assess the seriousness of an episode or the risk of repetition. Some acts of parasuicide do have a quite unintended fatal outcome. On the other hand, an individual who is quite determined to commit suicide may, unexpectedly, survive and conceal their continued determination to succeed at suicide by denying current or future suicidal intent. Attempts to define suicidal or self-harming behaviour will continue to raise difficulties because there will always be the possibility for an unintended victim to become a fatality and for a potential fatality to become a survivor.

COMPLETED SUICIDE

Suicide in children under 12 years of age is rare (Shaffer, 1974; Hawton and Goldacre, 1982) and is a relatively unusual event in the under 15s. However, suicide rates since the 1970s have shown a particular increase among 15–19 year-old men. This increase is also reflected in rates for 'accidental' and 'undetermined' deaths (McClure, 1994) and is associated with the increase in the use of more lethal methods such as hanging and poisoning by vehicle exhaust gas. Among young suicide completers, males outnumber females in the order of 3:1. In contrast, over the same period the rates for females have fallen by nearly a half. The reasons for these trends are unclear but social factors such as the increasing rate of divorce, and of unemployment, may be important, although suicide rates have continued to increase even at times, as occurred in the late 1980s, when unemployment rates were coming down.

Differences in rates may point to some gender-specific social changes. For example, the increasing numbers of women in the workforce suggest not only a change in the traditional view of women's roles, but also a change in gender attribution to roles. Traditionally, employment has been a major defining role for men but, it could be argued, increasing unemployment among young men will have generated role conflict by removing one of the major components of their 'identity'. While women have generally occupied, and combined, a number of diverse roles, the male role repertoire has tended to be quite limited, leaving them little scope for role substitution, or the creation of new, defining roles. Misuse of alcohol and drugs by young people has also increased, and both are related to suicide among the young, particularly among young men (Marttunen *et al.*, 1991). Antisocial behaviour in the year preceding suicide has been reported in half of the males and a third of the females in a Finnish study (Marttunen *et al.*, 1994). Depressive disorders were common among all suicide victims but young men with antisocial behaviour had more alcohol abuse alongside their mental disorder compared with those without antisocial behaviour. Separation from parents, parental alcohol abuse and parental violence were also common for young male victims with antisocial behaviour. Substance abuse, which is more common among young men than young women, is increasingly cited in reports as a serious risk factor for completed suicide and deliberate self-harm (Bukstein *et al.*, 1993). There is also increasing evidence to suggest an important link between psychiatric disorders, such as depression, and suicide in young people (Brent *et al.*, 1994).

Suicide among the young is often preceded by psychosocial difficulties of one kind or another. It is probably the culmination of chronic difficulties which include depression, drug or alcohol use, psychosocial stress and/or behavioural problems. The effects of suicide on family and friends have also been highlighted in research (Brent, 1992), where friends of young people who had killed themselves experienced significant psychiatric morbidity after the death, and grief reactions which persisted for some months. Indeed, the aftermath of suicide can be as traumatic as the event itself, for those who are close to the deceased. Where the deceased is a young person there is a particular poignancy about a life that has been wasted before it has hardly begun. In addition, the stigma associated with suicide means that families will tend to withdraw into their own private world, unable to deal with the event publicly until a private accommodation has been achieved. For most the event will be a traumatic, nightmarish experience, and one for which they could have had no preparation. In some families, however, the suicide of a young family member may be the culmination of a long period of problematic behaviour and deteriorating family relationships. Soul-searching, self-recrimination, rumination and guilt are all natural responses to trauma of this kind and some families can go through these processes together, sharing the grief and helping each other. In other families, the problems and issues may be more complex, particularly if a suicide note has directed the guilt explicitly towards a particular person or event.

At this time, the need within families is for safe and supportive professional intervention to help them explore their feelings and to address some difficult and often painful issues. Unfortunately, this kind of help is not readily available and families have very few opportunities open to them for gaining support and assistance. Those who are linked to a church or religious organisation will usually be offered support during the early days following a death, and this is often very welcome. If there are psychiatric problems for a family member following on from the suicide, then referral to mental health services may be possible. However, most families are unlikely to need psychiatric help but would benefit from having someone available, unconnected with the family, to talk to. It is the absence or unavailability of services of this kind that has led the voluntary sector to become a lead provider in this field. Organisations such as 'Compassionate Friends', and 'Papyrus', have grown from the efforts of those individuals who have struggled to come to terms with the suicide of someone close to them. It is the strengths and the insights gained from the 'struggle', and the desire to reduce the distress among others in similar circumstances by sharing these experiences, that has generated a growing network of self-help groups around the country.

Try to bring teens away from death.

ATTEMPTED SUICIDE

Suicidal behaviour is quite common among teenagers, with lifetime estimates ranging from 1.3 to 3.8% for males, and from 1.5 to 10.1% for females (Hawton and Goldacre, 1982; Centers for Disease Control, 1991; Lewinsohn *et al.*, 1994; Kienhorst *et al.*, 1995). Based on these and other studies of adolescents, this would give annual suicide attempt rates in the range of 1–3%. It should be noted, however, that rates are generally based on those young people who present to health services and do not include suicidal episodes dealt with outside of the formal health system. The extent of under-reporting is not known, but it does mean that official statistics need to be used with caution. On the basis of rates found in Oxford, Hawton and Fagg (1992) estimated that nearly 20 000 young people would be referred to general hospitals each year in England and Wales, as a result of deliberate self-poisoning or self-injury. Throughout early adolescence suicidal behaviour is relatively uncommon among males, with female attempters outnumbering males, usually in the order of 5:1. However, recent findings (Hawton *et al.*, 1997) suggest that, with increasing numbers of young men becoming vulnerable to suicidal behaviour, the sex differences in rates among older adolescents are becoming less marked.

Suicidal behaviour is frequently repeated and in some cases will lead to death. Estimates of repetition rates taken from a number of studies give a range of 10% at 6 months follow-up to 42% at 21 months follow-up, producing a median recurrence rate of 5–15% annually (Hawton and Catalan, 1987; Kerfoot, 1988; Pfeffer *et al.*, 1993; Brent *et al.*, 1993). The rates of subsequent completed suicide among attempters are around 0.5–1.0% per year and, although appearing to be low, this is a substantially higher rate than is found in the general population (Otto, 1972; Sellar, Hawton and Goldacre, 1990). Among suicide completers, the rate of attempts is twenty times higher than among non-completers (Shaffer *et al.*, 1988; Brent *et al.*, 1993).

ASSESSMENT OF SUICIDAL RISK

There are a number of issues that relate to 'risk' and these are associated with the particular characteristics of the suicidal episode, mental illness and proneness, psychological characteristics of the individual, and family and social factors. The characteristics of a suicide attempt can be subdivided into 'intent', 'lethality', 'precipitants' and 'motivation'.

Intent

The assessment of intent relies not only on self-report but also on the observed behaviour of the individual. Verbal accounts may be factually incorrect, or misleading, or may be difficult to obtain. With an uncommunicative young person, for example, or where there is persistent denial of suicidal intent in circumstances which appear to contradict this view, behavioural observation is clearly crucial. However, it is often the case with adolescents that the attempt shows very little evidence of planning or premeditation, and the circumstances invariably point to it having been a highly impulsive act.

Lethality

By far the most common method of deliberate self-harm in adolescents is self-poisoning, usually by an overdose of tablets. Frequently, these are tablets that can be bought over the counter, such as analgesics (Hawton and Goldacre, 1982) but in younger adolescents at least half of the overdoses that occur involve the use of prescribed medication (Kerfoot, 1988). Particularly worrying is the increased use of paracetamol because of the severe liver damage that can result. An earlier study (Kerfoot, 1988) found that only 17% of young adolescents had used paracetamol in overdose whereas a more recent study (Kerfoot *et al.*, 1996) found that 56% of a comparable sample used paracetamol in the attempt. Other forms of self-injury such as cutting of wrists and arms is more often seen in older adolescents and does not usually result in serious risk to life. Not surprisingly, episodes that reveal a high degree of lethality are associated with an increased risk of suicide (Brent *et al.*, 1988).

[handwritten margin note: Include Dr/Al/Aa etc. — LS.]

Precipitants

Adolescent suicidal behaviour is often linked to a clear and present precipitant, an event or circumstance which has provoked a crisis for the individual, and which can occur suddenly or may, on the other hand, have been building up over a period of time. For many of these young people, regular arguments between parent and child are a feature of family life, and interpersonal conflict of this kind is cited as the precipitating factor in 50–75% of cases (Brent *et al.*, 1994; Kerfoot *et al.*, 1996). Physical and/or sexual abuse has been associated with suicidal behaviour in between 5% and 20% of cases (Hibbard *et al.*, 1988; Kosky *et al.*, 1990) and it may be that for these victims of abuse admission to hospital following a suicide attempt provides an opportunity for escape from an abusing situation.

Motivation — *could be more than 1.*

Around one third of adolescents express 'a wish to die' as the principal motivation underlying their attempt, while the remaining two thirds convey more mixed reasons for their suicidal behaviour (Hawton *et al.*, 1982a, 1982b). These include 'a wish to escape' usually from a threatening or stressful situation, to 'express hostility', to 'make someone feel guilty', or to 'gain attention'. Those who express a wish to die often have a higher lethality rating and are at greater risk of repetition. Understanding the motivation which drives the attempt also gives important clues to treatment as in, for example, learning more appropriate ways of gaining attention from others, and more socially acceptable and safer ways of expressing hostility.

PSYCHOPATHOLOGY AND SUICIDALITY

In around 75% of adolescent suicide attempters, there is associated psychopathology, usually in the form of depressive, anxiety or conduct disorder, but the most significant association is with depressive disorder, which is seen in around 50% of those involved (Andrews and Lewinsohn, 1992; Kerfoot *et al.*, 1996). This is frequently linked to other conditions, and in older adolescents substance misuse and antisocial behaviour becomes more common. In this older age group, the co-existence of psychiatric disorder and serious personality problems highlights the crucial role of skilled assessment in ensuring that these young people access the most appropriate form of psychiatric or social intervention. If there is no formal psychiatric disorder then psychiatric services may be unable or unwilling to intervene. Young people, too, are often not the best users of these services when they are available and are put off by clinical settings. For reasons such as these, voluntary sector services are often more accessible and appropriate for young people who need counselling and support rather than psychiatric treatment.

Children and young people who have harmed themselves have many features in common with depressed individuals in the same age group (Pfeffer, 1992; De Wilde *et al.*, 1993). Moreover, some follow-up studies find that the outcome of childhood deliberate self-harm is similar to that of childhood depression (Lewinsohn *et al.*, 1994) and that repetition of deliberate self-harm is often linked to episodes of depression (Pfeffer *et al.*, 1993). These findings suggest that in many cases deliberate self-harm in young adolescents is best conceptualised as a symptom of major depressive disorder. It has been reported, however, that major depressive disorder in the young often remits very rapidly following deliberate self-harm (Kerfoot *et al.*, 1996), raising the possibility that depression has a different significance when it occurs in the context of deliberate self-harm. Deliberate self-harm in the young is strongly linked with family dysfunction, behavioural problems and psychosocial stressors such as poverty (Kerfoot, 1988; Kerfoot *et al.*, 1996).

Young people attempting suicide who persistently express suicidal ideas, particularly where there is evidence of planning and strong intent to die, are at increased risk of re-attempting suicide. In addition, those with a past history of suicide attempts are at greater risk for engaging in further suicide attempts (Pfeffer *et al.*, 1993; Lewinsohn *et al.*, 1994).

Substance misuse is becoming increasingly cited in research reports as a serious risk factor for completed suicide and deliberate self-harm. Bukstein *et al.* (1993) compared individuals who completed suicide with community controls who had a lifetime history of substance abuse. Those who completed suicide were more likely to have had active substance abuse (particularly alcohol), co-morbid major depression (usually antedating the substance misuse), suicidal ideation in the past week, a family history of depression and substance misuse, and legal problems. Depression in young people who abuse substances is often difficult to identify but important clues can be gained from an exploration of the family history of affective illness.

PSYCHOLOGICAL CHARACTERISTICS

The psychological characteristics of young people who make suicide attempts include such things as feelings of hopelessness, suicidal ideation and impulsivity. Hopelessness is an important feature to assess because it has been associated with suicide attempts and re-attempts, and also with completed suicide (Beck *et al.*, 1974; Hawton *et al.*, 1982a, 1982b; Kerfoot *et al.*, 1996). While features such as suicidal ideation may be much reduced at follow-up assessment, hopelessness can still be very prevalent (Kerfoot *et al.*, 1996). This is a worrying finding because in adults it may predict eventual suicide (Beck *et al.*, 1985). It should also be remembered that although levels of suicidal thinking can be reduced at follow-up, they are still far in excess of those found in community controls. Hopelessness and suicidal thinking also have implications for therapy because young people with high hopelessness scores may see little point or value to therapy, and be inclined to withdraw prematurely. Suicidal ideation often reduces following an attempt partly because it releases the accumulated pressure which has generated the attempt, but also because it induces a sense of relief that some positive therapeutic action will follow. This does not mean that the suicidal ideation is no longer present and the assessor or therapist should be vigilant about this.

Almost all studies of adolescent suicidal behaviour have noted impulsivity to be a common feature of attempts in this age group. Attempts are usually made with very little planning or forethought, and there is an immediacy about them which makes them very difficult to predict. Impulsivity can also override positive therapeutic intervention, even when the adolescent has been making considerable progress. This 'rush to action' takes on a 'dangerousness' in the suicidal adolescent which must be addressed in therapy, if re-attempts are to be avoided.

FAMILY AND SOCIAL FACTORS

The literature on suicidal behaviour indicates that young people who harm themselves may be particularly vulnerable to such behaviour because of a long-standing history of problems of varying degrees of seriousness. The behaviour and attitudes of parents and other family members are important here, as are the more overt signs of marital failure and family breakdown. Disturbed family functioning and the stress that disordered interaction produces have long been associated with behavioural and emotional difficulties in childhood and adolescence. Commonly the problem is one of continuing conflict between parent and child, often presenting as a series of disciplinary crises which fail to be resolved.

Stress within personal relationships is clearly important in the genesis of attempted and completed suicide at all ages, but for children and adolescents their parents, parental partners and siblings are the main vehicle for this. Stressful relationships with parents, particularly mother–adolescent relationships, have been shown to be significantly related to depression and suicidal ideation (Adams *et al.*, 1994), with families showing dysfunction in areas such as problem-solving and crisis avoidance. Fatherless families are greatly over-represented in statistics for suicidal adolescents and so the problems for unsupported mothers of teenage children are acute. Around 57% of suicidal adolescents come from homes where there has been parental separation or divorce (Kerfoot, 1988). Along with single-parent status these families experience a great deal of social disadvantage as evidenced by manual social class (67%), reliance on welfare benefits (55%), family history of delinquency (42%), family history of deliberate self-harm (49%), and increased contact with social welfare agencies (64%) (Kerfoot, 1988; Kerfoot *et al.*, 1996). In some families, physical or sexual abuse is also an important feature and highlights the need for comprehensive psychosocial assessment in all cases (Hibbard *et al.*, 1988).

INTERVENTION AND FOLLOW-UP

Despite the public health importance of suicidal behaviour in children and adolescents, and the heavy demands that these cases put on medical and mental health services, there is little consensus about what aftercare is needed for those individuals who do not require inpatient or other residential services. Although the Royal College of Psychiatrists (1982) has issued guidance in respect of such young people, aftercare arrangements vary considerably across the country. Thus far, the UK has not produced any controlled studies of intervention with this group, although there is a sizeable literature suggesting treatment methods and models of intervention (Deykin *et al.*, 1986; Shaffer *et al.*, 1988; Tolan *et al.*, 1988; Brent and Kolko, 1990; Allard *et al.*, 1992). Well-defined studies focusing on the efficacy of aftercare and its outcome are much needed, not only because of the dangers associated with acts of deliberate self-harm, but also because these episodes are often markers of severe social, interpersonal or psychiatric difficulties such as depression or behavioural problems. These concurrent problems frequently persist (Kerfoot and McHugh, 1992) and recent research suggests that poor social adjustment and mood disorder are the strongest risk factors for another episode of suicidal behaviour (Pfeffer *et al.*, 1993).

Previous research on the characteristics of young people with suicidal behaviour in the UK has generated important clues about the kinds of factor that might be relevant in designing and delivering interventions (Hawton *et al.*, 1982a, 1982b; Kerfoot, 1984; Taylor and Stansfield, 1984; Kerfoot, 1988; Hawton and Fagg, 1992). In particular, there has been general agreement that children and young people who engage in suicidal behaviour will, in most cases, come from families with disturbed relationships. These families are often coping with extremely high levels of interpersonal and social stress. The quality of communication within the family is often poor (Richman, 1979), and their problem-solving skills may be quite limited (Hawton, 1986). It becomes possible, therefore, to target interventions into specific areas of individual and family functioning, and to devise ways in which these interventions can be evaluated. It is known from studies of adults who attempt suicide, as well as from child and adolescent studies, that these individuals are difficult to engage in treatment and follow-up (Morgan, 1979; Taylor and Stansfield, 1984; Kerfoot and McHugh, 1992) and that it is an under-resourced area of work in the UK generally (Black, 1992). These factors also need to be taken into account when planning and designing interventions.

An episode of suicidal behaviour is a highly emotive issue for most families. Feelings of guilt, blame or embarrassment are often prominent and the family may, paradoxically, withdraw from contact with the very services that have the potential to help them. Follow-up, therefore, may present particular problems where families deny the seriousness of what has happened and regard a commitment to therapeutic intervention as an unwelcome and painful reminder of the suicidal episode. It is for reasons of this kind that motivation in some of these families fluctuates quite markedly, and why withdrawal from, or failure to comply with, intervention is common. Any model of intervention must take these factors into account if it is to maximise the chances of a positive therapeutic outcome.

A variety of treatment approaches have been reported in the literature and some of these have been subject to scientific evaluation. Offers of treatment must always follow a rigorous psychosocial assessment of the individual, and their immediate family or caretakers. The PATHOS screening interview provides a useful shorthand for the assessment of suicidal adolescents and includes the most important components for making judgments about intent and risk (Kingsbury, 1993). The assessment enables judgments to be made about the risk of further episodes, and the problems or issues which have generated the suicide attempt will also give clues to, and provide a focus for, treatment. The assessment stage will also provide an opportunity for the negotiation of a 'no suicide' contract, which is a necessary precursor of therapeutic intervention. The contract, which can be written or verbal, is designed to focus attention on positive action rather than negative withdrawal so that the individual can feel free to express recurrent suicidal ideas, or to let people know when his or her motivation is decreasing. This is important because having an agreement which requires the young person to share his or her most depressing thoughts openly, but in confidence, with identified others rather than to harbour them secretly, gives an impetus to the treatment process. The 'no suicide' contract is a shared responsibility since it requires not only positive action on the part of the adolescent, but also that others be available consistently so that there is ready access to a sympathetic listener when required.

A more formalised version of the 'no suicide' contract is the 'green card' system, which was set up within a service for adults with suicidal behaviour (Morgan and Owen, 1990). In return for agreeing to a 'no suicide' contract, the individual is given a green card which gives immediate access to professional help and advice in specified clinical settings. The green card acts as a lifeline for the suicidal individual, it is carried on the person at all times, and is a reassurance that help is on hand should it be needed. The provision of 24-hour access to professional help via the green card has been shown to reduce suicide attempts and threats in an adult population (Morgan et al., 1993). A similar study based on readmission to hospital on demand, which was conducted with a younger age group, had a negative result (Cotgrove et al., 1995).

Since there has been little empirical work so far on the efficacy of treatment to adolescent suicide attempters, it is difficult to give therapeutic direction to interested professionals. However, what studies there have been suggest that treatments that engage the individual in an active and challenging way, and are flexible with regard to timing and setting, are likely to have more success than more traditional approaches. Research also indicates that treatment programmes that are focused on specific difficulties such as poor problem-solving, dysfunctional family communication and negative cognitions are more likely to increase treatment compliance and to reduce suicidal ideas than traditional approaches.

One of the key questions in providing treatment relates to those individuals who will be involved in the treatment process. Broadly speaking, treatments fall either into individual or group therapy programmes, or into family treatments, but with adolescents it is likely that a combination of these approaches may be required. Young people who make suicide attempts often do so in response to stresses that are generated within the family. Since most young people will generally return to their families following hospital treatment for a suicide attempt, the family context becomes a significant issue in aftercare and follow-up. While a family approach would appear to be the most logical and appropriate therapeutic direction, it should be remembered that many of those who attempt suicide will require some form of individual intervention as well. The physical and emotional changes that take place during adolescence frequently produce greater self-consciousness, and marked differences in ways of thinking and behaving when compared to adults. When not in the company of their peers, young people may handle these difficulties by demanding greater privacy and their own personal space within the family. There are, therefore, parts of adolescent life and experience from which 'family' are excluded. This is why an individual treatment approach may be more attractive to the adolescent than a family approach but because of the family context of adolescent suicidal behaviour, it would make sense to have the family engaged in the treatment process at some point.

Social problem-solving therapy has been used to good effect with groups of college students scoring significantly for suicidal ideation (Lerner and Clum, 1990). Compared with supportive group therapy, social problem-solving therapy proved to be superior in reducing depressive symptoms and hopelessness, but was no more effective than supportive therapy in reducing suicidal ideation. Interpersonal problem-solving skills training (McLeavey et al., 1994) produced sustained improvement over a one year period in a group of suicidal adolescents, when compared with a control treatment. The young people involved showed greater self-perception and interpersonal skills in problem-solving situations, and there was a clear though non-significant trend towards fewer repeat suicidal episodes, when compared with treatment controls.

Cognitive behavioural therapy is an individual approach which specifically addresses hopelessness, and has been used successfully in the treatment of depression in children and adolescents (Wood et al., 1996) and in treating depression and suicidality (Lewinsohn and Clarke, 1990). However, cognitive dialectic therapy, which is another cognitive behavioural approach, proved no more effective than 'routine treatment' in reducing depression, hopelessness and suicidal ideation scores in young adults (Linehan *et al.*, 1991), but did produce fewer and less lethal attempts.

A number of family approaches are currently being employed and evaluated in clinical and community settings, and preliminary findings from these are encouraging. Family approaches are important because it is dysfunctional interactions, particularly between parents and children, that are most frequently identified as precipitating suicidal behaviour. A recent programme of Brief Family Intervention has used insights from research and clinical practice to develop an approach which is brief, focused, intensive, action-oriented and home-based (Kerfoot *et al.*, 1994). Within the sessions, the meaning and significance of the suicidal episode is explored both as a personal event for the individual and as a phenomenon involving family, peers and others. The session provides knowledge and information for those family members who do not have it, but also corrects misunderstandings and wrong information. Other sessions are dedicated to exploring, understanding and improving dysfunctional family communication, improving and expanding family problem-solving skills, and helping family members become knowledgeable about adolescent development and the particular problems and issues that may arise during this period. The Brief Family Intervention is currently being evaluated in a randomised controlled trial, using 'routine clinical intervention' as the control treatment. Preliminary results indicate significantly greater compliance with the Brief Family Intervention than with routine treatment, and significant and sustained improvement for non-depressed suicidal adolescents. It appears likely that adolescents who score for major depression will need an individual approach such as cognitive behaviour therapy to reduce cognitive distortions and hopelessness, and to promote assertiveness and self-esteem. Individual interventions of this kind, which target specific psychological characteristics in the individual, can be offered as part of a treatment package which will also include Brief Family Intervention. A number of other programmes have been constructed using similar insights (Brent *et al.*, 1993; Rotheram-Borus *et al.*, 1994) and are currently undergoing scientific evaluation.

FUTURE PRIORITIES

There are a number of issues raised in past and current research into suicide and attempted suicide in the younger age groups which indicate possible priorities and directions for future research activity. An important issue is that of identifying and treating psychiatric disorders in children and adolescents. Many professionals can readily confirm that emotional and behavioural problems in the young are real, and demand careful investigation. They cannot be dismissed as temporary or self-remitting phenomena which are of little significance or importance. The growing evidence of clear links between depression, antisocial behaviour and substance abuse, and suicidal risk is well documented and it is important that these disorders are recognized and treated.

Primary and secondary prevention are additional research priorities and highlight the need for developing screening instruments for at-risk populations. Work by Shaffer *et al.* (1988), for example, has shown that preventive initiatives in schools or elsewhere could more profitably be focused on screening for vulnerable populations as opposed to peer group 'buddying' schemes, or peer surveillance. The continued development of effective methods of intervention, and their evaluation in randomised controlled treatment trials should provide an effective means of secondary prevention. Interventions can be specifically targeted at those who are at most risk for repeated attempts, ensuring that resources are prioritised in relation to risk.

There is also a clear need for child to adult follow-up studies. Children who have harmed themselves have many risk factors for later personality disturbance, such as repeated separations, poor social problem-solving and impaired peer relationships (Sadowski and Kelly, 1991; Andrews and Lewinsohn, 1992; Kerfoot *et al.*, 1996). It is only in adulthood that certain aspects of outcome can be adequately assessed. To separate personality dysfunction, for example, from episodic disorders such as depression, it is necessary to obtain information on functioning over several years of adult life.

Finally, the risk of repetition calls for increased efforts to develop interventions that are geared to the specific needs of young people and their families, and controlled studies to evaluate the effectiveness of these. Targeted developments of this kind are likely to increase compliance among service users, and to give greater cost effectiveness to purchasers of services. This is particularly important in the current economic climate where there is considerable pressure to achieve the most efficient use of scarce resources.

REFERENCES

Adams, D.M., Overholser, J.C. and Spirito, A. (1994) Stressful life events associated with adolescent suicide attempts. *Canadian Journal of Psychiatry*, 39, 43–48.

Allard, R., Marshall, M. and Plante, M.C. (1992) Intensive follow-up does not decrease the risk of repeat suicide attempts. *Suicide and Life Threatening Behaviour*, 22, 303–314.

Andrews, J.A. and Lewinsohn, P.M. (1992) Suicide attempts among older adolescents: prevalence and co-occurrence with psychiatric disorders. *Journal of the American Academy of Child and Adolescent Psychiatry*, 31, 655–662.

Beck, A., Schuyler, D. and Herman, I. (1974) Development of suicidal intent scales. In A.T. Beck, D.J. Lettieri and H.L.P. Resnick (Eds) *The Prediction of Suicide*. Baltimore, Maryland: Charles Press.

Beck, A.T., Steer, R.A., Kovacs, M. and Garrison, B. (1985) Hopelessness and eventual suicide: a 10 year prospective study of patients. *American Journal of Psychiatry*, 142, 559–563.

Black, D. (1992) Mental health services for children. *British Medical Journal*, 305, 971–972.

Brent, D.A. (1992) Psychiatric effects of exposure to suicide among the friends and acquaintances of adolescent suicide victims. *Journal of the American Academy of Child and Adolescent Psychiatry*, 31, 629–640.

Brent, D.A. and Kolko, D.J. (1990) Suicide and suicidal behaviour in children and adolescents. In B.D. Garfinkel, G. Carlson and E. Weller (Eds) *Psychiatric Disorders in Children and Adolescents*. Philadelphia: W.B. Saunders.

Brent, D.A., Perper, J.A., Goldstein, C.E., Kolko, D.J., Allan, M.J., Allman, C.J. and Zelenak, J.P. (1988) Risk factors for adolescent suicide: a comparison of adolescent suicide victims with suicidal inpatients. *Archives of General Psychiatry*, 45, 581–588.

Brent, D.A., Kolko, D.J., Wartella, M.E., Boylan, M.B., Moritz, G., Baugher, M. and Zelanek, J.P. (1993) Adolescent psychiatric inpatients' risk of suicide attempt at 6-month follow-up. *Journal of the American Academy of Child and Adolescent Psychiatry*, 32, 95–105.

Brent, D.A., Perper, J.A., Moritz, G., Baugher, M., Schweers, J. and Roth, C. (1994) Suicide in affectively ill adolescents: a case control study. *Journal of Affective Disorders*, 31, 193–202.

Bukstein, O.G., Brent, D.A., Perper, J.A., Moritz, G., Baugher, M., Schweers, J., Roth, C. and Balach, L. (1993) Risk factors for completed suicide among adolescents with a lifetime history of substance abuse: a case control study. *Acta Psychiatrica Scandinavica*, 88, 403–408.

Centers for Disease Control (1991) Attempted suicide among high school students: United States 1990. *Morbidity and Mortality Weekly Report*, 40, 633–635.

Cotgrove, A., Zirinsky, L., Black, D. and Weston, D. (1995) Secondary prevention of attempted suicide in adolescence. *Journal of Adolescence*, 18, 569–577.

De Wilde, E.J., Kienhorst, I.C.W.M., Diekstra, R.F.W. and Wolters, W.H.G. (1993) The specificity of psychological characteristics of adolescent suicide attempters. *Journal of the American Academy of Child and Adolescent Psychiatry*, 32, 51–59.

Deykin, E.Y., Chung-Chen, H., Joshi, N. and McNamarra, J.J. (1986) Adolescent suicidal and self-destructive behaviour: results of an intervention study. *Journal of Adolescent Health Care*, 7, 88–95.

Harrington, R.C. and Dyer, E. (1993) Suicide and attempted suicide in adolescents. *Current Opinion in Psychiatry*, 6, 467–469.

Hawton, K. (1986) *Suicide and Attempted Suicide Among Children and Adolescents*. Beverly Hills: Sage.

Hawton, K. and Catalan, J. (1987) *Attempted Suicide: A Practical Guide to its Nature and Management*. New York: Oxford University Press.

Hawton, K. and Fagg, J. (1992) Deliberate self-poisoning and self-injury in adolescents: a study of characteristics and trends in Oxford 1976–1989. *British Journal of Psychiatry*, 161, 816–823.

Hawton, K. and Goldacre, M. (1982) Hospital admissions for adverse effects of medicinal agents (mainly self-poisoning) among adolescents in the Oxford region. *British Journal of Psychiatry*, 141, 166–170.

Hawton, K., Osborn, M., O'Grady, J. and Cole, D. (1982a) Adolescents who take overdoses: their characteristics, problems and contacts with helping agencies. *British Journal of Psychiatry*, 140, 118–123.

Hawton, K., Osborn, M., O'Grady, J. and Cole, D. (1982b) Classification of adolescents who take overdoses. *British Journal of Psychiatry*, 140, 124–131.

Hawton, K., Fagg, J., Simkin, S., Bale, E. and Bond, A. (1997) Trends in deliberate self-harm in Oxford 1985–1995. Implications for clinical services and the prevention of suicide. *British Journal of Psychiatry*, 171, 556–560.

Hibbard, R.A., Brack, C.J., Rauch, S. and Orr, D.P. (1988) Abuse, feelings, and health behaviours in a student population. *American Journal of Diseases in Children*, 142, 326–330.

Kerfoot, M. (1984) Assessment of young adolescents and the family. In C.L. Hatton and S.M. Valente (Eds) *Suicide: Assessment and Intervention*, 2nd edn. Norwalk, Connecticut: Appleton-Century-Crofts.

Kerfoot, M. (1988) Deliberate self-poisoning in childhood and early adolescence. *Journal of Child Psychology and Psychiatry*, 29, 335–343.

Kerfoot, M. and McHugh, B. (1992) The outcome of childhood suicidal behaviour. *Acta Paedopsychiatrica Scandinavica*, 55, 141–145.

Kerfoot, M., Harrington, R. and Dyer, E. (1994) Brief home-based intervention with young suicide attempters and their families. *Journal of Adolescence*, 18, 557–568.

Kerfoot, M., Dyer, E., Harrington, V., Woodham, A. and Harrington, R. (1996) Correlates and short-term course of self-poisoning in adolescents. *British Journal of Psychiatry*, 168, 38–42.

Kienhorst, I., de Wilde, E.J., Diekstra, R.F.W. and Wolters, W. (1995) Adolescents' image of their suicide attempt. *Journal of the American Academy of Child Adolescent Psychiatry*, 34, 623–628.

Kingsbury, S. (1993) Parasuicide in adolescence: a message in a bottle. *ACCP Review and Newsletter*, 15(6), 253–259.

Kosky, R., Sulburn, S. and Zubrick, S.R. (1990) Are children and adolescents who have suicidal thoughts different from those who attempt suicide? *Journal of Nervous and Mental Disease*, 178, 38–43.

Lerner, M.S. and Clum, G.A. (1990) Treatment of suicide ideators: a problem-solving approach. *Behaviour Therapy*, 21, 403–411.

Lewinsohn, P.M. and Clarke, G.N. (1990) Cognitive-behavioural treatment for depressed adolescents. *Behaviour Therapy*, 21, 385–401.

Lewinsohn, P.M., Rohde, P. and Seeley, J.R. (1994) Psycho-social risk factors for future adolescent suicide attempts. *Journal of Consulting and Clinical Psychology*, 62, 297–305.

Linehan, M.M., Armstrong, H.E., Suarez, A., Allmon, D. and Heard, H.L. (1991) Cognitive-behavioural treatment of chronically parasuicidal borderline patients. *Archives of General Psychiatry*, 48, 1060–1064.

Marttunen, M.J., Aro, H.M., Henriksson, M.M. and Lonnqvist, J.K. (1991) Mental disorders in adolescent suicide: DSM-III-R axes I and II diagnoses in suicides among 13–19 year olds in Finland. *Archives of General Psychiatry*, 48, 834–839.

Marttunen, M.J., Aro, H.M., Henriksson, M.M., Lonnqvist, J.K. (1994) Anti-social behaviour in adolescent suicide. *Acta Psychiatrica Scandinavica*, 89, 167–173.

McClure, G.M.C. (1994) Suicide in children and adolescents in England and Wales. *British Journal of Psychiatry*, 165, 510–514.

McLeavey, B.C., Daly, J.D., Ludgate, J.W. and Murray, C.M. (1994) Inter-personal problem-solving skills training in the treatment of self-poisoning patients. *Suicide and Life Threatening Behaviour*, 24, 382–394.

Morgan, H.G. (1979) *Death Wishes? The Assessment and Management of Deliberate Self-Harm*. London: Wiley.

Morgan, H.G. and Owen, J.H. (1990) *Persons At Risk of Suicide: Guidelines on Good Clinical Practice*. Nottingham: Boots.

Morgan, H.G., Jones, E.M. and Owen, J.H. (1993) Secondary prevention of non-fatal self-harm: the green card study. *British Journal of Psychiatry*, 163, 111–112.

Office of Population Census and Surveys (1990) *Mortality Statistics. Causes: England and Wales*. London: HMSO.

Otto, U. (1972) Suicidal acts by children and adolescents: a follow-up study. *Acta Psychiatrica Scandinavica*, Suppl. 233.

Pfeffer, C.R. (1992) Relationship between depression and suicidal behaviour. In M. Shafii and S.L. Shafii (Eds) *Clinical Guide to Depression in Children and Adolescents*. Washington, DC: American Psychiatric Press.

Pfeffer, C.R., Klerman, G.L., Hurt, S.W., Lesser, M., Peskin, J.R. and Siefker, C.A. (1993) Suicidal children grow up: demographic and clinical risk factors for adolescent suicide attempts. *Journal of the American Academy of Child and Adolescent Psychiatry*, 30, 609–616.

Richman, J. (1979) The family therapy of attempted suicide. *Family Process*, 18, 131–142.

Rotheram-Borus, M.J., Piacentini, J., Miller, S., Graae, F. and Castro-Blanco, D. (1994) Brief cognitive-behavioural treatment for adolescent suicide attempters and their families. *Journal of the American Academy of Child and Adolescent Psychiatry*, 33, 508–517.

Royal College of Psychiatrists (1982) The management of parasuicide in young people under sixteen. *Bulletin of the Royal College of Psychiatrists*, 6, 182–185.

Sadowski, C. and Kelly, M.L. (1991) Social problem-solving in suicidal adolescents. *Journal of Consulting and Clinical Psychology*, 61, 121–127.

Sellar, C., Hawton, K. and Goldacre, M.J. (1990) Self-poisoning in adolescents: hospital admissions and deaths in the Oxford Region 1980–85. *British Journal of Psychiatry*, 156, 866–870.

Shaffer, D. (1974) Suicide in childhood and early adolescence. *Journal of Child Psychology and Psychiatry*, 15, 275–291.

Shaffer, D., Garland, A., Gould, M. and Fisher, P. (1988) Preventing teenage suicide: a critical review. *Journal of the American Academy of Child and Adolescent Psychiatry*, 27, 675–687.

Taylor, E.A. and Stansfield, S.A. (1984) Children who poison themselves: a clinical comparison with psychiatric controls. *British Journal of Psychiatry*, 145, 127–132.

Tolan, P., Ryan, K. and Jaffe, C. (1988) Adolescents' mental health service use and provider process, and recipient characteristics. *Journal of Clinical and Child Psychology*, 17, 229–236.

Wood, A.J., Harrington, R.C. and Moore, A. (1996) Controlled trial of a brief cognitive-behavioural intervention in adolescent patients with depressive disorders. *Journal of Child Psychology and Psychiatry*, 37, 737–746.

Part II
SPECIAL GROUPS AND SPECIAL NEEDS

Chapter 8

Sexuality and Mental Health Promotion: Lesbian and Gay Young People

Ian Warwick, Christine Oliver and Peter Aggleton

There is an increasing awareness among many adults of the need to work together to promote the physical and emotional well-being of young people. Parents, teachers, youth workers and social workers all have an interest in shaping and influencing the lives of young people with whom they live and work, and for whom they care and love. Policy makers too are coming to realise that they can support such work to enhance the lives of young people as sons and daughters, as pupils in school, as clients and as citizens.

In Britain and many other countries, government policies often emphasise the importance of collaborative work. 'Joined up' thinking, for example, between government departments, and between local authorities, health authorities and the voluntary sector, seeks to provide the framework for joined up actions. Such an approach aims to ensure that the health concerns and needs of young people and their families are better addressed by statutory and non-governmental organisations (Department of Health, 1997). This is not to say that working in partnership is an easy achievement. As adults we have different personal aptitudes and values. As professionals, we can have more or less competing perspectives of the world, different degrees of autonomy and conflicting lines of responsibility.

Alongside the encouragement provided to adults to work together better is a renewed interest in enabling young people to express their views on matters of concern to them. Furthermore, their views on,

Young People and Mental Health. Edited by P. Aggleton, J. Hurry and I. Warwick.
© 2000 John Wiley & Sons Ltd.

among other things, education, health services, non-discrimination, abuse, culture, access to information as well as recreation should be given
proper consideration by adults. Stimulated by the UN Convention on
the Rights of the Child, the right to express one's views and have them
considered should apply to all young people regardless *inter alia* of
poverty, class, race, gender or sexuality.

In practice, it is perhaps easier for some young people than others to
make their views known, and to have them properly considered by
adults. Black young men, for example, may find their views regarding
education taken less seriously by adults than those of their white male
friends. Young disabled women may have fewer opportunities to articu-
late their sexual needs than more able-bodied women of the same age.
Young people who are sexually attracted to others of the same sex may
feel it difficult, if not at times impossible, to talk about their own needs
for a girlfriend or boyfriend in a broader context where lesbian and gay
relationships are not recognised and valued. Involving young people in
service development, implementation and evaluation can be more or
less challenging depending on the groups worked with or the issues
addressed (see Cohen and Emanuel, 1998).

With a diverse range of adults and professionals, a diverse range of
young people, and a series of issues as emotive as mental health and
lesbian and gay sexuality, this might disorient even the best intentions
to work in partnership. However, and as we shall see, the mental health
needs of lesbian and gay young people cannot be addressed simply by
setting up a youth group here or there, by providing individual counselling, or by the brief inclusion of related issues in personal and social
education in schools. While all of these may be welcome, the development of services should be more strategic and aim to operate across a
number of different levels and contexts which shape the lives of young
people in general, and lesbian and gay young people in particular.

This chapter seeks to provide those with an interest in lesbian and gay
young people's mental health and emotional well-being with an outline of
some important issues. It highlights how lesbian and gay young people's
needs are influenced by the contexts, often discriminatory, in which they
live. We conclude by highlighting some of the issues facing professionals
if they are to promote the mental health and emotional well-being of
lesbian and gay young people, rather than solely prevent mental illness.

MENTAL ILLNESS, MENTAL HEALTH AND MENTAL HEALTH PROMOTION

With the publication of the White Paper *Saving Lives: Our Healthier
Nation* (Department of Health, 1999), a new national contract on mental
health is being developed in the UK (Secker, 1998a). Among other
things, this seeks to:

- Encourage the development of mental health services
- Create job opportunities for people with mental ill-health
- Reduce the incidence of mental ill-health
- Prevent suicide
- Address the socio-economic causes of mental ill-health

However, these aims appear to be based chiefly on the avoidance of mental illness and display something of a preoccupation with primary and secondary prevention (that is, preventing and treating mental illness). While mental health might be thought of as the absence of mental illness, it can also be defined more positively (Secker, 1998b) as,

> '. . . the emotional and spiritual resilience which enables us to enjoy life and to survive pain, suffering and disappointment. It is a positive sense of well-being and an underlying belief in our own and others' dignity and worth.' (HEA, 1997: 7)

Notwithstanding the need to develop a shared understanding of terms such as 'emotional and spiritual resilience', the distinctions between different types of definitions are important to bear in mind. While reducing rates of suicide among lesbians and gay young people is an important priority, other initiatives are needed to address in a more holistic way the emotional well-being of young lesbians and gay men.

MENTAL HEALTH ISSUES FACING LESBIAN AND GAY PEOPLE

It would be a mistake to assume that the mental health issues facing young lesbians and gay men are unique. Many other young people are likely to face, for example, discrimination at home, at school or at work. And discrimination against lesbians and gay men can follow them throughout their adult lives. When identifying the specific issues facing lesbian and gay youth, it is important to keep firmly in mind the other groups against which comparisons are being made. To put the needs of lesbian and gay young people in context, we will outline some issues facing young people in general as well as those encountered by adult lesbians and gay men.

The Mental Health Foundation reports that as many as 49% of children and young people will at some time meet the criteria for at least one psychiatric disorder. This figure, however, is thought to be unrealistically high (being based on the presence of any signs or symptoms rather than the impact it has on young people's lives). Specific mental illnesses among young people include anxiety disorder, depression, eating disorders, schizophrenia, self-harm and suicide (Mental Health Foundation, 1998; and see elsewhere in this book).

While lesbian and gay adults are often said to experience mental health problems to a greater degree than heterosexuals, the situation is rather more complex than this. Experiences vary according to the type of mental health problem or issue, and with gender, ethnicity and HIV status among other factors. Furthermore, almost all studies sample lesbians and gay men, be they younger, older or in their middle years, from community services (such as support groups), community events (such as lesbian and gay Pride), specialised provision (such as mental health services), or through the lesbian and gay media (such as targeted newspapers and magazines). As it is not possible to draw a representative sample of all lesbians and gay men, comparisons with general population samples must be made with some caution.

In a major national survey of adult lesbians in the USA which focussed specifically on mental health, key issues identified included: depression, sexual abuse, eating disorders, use of counselling services and suicide (Bradford et al., 1994). A broad definition of depression was used, with 33% of lesbian respondents indicating they had been depressed at some point in their lives. This was reported as being similar to that obtained for heterosexual woman in community surveys using a similar definition of depression. There were also few differences between lesbians in this survey and heterosexual women in other broadly similar surveys with regard to sexual abuse and eating disorders. Lesbians were, however, reported to be more likely to be the recipients of counselling than heterosexual women.

In contrast to this situation, higher rates of eating disorders have been reported among gay men than their heterosexual male counterparts (Harrison and Silenzio, 1996). Studies which have examined depression also suggest that this condition is more common among gay male populations than heterosexual ones (Harrison and Silenzio, 1996). In another study, again conducted in the USA, there were reported to be higher rates of 'depressive distress' among adult lesbians and gay men (some of whom were living with HIV) from black and minority ethnic communities (Cochran and Mays, 1994). Figures from earlier investigations indicated that 23% of black men and 26% of black women from the general population reported depressive distress compared with 33% of black gay men and 38% of black lesbians in the Cochran and May's study. Men with symptomatic HIV disease reported higher levels of depressive distress than those who were unsymptomatic or who were not living with HIV.

DRUG USE

Although not a mental health issue in itself, drug use among lesbians and gay men is often thought of as a symptom of an underlying problem, such as coping with psychological issues or low self-esteem (AMA Council on Scientific Affairs, 1996; Rosario et al., 1997). It has been suggested that lesbians are more likely to use alcohol than heterosexual women (Bradford et al., 1994) and there are also reported elevated rates of alcohol use among gay men when compared to population as a whole (Harrison and Silenzio, 1996).

A recent study of alcohol use, smoking and illicit drug use among young 'lesbian, gay and bisexual youth' living in an inner city in the USA reported mixed findings. When compared to national undifferentiated (presumably heterosexual) samples of other young people, lesbians were about twice as likely to have used drugs, with lifetime prevalence rates for young gay men being similar to those of men drawn from the undifferentiated sample. When compared to inner city samples, drug use was similar among all young people, although young lesbians and gay men were reported to have used marijuana to a greater extent (Rosario et al., 1997).

In two studies drawing young gay and bisexual men from specialist youth provision, alcohol and other drug use correlated with unsafe sex (Rotheram-Borus et al., 1994; Winters et al., 1996). Whether a causal mechanism exists, or whether both unsafe sex and drug use are indications of, for example, an underlying problem is left open to interpretation.

Indeed, it is somewhat unclear whether drug use was actually problematic for the young people concerned. These studies did not enable young people to talk about their drug use, their reasons for taking drugs, or their perceptions of problems or difficulties. As such, it is left to adult researchers to determine, for example, that 'frequent use'consisted of having used a drug (such as alcohol, cigarettes or marijuana) more than five times in one's life (Rosario et al., 1997).

SUICIDE

Many studies of lesbians' and gay men's mental health problems concern suicide, whether this be in the form of suicidal thoughts, suicide attempts or completed suicide. Adult lesbians differ only marginally from heterosexual women in relation to having suicidal thoughts or attempted suicide (Bradford et al., 1994). There were indications in this study, though, that a higher percentage of younger lesbians surveyed had suicidal thoughts and had made more suicide attempts than older lesbians. A considerably increased risk for suicide is said to exist for lesbians and gay men from Black and minority ethnic communities (Harrison and Silenzio, 1996).

Numerous US studies have reported considerably higher rates of suicide among young lesbians and gay men when compared to other young people of broadly similar ages. A study commissioned by the US Government concluded that lesbian and gay young people were two to three times more likely to attempt suicide than other young people and may account for 30% of all suicides among young people (reported in Mental Health Foundation, 1997). Although exceedingly difficult to estimate, around 2–6% of young people are likely to be lesbian or gay, highlighting the disproportionately high suicide rate.[1]

The figures for rates of suicidal ideas or actions vary. While one review has noted that 7% of all 13–18 year olds report having ideas about suicide (Aggleton, 1996), other studies have found rates of around 15% to as high as 63% (Garland and Zigler, 1993; Diekstra *et al.*, 1995). It is reported that between 6% and 20% of young people in general have attempted suicide (Garland and Zigler, 1993; Diekstra *et al.*, 1995). These variations highlight difficulties in recording and reporting rates of attempted suicide or suicidal ideas, a problem shared with studies of lesbians and gay men. This has led some to suggest that there are not elevated rates of suicidal thoughts or suicide attempts among lesbians and gay men (Muerher, 1995). Muerher appears right to note that accurate comparisons across lesbian, gay and heterosexual populations are exceedingly difficult to make. Nevertheless, many other studies are suggestive of the need to address suicide-related issues among young lesbians and gay men. While the level of suicidal thoughts may indeed be no higher among samples of lesbian and gay youth than among undifferentiated samples of young people, studies with lesbian and gay young people have typically shown rates of attempted suicide of between 19% and 50% (Proctor and Groze, 1994; Hershberger *at al.*, 1997; Mental Health Foundation, 1997). This suggests an elevated risk of attempted suicide among young lesbians and young gay men compared to young people in general.

FACTORS ASSOCIATED WITH MENTAL HEALTH PROBLEMS AMONG LESBIAN AND GAY YOUNG PEOPLE

It is not unusual for young people to be thought of as intrinsically mad, bad or sad (see Aggleton and Warwick, 1997) However, as Aggleton (1996) concludes in his recent review of health issues facing young people, it is perhaps more useful to think of young people moving in an out of different *cultures* and *contexts* of health. Young people, he suggests, may engage with, and disengage from, multiple health risks associated with these cultures at different points in their lives. This, rather usefully, helps us move away from an individualised perspective of risk, to think about the contexts within which young lesbians and young gay men, indeed all young people, live their lives. While not denying the importance of genetics in mental illness (Mental Health Foundation, 1998), it is often specific contexts and circumstances that promote, or otherwise, young people's sense of mental health and well-being. While such a view raises questions about the inevitability of the relationship between specific actions that take place in certain settings (such as bullying at school) and mental health problems (such as suicide), it is nonetheless important to keep in mind the often violently challenging circumstances in which lesbian and gay young people find themselves.

Young lesbians and young gay men face many of the same sorts of stresses as most other young people: the everyday stresses such as moving to a new school, moving house, dealing with new social situations; the severe acute stresses such as the loss of family and friends as well as parental divorce; and severe chronic stresses such as those related to poverty, persistent family discord, racism, depression and/or a parent's alcoholism. All of these factors have been shown to be associated with mental health problems among young people (Aggleton, 1996).

For young as well as older lesbians and gay men, victimisation and bullying, low self-esteem, and social support have all been particularly studied as possible contributors to mental health problems. Because of the stigma associated with being lesbian or gay, many young people and adults are confronted with additional challenges that others of the same age may not experience.

Among young people in general, depression and anxiety can be related to bullying. In one study, 10% of secondary school students reported being bullied 'sometimes', and 4% reported being bullied once a week (reported in Douglas et al., 1999). Bullying was the most frequently mentioned problem for callers to Childline.[2] Of 115 146 first time callers, 17% were concerned with bullying. Longer term effects of bullying can include depression and anxiety, feelings of guilt and shame, social isolation and exceptional timidity (Elliot and Kilpatrick, 1994).

To date, there has been no systematic survey of homophobic bullying.[3] In an early study involving young lesbian and gay respondents in the UK, 12% reported having been beaten at school and 21% had been verbally abused (Trenchard and Warren, 1984). In a more recent survey of 'hate crimes' against lesbians and gay men, of those respondents aged under 18, 79% reported that they had been subject to homophobic verbal bullying, 24% that they had been subject to homophobic physical bullying, and 19% that they had been subject to severe homophobic physical bullying (Mason and Palmer, 1996). Rivers' (1996) study describes some of the sorts of bullying and attacks reported by respondents: having clothes set alight; having chemicals thrown on them during science classes; being urinated upon; being burned with cigarettes while being held down; being dragged across the school playing field by the hair; and being raped by teachers or pupils (Rivers, 1996). A recent UK survey of secondary school teachers' perceptions of bullying reported that 97% were aware of general bullying having taken place in their schools, 82% were aware of homophobic verbal bullying, and 26% were aware of homophobic physical bullying (Douglas et al., 1999).

While bullying may often be linked to school settings, a number of studies have examined the effects of victimisation of lesbian and gay adults and young people. Pilkington and D'Augelli (1995) note that none of the social contexts in which young lesbians and young gay men live were risk-free. Whether at home, at school, at work or in the community, lesbian and gay young people to varying degrees feared for their safety, concealed their sexual orientation, and incurred verbal and/or physical violence. Of 194 respondents, more than 80% had experienced some form of victimisation based on their sexual orientation alone.[4] The younger the age at which young people had self-labelled themselves as lesbian or gay the higher the level of victimisation. This association was also found among those young people who were more open about their sexuality and more 'obviously' lesbian or gay in appearance or conduct.

Young lesbians and gay men from black and minority ethnic communities have been said to experience fewer instances of homophobic victimisation. This may well relate to common assumptions about ethnicity and sexuality, that is, that a young man could not be African-Caribbean and gay, or a young woman could not be Asian and lesbian. Young people from black and minority ethnic communities may, however, be more fearful than young white people of the reactions to their feelings of attraction to people of the same sex were it to be disclosed (Pilkington and D'Augelli, 1995). At least one author has suggested that lesbians and gay men from black and minority ethnic communities are subject to multiple forms of discrimination, not only those relating to sexuality, but also those linked to race and ethnicity as well as, for women, to gender (Greene, 1994). Whether this means that discrimination is additive in its effects remains an open question.

Otis *et al.* (1996) note that physical harm, the threat of such harm, verbal abuse, male sexual assault and multiple victimisation (rather than experiencing theft or robbery) were associated with depression among lesbian and gay adults. And while lower self-esteem correlated with higher levels of depression, the support of partners reduced levels of depression—particularly among lesbians.[5]

With regard to suicide, a weak, although not absent, association has been identified between levels of victimisation and having ideas about suicide and attempting suicide (Hershberger and D'Augelli, 1995). In a further article, respondents who had attempted suicide had disclosed more completely their sexual orientation and, because of disclosures, had lost more friends. Furthermore, those young people who had attempted suicide had lower self-esteem and more mental health problems. Both the loss of friends (due to 'coming out' about one's sexuality) and contemplating suicide were among the strongest predictors of suicide attempts (Hershberger *et al.*, 1997).

Protective factors related to social support were also identified in a study of lesbian and gay young people. Perceptions of having support from one's family buffered these young people against mental health problems (as measured by the Brief Symptom Inventory). But this held true only on those occasions where family support was perceived to be high and victimisation was low. One apparent effect of family support was to increase levels of self-acceptance which, in turn, appeared to relate to fewer mental health problems (Hershberger and D'Augelli, 1995).

Savin-Williams and Dubé (1998) have noted that parental reactions have been assumed to follow a series of stages following disclosure that their child may be lesbian or gay. These steps are shock, denial, anger, bargaining, depression and acceptance. However, the authors note that the empirical support for such a stage theory is weak. Some parents may react immediately with shock, others will not. Some parents may react angrily, others will not. On the whole, the authors indicate, parents will become more or less accepting of their child—even though their son or daughter may not perceive their parents as expressly accepting.

One study, examining protective factors among mainly black and Latino/a respondents, considered the associations between self-esteem, supportiveness and emotional distress (Grossman and Kerner, 1998). Higher self-esteem, it was reported, correlated with lower levels of emotional distress, especially for young lesbians. In this study, social support was not related to levels of emotional distress. However, the authors caution that a global measure of satisfaction with social support was used, rather than a specific appraisal of different types of support (such as that from family, from friends, from work colleagues). As noted already, the effects of support from different people may have different consequences for mental health.

INTERVENTIONS

It is routine for authors of articles on the mental health of lesbian and gay young people to conclude with calls for a series of actions to be taken— whether related to service provision or further research. However, rather than calling for one or another type of specialised provision, or a series of *ad hoc* services targeted towards young lesbians and young gay men, or more of the same types of research, a more inclusive and strategic approach to mental health promotion might be timely.

There are plenty of suggestions for the development of initiatives aiming to promote mental health and mental well-being among young lesbians and gay men (although there are few, if any, evaluations of these). For adults, Garnets and D'Augelli (1994) note that promoting the civil rights of lesbians and gay men is likely to support their emotional well-being. Resonating with this, as well as some of the themes contained in the UN Convention on the Rights of the Child, Martin (1996) emphasises that children should have a right to be lesbian or gay, if that is the way they wish to define themselves. Some adults may question young people's capacity to define their own sexuality, or believe it to be desirable that young people at least attempt to achieve adult heterosexual status. However, as Martin argues, trying to re-orient a young person's self-defined sexuality should be seen as a form of emotional abuse.

D'Augelli and Hershberger (1993) suggest that while crisis intervention services exist in some areas of the USA, more should be done to provide support and combat discrimination among parents and in schools. For parents, Savin-Williams and Dubé (1998) note that information, education and support, from individuals or through self-help parents' groups, are important resources. These can help parents discard their previous heterosexual hopes for their child and their fears about homosexuality. A positive family relationship, prior to learning that a son or daughter is attracted to someone of the same sex, is a good indicator that a child's sexuality will be more or less accepted. Nonetheless, they caution that recognising and being comfortable with a lesbian daughter or gay son requires of a family 'time, trust and stamina' (Savin-Williams and Dubé, 1998: 11).

With a primary focus on schools, Treadway and Yoakam (1992) note that these settings are often an unsafe place for lesbian and gay pupils. Telljohann and Price (1993) highlight the isolation of lesbian and gay pupils in schools, and Walters and Hayes (1998) report that homophobia has a negative impact on learning. Each make suggestions for improvement which include: being aware of and ceasing to use homophobic language and terms; setting up support groups for lesbian and gay pupils; providing realistic information about same sex sexual feelings; providing a referral system for lesbian and gay pupils with mental health problems; re-orienting initial teacher training; and providing training on issues related to same sex sexuality for practising teachers. While not attempting to address all of these issues, Forrest *et al.* (1997) provide information, as well as a series of structured exercises, which school staff can use to promote discussion of lesbian and gay issues in secondary schools among colleagues, parents, governors and pupils.

The need for professional development in the field of sexuality is not limited to teacher training. 'Homosexuality' was not declassified as a mental illness in the UK until the early 1990s, and there still remains the mental 'disorder' of 'ego-dystonic' homosexuality, that is, being confused about one's sexual identity (MIND, no date). One legacy of this is the experience of sexuality-related discrimination against lesbians and gay men while undergoing therapy and counselling (McFarlane, 1998; MIND, no date). Various authors have called for the development of therapeutic services to take into account issues related to same sex sexual attraction (McHenry and Johnson, 1993; Kottman *et al.*, 1995; Baron, 1996; Crosbie-Burnett *et al.*, 1996; Fontaine and Hammond, 1996; Clark and Serovich, 1997; Townsend *et al.*, 1997). Other writers, after noting that lesbians can have difficulty discussing health-related problems with general medical professionals, suggest that initiatives should involve primary care staff to ease communication problems (White and Dull, 1997; Lehmann *et al.*, 1998.)

With regard to out-of-school services, there are a number of lesbian and gay youth groups and telephone helplines in the UK, most often in cities and large towns, but also occasionally in more rural areas. National helplines, such as London's Lesbian and Gay Switchboard in the UK, can provide information about these.[6] Local groups and helplines (unless they have a specific youth focus) seek to provide a general support service for all lesbians and gay men. The development of one specific service to promote the emotional well-being of young lesbians is reported by Bridget and Lucille (1996). Called the 'Lesbian

Youth Support Information Service' (LYSIS), this was set up following a small-scale study with young lesbians which highlighted (in line with findings from many other pieces of work) problems related to their mental health (including depression), suicide, self-harming behaviours and alcohol use. LYSIS offers support through correspondence counselling, telephone counselling, peer support and information.

Phillips *et al.* (1997) report on the re-orientation of out-of-school services for young people in general, rather than the setting up of specific services for lesbian and gay youth. This, they suggest, may require members to reflect on and change the underlying values or philosophies of their agency (so that it is inclusive of young lesbians and young gay men), to put in place an equal opportunities policy which makes reference to sexuality, to provide in-service training for staff, and to be conscious of the images used in a setting (so that posters do not only show images of heterosexual people). The authors warn that organisational change can often be dependent on the efforts of key individuals whose departure can impede further development. Initiatives should be institutionalised through policy development and implementation which would include a commitment to staff training.

DISCUSSION AND IMPLICATIONS

It is unquestionable that many young people are attracted to others of the same sex. From the studies reported here, it is beyond doubt that many of those who are, encounter discrimination, are victimised, and are confronted with homophobic verbal and physical bullying. Some will experience mental health problems, some will not. And, to a greater extent than young people in general, some will attempt and commit suicide.

Calls have been made to re-orient education and support services, set up new information and support services for young people and their parents, and create supportive family networks. All these have been suggested as ways by which young people's self-esteem might be raised and their social networks (including, importantly, family relationships) made more supportive.

There is, however, an unresolved difficulty running through many of the papers and articles described in this chapter. It is not clear whether the authors are concerned to address mental illness or mental health and emotional well-being, or are interested in the prevention of mental illness or the promotion of mental health. Where there is an interest in what might be termed 'mental illness' such as depression or suicide, much research has attempted to find specific emotional or mental attributes which correlate with, and perhaps cause, such illness. It is hoped that altering these attributes may reduce mental illness.

This appears to have led many researchers to use pre-determined scales to measure particular aspects of young people's lives, be this self-esteem, anxiety, mental health, suicidal ideas or social support. Just possibly, this could facilitate comparisons across different samples of young lesbians and gay men, even though in actuality this is rarely the case. More worryingly, it only allows certain aspects of young people's lives to become known about. Young lesbians and gay men often have concerns which may not be immediately related to their sexuality. And young people who do not identify as lesbian or gay may nonetheless have concerns about issues related to same sex attraction. Enabling young people to talk about these issues in a rather more open-ended way than has hitherto been attempted may allow new sets of under-standings to emerge about young people's feelings and experiences. On the one hand, this may lead us to question the utility of measures of 'psychiatric disorder' such as 'depression' and 'anxiety'. On the other, it is likely to provide a rather more holistic understanding of young people's lives—one which is less concerned about the prevention of mental illness and more attuned to overall emotional well-being.

Even though there have been calls for a broad range of actions, such as providing individualised support and changing the context (such as families and schools) within which young people live, the issues ad-dressed often relate to alleviating specific mental health problems. As the Health Education Authority in England has cautioned, activities to promote mental health are frequently strategies to prevent mental ill-ness. By way of contrast, it is suggested that,

> 'Mental health promotion (should) include any activity which fosters good mental health . . . Activities which promote mental health may also pre-vent mental illness . . . Mental health promotion strategies . . . should cover the needs of individuals and communities, and incorporate different types of activities, from primary prevention to the delivery of services in the most extreme need.' (HEA, 1997: 9)

Activities embedded within a wider mental health promotion pro-gramme might usefully be undertaken within and across three different levels:

- At the structural level, such as making changes to national policy
- At the organisation or community level, such as re-orienting existing services and setting up new ones
- At the personal or individual level, such as providing individualised support (HEA, 1997)[7]

The all encompassing nature of this work may seem somewhat daunt-ing to professionals involved in small-scale projects. However, those taking a strategic view at a national, regional or local/health authority level may have these as features of an overall programme of work, with local initiatives being narrower in focus.

At the beginning of this chapter, we noted the importance of working collaboratively and within a framework which provides children and young people with the right to express their views and have them considered. As we have attempted to highlight, both differences and commonalities exist among young lesbians and young gay men, and between them and lesbian and gay adults and other young people. As such, programmes and interventions that seek to promote mental health and emotional well-being among all young people should be sensitive to issues of sexuality. Similarly, initiatives which seek to promote the mental health and emotional well-being of adult lesbians and gay men should be sensitive to age-related concerns.

Important as it is to combat discrimination and homophobic bullying, important as it is to alleviate anxiety and depression, and important as it is to prevent suicide, this should not be our horizon. If we are to help all young people develop 'a positive sense of well-being and an underlying belief in [their] own and others' dignity and worth' (HEA, 1997: 7), there will be both personal and professional challenges ahead. We will, ourselves, need to feel truly comfortable in supporting young people of the same sex in forming caring, desiring, sexual and loving relationships.

ENDNOTES

1. This figure is drawn from an interpretation of data offered by Johnson *et al.* (1994).
2. Childline is a children's charity that operates a national freephone telephone helpline for children and young people.
3. Homophobic bullying is said to have taken place where incidents of verbal or physical bullying are accompanied by, or consist of, derogatory or abusive use of terms such as lesbian, gay, queer or lezzie.
4. In addition to homophobic victimisation, young lesbians and young gay men are, like other young people, likely to be victimised for other reasons related to their ethnic background, their gender, their way of speaking, and so on.
5. While having partner support was associated with lower depression, having contact with lots of friends related to higher levels of depression.
6. The contact number for London Lesbian and Gay Switchboard from the UK is 020 7837 7234.
7. This threefold classification can be used to identify the primary focus of work. Work undertaken at the individual level may have an impact on an organisation, and work at the structural level may impact on an individual's sense of well-being.

REFERENCES

Aggleton, P. (1996) *Health Promotion and Young People*. London: Health Education Authority.

Aggleton, P. and Warwick, I. (1997) Young people, sexuality and HIV and AIDS education. In L. Sherr (Ed.) *AIDS and Adolescents*. Amsterdam: Harwood Academic.

American Medical Association, Council on Scientific Affairs (1996) Health care needs of gay men and lesbians in the United States. *Journal of the American Medical Association*, 275(17), 1354–1359.

Baron, J. (1996) Some issues in psychotherapy with gay and lesbian clients. *Psychotherapy*, 33(4), 611–616.

Bradford, J., Ryan, C. and Rothblum, E.D. (1994) National lesbian health care survey: implications for mental health care. *Journal of Consulting and Clinical Psychology*, 62(2), 228–242.

Bridget, J. and Lucille, S. (1996) Lesbian youth support information service (LYSIS): developing a distance support agency for young lesbians. *Journal of Community and Applied Psychology*, 6, 355–364.

Clark, W.M. and Serovich, J.M. (1997) Twenty years on and still in the dark? Content analysis of articles pertaining to gay, lesbian and bisexual issues in marriage and family therapy journals. *Journal of Marital and Family Therapy*, 23(3), 239–253.

Cochran, S.D. and Mays, V.M. (1994) Depressive distress among homosexually active African American men and women. *American Journal of Psychiatry*, 151(4), 524–529.

Cohen, J. and Emanuel, J. (1998) *Positive participation. Consulting and involving young people in health-related work: a planning and training resource*. London: Health Education Authority.

Crosbie-Burnett, M., Foster, T.L., Murry, C.I. and Bowen, G.L. (1996) Gays' and lesbians' families-of-origin. A social-cognitive-behavioural model of adjustment. *Family Relations*, 45(4), 397–403.

D'Augelli, A.R. and Hershberger, S.L. (1993) Lesbian, gay and bisexual youth in community settings: personal challenges and mental health problems. *American Journal of Community Psychology*, 21(4), 421–448.

Department of Health (1997) *Press release—public health strategy launched to tackle root causes of ill-health*. 7 July, Department of Health, London.

Department of Health (1999) *Saving Lives: Our Healthier Nation*. London: Stationery Office.

Diekstra, R.F.W., Kienhorst, C.W.M. and de Wilde, E.J. (1995) Suicide and suicidal behaviour among adolescents. In M. Rutter and D.J. Smith (Eds) *Psychosocial Disorders in Young People. Time Trends and Their Causes*. Chichester: John Wiley.

Douglas, N., Warwick, I., Kemp, S., Whitty, G. and Aggleton, P. (1999) Homophobic bullying in secondary schools in England and Wales—teachers' experiences. *Health Education*, 99(2), 53–60.

Elliot, M. and Kilpatrick, J. (1994) *How to Stop Bullying. A Kidscape guide to training*. Stoke-on-Trent: Trentham Books.

Fontaine, J.H. and Hammond, N.L. (1996) Counselling issues with gay and lesbian adolescents. *Adolescence*, 31(124), 817–830.

Forrest, S., Biddle, G. and Clift, S. (1997) *Talking about homosexuality in the secondary school*. Horsham: AVERT.

Garland, A.F. and Zigler, E. (1993) Adolescent suicide prevention. Current research and social policy implications. *American Psychologist*, 48(2), 169–182.

Garnets, L.D. and D'Augelli, A.R. (1994) Empowering lesbian and gay communities: a call for collaboration with community psychology. *American Journal of Community Psychology*, 22(4), 447–470.

Greene, B. (1994) Ethnic-minority lesbians and gay men: mental health and treatment issues. *Journal of Consulting and Clinical Psychology*, 62(2), 243–251.

Grossman, A.H. and Kerner, M.S. (1998) Self-esteem and supportiveness as predictors of emotional distress in gay male and lesbian youth. *Journal of Homosexuality*, 35(2), 25–39.

Harrison, A.E. and Silenzio, V.M.B. (1996) Comprehensive care of lesbian and gay patients and families. *Primary Care*, 23(1), 31–46.

Health Education Authority (1997) *Mental Health Promotion. A quality framework*. London: Health Education Authority.

Hershberger, S.L. and D'Augelli, A.R. (1995) The impact of victimization on the mental health and suicidality of lesbian, gay and bisexual youths. *Developmental Psychology*, 31(1), 65–74.

Hershberger, S.L., Pilkington, N.W. and D'Augelli, A.R. (1997) Predictors of suicide attempts among gay, lesbian, and bisexual youth. *Journal of Adolescent Research*, 12(4), 477–497.

Johnson, A.M., Wadsworth, J., Wellings, K. and Field, J. (1994) *Sexual Attitudes and Lifestyles*. London, Blackwell Scientific Press.

Kottman, T., Lingg, M. and Tisdell, T. (1995) Gay and lesbian adolescents—implications for Adlerian therapists. *Individual Psychology—The Journal of Adlerian Theory, Research and Practice*, 51(2), 114–128.

Lehmann, J.B., Lehmann, C.U. and Kelly, P.J. (1998) Development and health care needs of lesbians. *Journal of Women's Health*, 7(3), 379–387.

Martin, S.R. (1996) A child's right to be gay: addressing the emotional maltreatment of queer youth. *Hastings Law Journal*, 48, 167–196.

Mason, A. and Palmer, A. (1996) *Queer bashing. A national survey of hate crimes against lesbians and gay men*. London: Stonewall.

McFarlane, L. (1998) *Diagnosis: homophobic. The experiences of lesbians, gay men and bisexuals in mental health services*. London: Project for Advice Counselling and Education.

McHenry, S.S. and Johnson, J.W. (1993) Homophobia in the therapist and gay or lesbian client—conscious and unconscious collusions in self-hate. *Psychotherapy*, 30(1), 141–151.

Mental Health Foundation (1997) Suicide and deliberate self-harm. The fundamental facts. *Mental Health Foundation Briefing, No. 1*. London: Mental Health Foundation.

Mental Health Foundation (1998) Facts not fairy tales: mental health and illness in children and young people. *Mental Health Foundation Briefing, No. 15*. London: Mental Health Foundation.

MIND (no date) Mind's policy on lesbians, gay men, bisexual women and men and mental health. *MINDfile Policy 1*. London: MIND.

Muerher, P. (1995) Suicide and sexual orientation: a critical summary of recent research and directions for future research. *Suicide and Life Threatening Behaviour*, 25, Supplement, 72–81.

Otis, M.D. and Skinner, W.F. (1996) The prevalence of victimization and its effect on mental well-being among lesbian and gay people. *Journal of Homosexuality*, 30(3), 93–121.

Phillips, S., McMillen, C., Sparks, J. and Ueberle, M. (1997) Concrete strategies for sensitizing youth-serving agencies to the needs of gay, lesbian, and other sexual minority youths. *Child Welfare*, 76(3), 393–409.

Pilkington, N.W. and D'Augelli, A.R. (1995) Victimization of lesbian, gay and bisexual youth in community settings. *Journal of Community Psychology*, 23(1), 34–56.

Proctor, C.D. and Groze, V.K. (1994) Risk factors for suicide among gay, lesbian and bisexual youths. *Social Work*, 39(5), 504–513.

Radowsky, M. and Siegal, L.J. (1997) The gay adolescent: stressors, adaptations, and psychosocial interventions. *Clinical Psychology Review*, 17(2), 191–216.

Rivers, I. (1996) Young, gay and bullied. *Young People Now*, January, 18–19.

Rosario, M., Hunter, J. and Gwadz, M. (1997) Exploration of substance use among lesbian, gay and bisexual youth: prevalence and correlates. *Journal of Adolescent Research*, 12(4), 454–476.

Rotheram-Borus, M.J., Rosario, M., Meyer-Bahlburg, H.F.L., Koopman, C., Dopkins, S.C. and Davies, M. (1994) Sexual and substance use acts of gay and bisexual male adolescents in New York city. *Journal of Sex Research*, 31(1), 47–57.

Savin-Williams, R.C. and Dubé, E.M. (1998) Parental reactions to their child's disclosure of a gay/lesbian identity. *Family Relations*, 47, 7–13.

Secker, J. (1998a) Mental health promotion theory and practice: implications for implementation of Our Healthier Nation. *Mental Health Review*, 3(2), 5–12.

Secker, J. (1998b) Current conceptualisations of mental health and mental health promotion. *Health Education Research*, 13(1), 57–66.

Telljohann, S.K. and Price, J.H. (1993) A qualitative examination of adolescent homosexuals' life experiences: ramifications for secondary school personnel. *Journal of Homosexuality*, 26(1), 41–56.

Townsend, M.H., Wallick, M.M., Pleak, R.R. and Cambre, K.M. (1997) Gay and lesbian issues in child and adolescent psychiatry training as reported by training directors. *Journal of the American Academy of Child and Adolescent Psychiatry*, 36(6), 764–768.

Treadway, L. and Yoakam, J. (1992) Creating a safer school environment for lesbian and gay students. *Journal of School Health*, 62(7), 352–357.

Trenchard, L. and Warren, H. (1984) *Something to tell you*. London: London Gay Teenage Group.

Walters, A.S. and Hayes, D.M. (1998) Homophobia within schools: challenging the culturally sanctioned dismissal of gay students and colleagues. *Journal of Homosexuality*, 35(2), 1–23.

White, J.C. and Dull, V.T. (1997) Health risk factors and health-seeking behaviours in lesbians. *Journal of Women's Health*, 6(1), 103–112.

Winters, K.C., Remafedi, G. and Chan, B.Y. (1996) Assessing drug abuse among gay-bisexual young men. *Psychology of Addictive Behaviours*, 10(4), 228–236.

Chapter 9

Young People with Learning Difficulties

Jenny Corbett

This chapter will focus upon the concept of challenging behaviour as it exists in a continuum of degrees of severity and in relation to a variety of forms of intervention strategies. The term *learning difficulties* covers a wide range of special educational needs, which includes those of young people diagnosed as experiencing the following conditions: attention deficit and hyperactivity disorder (ADHD); autism; Tourette's syndrome; profound and complex disabilities. When teachers and care staff refer to behaviour as being challenging, they tend to mean that it causes them problems in daily management and is a potential hazard both to the individual and to others, although what different managers define as challenging service providers will vary according to individual perceptions (Qureshi, 1994).

Learning difficulties have become a considerable cause for concern as recent care in the community initiatives have brought more people with difficult behaviours into a social context in which both their safety and that of others may be a significant care issue. Mansell (1994) defined *challenging behaviour* as that 'which presents a serious risk to the physical safety of the individual or others around them, or which prevents the individual taking part in everyday life in the community' (Mansell, 1994: 2). He suggests that challenging behaviour is socially constructed, being the product of both individual and environmental characteristics. He stresses that the goal of intervention should be to build up useful or constructive skills and behaviours rather than just to focus on eliminating unwanted ones. One of the key themes of his analysis is that the best intervention methodologies are those that conceptualise assessment and

Young People and Mental Health. Edited by P. Aggleton, J. Hurry and I. Warwick.
© 2000 John Wiley & Sons Ltd.

intervention as involving a much wider range of issues than simply the behaviour in question.

Moss (1997) has recently suggested that improving the mental health of people with learning disabilities can significantly enhance their quality of daily life. Diagnosis is problematic, however, as the person concerned often has difficulty in expressing themselves verbally. Moss reflected that there could be real problems for practitioners in assessing needs accurately. Traditionally, psychiatrists have been used to learning about symptoms through discussion, which is usually difficult for the person with learning difficulties. A behaviour modification approach, on the other hand, might observe the behaviours but not take past history into account. Moss asked whether what is called challenging behaviour is really a mental health problem relating to quality of life issues. He asked how many young people with learning difficulties could be said to have satisfactory relationships, achievements and living conditions. They are likely to have low social esteem, unlikely to have a partner and may have few friends and support networks.

In its exploration of the wide range of issues within a broad continuum, this chapter will include: an evaluation of the extent to which challenging behaviours are socially constructed; suggestions regarding the concept of *quality of life* for young people with learning difficulties and mental health problems; and examples of effective intervention strategies.

THE NATURE OF CHALLENGING BEHAVIOURS: DEGREES ON A CONTINUUM

All schools contain some challenging young people. Those who are now labelled as having attention deficit and hyperactivity disorder (ADHD) or Asperger's syndrome may be found in mainstream schools and colleges, often on medication and/or participating in behaviour modification programmes. Where the degree of challenge relates to severe learning disability, intervention strategies are likely to be highly structured and carefully monitored.

The diagnosis of ADHD has proliferated in the USA and Australia over recent years and has now become prevalent in Britain. The American Psychiatric Association (1987) has identified two categories: attention deficit disorder with hyperactivity syndrome (ADDHS) and attention deficit disorder without hyperactivity syndrome (ADDS). Bowley and Walter (1992) describe the syndrome as involving 'an imbalance or deficiency of one or more neurotransmitters in the brain' (Bowley and Walter, 1992: 39). The drug that is commonly prescribed to treat ADDS is methylphenidate (proprietary name Ritalin) and is a form of central nervous system stimulant which acts on the cerebral cortex to repress the child's hyperactivity, disruption or inattention. Whilst there is strong medical evidence to support the success of this chemical therapy, there are also noted side effects such as dizziness, drowsiness, blurred vision, depression, anorexia, nausea and growth suppression.

Slee (1995) suggests that ADDS has become so popular as a diagnosis because it does not blame parents for their child's bad behaviour but instead presents it as a sickness. He says that 'having one's child classed as special or deviant may well become tolerable if the attention now changes from the ire of school administration and teachers to the concern of guidance and medical personnel expert in this area' (Slee, 1995: 75). The contrast Slee observes between 'ire' and 'concern' is interesting because it implies that attitudinal aspects of the social context are major factors in the promotion of one form of challenging label over another. Being labelled 'delinquent' is more uncomfortable as it indicates that the individual and the family share responsibility for behaviours, while the term 'mentally disordered' suggests that neurological damage is largely responsible.

There has long been controversy over the diagnosis of autism. For many years the psychoanalytic view that autism was the result of cold, emotionless parenting was influential (e.g. Kanner and Eisenberg, 1956; Kanner, 1973). Recent research suggests that evidence of organic abnormality is almost always discovered (e.g. Steffenberg, 1991). As Trevarthen *et al.* (1996) imply, there is a very wide range of autistic conditions varying from the most extreme forms to the relatively mild. Diagnosis tends to focus upon classic symptoms like social detachment and obsessional behaviour, a ritualistic stereotyped exploration of objects and an insistence on everything being the same. In recent years there has been a new emphasis upon a mild form of autism, called Asperger's syndrome after Hans Asperger who first described children with these symptoms at about the same time as Leo Kanner was describing autistic children in the mid 1940s. Asperger's syndrome is defined in Burgoine and Wing (1983) as showing features of the following: a lack of empathy; naive, inappropriate interaction; little ability to form friendships; poor non-verbal communication and pedantic, repetitive speech. Attwood (1998) suggests that Asperger's syndrome is now best considered as a subgroup within the autistic spectrum, with its own diagnostic criteria and that it is far more common than classic autism.

When behaviours are described as 'challenging', they are usually presented as violent, destructive, self-injurious and antisocial. Those behaviours which remain unchanged in form may become increasingly challenging to services because of the gain in physical strength of the individual concerned or because of reduction in staff services or the loss of staff with particular skills. Philippa Russell, who chaired the recent Mental Health Foundation Committee on Services for Children with Learning Disabilities and Severe Challenging Behaviour in the UK, made the following observations about the adverse consequences of such behaviour for the following people:

- For the *child*. Some behaviours, such as self-injuries, can threaten health, even life, and may rapidly lead to rejection and exclusion. Behaviours such as overactivity or stereotypical behaviours may restrict personal growth and seriously impair personal relationships.
- For the *family*. Caring for a child with severe challenging behaviour is likely to have a profound impact upon day-to-day lives. The Committee heard powerful messages from families who felt isolated and exhausted, and often saw residential provision as the only solution.
- For *education, health and social services*. Children who pose a danger to themselves or others often challenge schools and other services. All too often, the response to the child's demands is exclusion and the use of a specialist residential provision. The current debate about the legality of the use of certain controls and treatments has further reduced the confidence of many professionals in actively working with children who challenge.
- For *the wider community*. Socially unacceptable behaviours are likely to elicit avoidance by and exclusion from the community (Russell, 1997: p. 61).

Learning how to respond to challenging behaviour among children with learning disabilities is a cause for social, political, ethical and economic concern. The prevalence of challenging behaviours and health and safety risks has to be understood within the context of broader social and ethnographic issues.

PREVALENCE AND INCIDENCE

In a controversial area like ADHD, there is a marked variation in prevalence within different countries. Recent estimates suggested that 1 child in 100 was diagnosed as having ADHD in the USA whereas it was only 1 in 2000 in the UK (Slee, 1995). With the increased publicity given to the use of the 'wonder' drug, Ritalin, and the popular impetus for parents to seek out a 'brain-damaged' label for their child's behaviour, these figures are currently at about 1 in 40 in the USA and 1 in 400 in the United Kingdom. The boy to girl ratio is about 5 to 1. This suggests that ADHD has increasingly become a socially constructed disorder in which elements of chaotic, essentially aggressively masculine behaviours are treated with drugs rather than confronting the wider social issues. In the current climate in which boys' underachievement is seen as a social crisis, ADHD contributes to a scare scenario of disturbed and disruptive boys unable to learn effectively.

Trevarthen *et al.* (1996) suggest that the apparent increase in the number of children diagnosed with autism in the UK population in general (from 4.5 to 6 cases per 10 000 population in earlier studies to 10 to 14 cases per 10 000 population in recent studies) is misleading. They imply that it is a consequence of a weakening of the definition since 1987 when the American Psychiatric Association *Diagnostic and Statistical Manual of Mental Disorders* (DSM III-R) classified 'autistic disorder' as a 'pervasive developmental disorder'. This included more so-called 'non-nuclear autistic' children whose difficulty lies mainly with language and not with behaviour. This is now being adjusted and the incidence appears to be levelling although the nature of autism has become a topic which many educationists are expressing interest in as more children diagnosed with this condition are being integrated into mainstream schools and colleges. Gillberg and Gillberg (1989) found a prevalence rate of 26 per 10 000 population for Asperger's syndrome, which is by far the most numerous of the autistic type of disorders. Most studies report about 4 males to 1 female with autism, but the inclusion of Rett's syndrome within a spectrum of autistic behaviours influences figures for those who combine the lowest intellectual ability with autism, as Rett's syndrome involves this group and exclusively affects girls. In those with the highest intellectual ability and autism (classic Kanner autism), the ratios are as high as 13 boys to 1 girl (Gillberg *et al.*, 1991). While it was assumed from Kanner's earlier work that autism was found more commonly among middle-class, professional families, this is now disputed. As developmental disorders in general occur most frequently in lower social classes, the fact that there seems to be no specific effect of social class suggests that there may be a genetic rather than an environmental cause.

Tourette's syndrome, in which multiple motor tics and one or more vocal tics are present at some time, is estimated to affect 5 people per 10 000 of the population although the number is considered to be higher in the special school population (Robertson, 1994).

Russell (1997) reports that recent research conducted in special schools for children with severe learning disabilities (Kiernan and Kiernan, 1994) suggests that approximately 2000 pupils in England and Wales present a serious challenge in their behaviours and a further 3400 a lesser challenge. These figures could be seen to reflect the extreme end of the continuum which contains much higher numbers of children being excluded from mainstream schooling because their behavioural difficulties disrupt the learning of others. Whether in mainstream or special schooling, behaviours which challenge are usually seen to place others at risk and are therefore presented as a health and safety hazard.

RISK FACTORS AND HEALTH PROTECTING BEHAVIOURS

It might be assumed that the major risk factors in relation to challenging behaviours in young people with learning disabilities are those of physical injury and coping with conflict. However, there are significant ethical and ideological dilemmas at both the high and the low risk ends of the continuum. The degree of physical intervention which is appropriate and legally acceptable is a key issue in relation to coping with challenging behaviours in young people with profound and multiple disabilities (Harris *et al.*, 1996). At the other end of the continuum, young people who are placed in special schooling and in off-site provision for pupils with emotional and behavioural difficulties may include a disproportionately high number from certain ethnic minority groups. In assessment procedures, allocation of placements and intervention strategies, there are moral judgements being made and prejudices perpetuated. It is important, therefore, that it is not just the more obvious physical risks which are considered but also the ethical risks which describing certain behaviours as 'challenging' can involve.

Peagam (1994) has made a study of the referral rates by teachers in a large Midlands education authority in which they identified primary school children whom they saw as having emotional and/or behavioural difficulties which led to their having difficulties in learning. While Afro-Caribbean children were over-represented by a factor of three, black Asian children were under-represented by a factor of four. Peagam was particularly concerned to learn if there were distinct differences in the way that teachers perceived 'disturbance' in children from different ethnic groups. His research suggested that Afro-Caribbean children were more likely to be described as 'reacting badly' to discipline and as 'unpredictable' than other groups. The research confirmed findings that there is a significant socio-economic bias in relation to the categorisation of emotional and behavioural difficulty (EBD), with many children coming from poor homes. There were also important differences between ethnic groups. Afro-Caribbean children were more likely to have a single parent (54.1%) than to be living with both parents (29.1%), while for children of Asian origin the pattern was reversed, with a significant majority (74.5%) living with both parents. Free-dinner rates were higher for Afro-Caribbean children (70.5%) and a larger proportion lived in council housing (84.3%). Peagam suggests that this situation merits urgent attention if 'EBD schools, particularly in our larger cities, are not to become ghettos for Afro-Caribbean children' (Peagam, 1994: 38), forecasting the current concern expressed by Sir Herman Ouseley, Chairman of the Commission for Racial Equality. He recently said that the White Paper on Education, 'Excellence for All', would instigate a fractured education system, with resources located in high status schools and concentrating those with greatest need in the low status provision, compounding the underperformance of Afro-Caribbean boys who have already been found to be six times as likely as white pupils to be excluded from school (Carvel, 1998). What Ouseley calls 'a system of educational apartheid', in which certain categories of school are divided on grounds of race and class, is a serious ethical dilemma in relation to defining what constitutes a learning difficulty and what 'challenging' behaviour really means. Peagam found that behaviours which provoked teachers were often ignored by peers, many

Afro-Caribbean boys being unpopular with their teachers but popular with their peers. The labelling of certain behaviours as challenging may reflect prejudices and stereotypes which influence responses and class-room management to the detriment of certain groups of children.

In recent years, there has been increased emphasis on schools teaching moral values so as to counteract the effects of social and family instability and address youth crime. Within this context, there are new dilemmas for schools in evaluating the extent to which certain be-haviours can be termed delinquent or disturbed. It is interesting to contrast the situation in the UK with that in the USA where Public Law 94–142 provides certain safeguards for students whose learning diffi-culties place them in the category of 'emotional disturbance'. Howe and Miramontes (1992) record the case of a boy whose violent and unpre-dictable behaviour threatened others in his high school but who could not be expelled because he experienced what was defined as a medical condition within the legislation. The authors point to the distinction between moral language and therapeutic language, between the use of 'delinquent' and 'disturbed' and 'disciplinary action' and 'behaviour modification'. As the culture of the UK is becoming more like the USA with its eagerness to take issues to court, the use of the tribunal system in special education has led to more middle-class parents confronting local authorities and demanding specific resources and placements. This can mean that, as the power of governing bodies can over-ride teachers' wishes, some children whose behaviour is disturbing to others are being returned to schools from which they have been expelled. As Gray et al. (1994) note, challenging behaviour can threaten the authority of teachers, causing them to become distressed themselves, defensive in their actions and unwilling to be flexible in their approaches. Thus, a circle of mistrust and hostility can be perpetuated.

With a focus upon the more severe end of the continuum, one of the major risk factors with people whose profound learning disabilities make communication difficult is that diagnosis may be inaccurate and lead to inappropriate treatment. By taking examples of individuals with Tourette's syndrome, Down's syndrome and schizophrenia, the com-plexity of coping with multiple disabilities can be clearly illustrated.

Tourette's syndrome is one of the remediable causes of challenging behaviour, although it often goes undiagnosed. Finlay (1995) suggests that it is vital that professionals working with people with learning disabilities are aware of Tourette's syndrome since many of the behaviours associated with it are similar to challenging and stereotypi-cal behaviours caused by other factors in their client group and can usually be treated by medication and social intervention. The case study described by Finlay is that of a young man with learning disabilities who had only been discovered to experience bouts of tics 'such as re-peated blinking, hand clenching, grimacing, shoulder shrugs, head jerks, snorts and sudden exclamations' (Finlay, 1995: 81) when living in a hostel, while during his schooldays he had been diagnosed variously as schizophrenic, autistic, or as having obsessive-compulsive disorder and depression. The correct diagnosis led to medication which gave him more control and confidence and helped staff to see a reason for his past behaviour.

Children with Down's syndrome are often stereotyped as being happy, good-natured and co-operative. This is not always the case, as Prasher and Clarke (1996) record in their case study of a 17 year old male with Down's syndrome, autism and challenging behaviour. They say that he was referred for assessment because of his difficult behaviour, which included 'throwing objects, taking off his clothes, smearing, unprovoked aggression, head banging and sexually disinhibited behaviours' (Prasher and Clarke, 1996: 167). They note that it is difficult to diagnose autism in people with Down's syndrome because some stereotyped behaviours and stubbornness are common in those with Down's syndrome but without autism. What is particularly important is that a diagnosis of autism can then lead to improved provision of care and access to specialist services.

Recent research in Cornwall has explored the issue of the dual diagnosis of schizophrenia and learning disability (James *et al.*, 1996). It reveals that a delay in starting treatment can often result from the complexity of diagnosis. Taking a series of case studies, the authors show that hallucinations, delusions and loss of self-esteem can also be experienced by people with learning disabilities, albeit at more basic levels. Sometimes psychiatrists mistakenly diagnose people who have chronic schizophrenia as having learning disabilities because their intellectual functioning is influenced by their illness. The difficulty in making a correct diagnosis can lead to people with learning disabilities and mental illness not receiving the psychiatric treatment which might help them and their families.

An on-going tension in relation to diagnosis concerns whether to take a mainly neurological approach or adopt a more holistic emphasis. The laboratory-based assessment of disturbed children was common practice in US clinics in the 1960s (e.g. Menninger Clinic, 1969), and is again seen as useful in relation to the assessment of neurological signs in the diagnosis of ADHD in the USA (Wodrich, 1994). This renewed emphasis upon neurological testing and medical categorisation can be seen to have influenced intervention strategies, particularly in relation to the use of medication.

EFFECTIVE INTERVENTIONS

During the 1990s, there has developed an emphasis upon teaching positive behaviour rather than punishing negative behaviours (Rogers, 1994). Using the term 'behaviour recovery' in the context of a whole-school approach, children whose behaviour is seen to be creating learning difficulties for them are helped to see what it does to other people and how they can develop more control. The sequences which Rogers describes of mirroring, modelling and rehearsing, based on individual programmes and target behaviour, are in the tradition of behaviour modification used extensively for children with learning disabilities. Whilst some may regard this approach in the mainstream schools of the late 1990s as retrograde, others will see the defining of 'behaviour disabled' pupils as having a distinct form of learning difficulty as a positive way of no longer treating them as intrinsically 'bad' but as able to improve. Rogers suggests that a behaviour-teaching programme can increase the child's self-esteem and peer acceptance, encouraging them to use self-guiding speech like 'I can put my hand up without calling out', 'I can move through the room without disturbing others', 'I can speak in a quiet voice' (Rogers, 1994: 170). This positive approach is essentially interactional, depending upon the social climate of a school and classroom.

Cooper (1993) recognises the value of addressing individual needs within an ecosystemic approach in which human behaviour is seen as the product of an ongoing interaction between influences in the social environment and internal motivations from prior social experiences. As Cooper says of boys exhibiting disturbed behaviour and underachievement,

'It is often difficult to say which comes first, the family problems or the school problems. What is clear, however, is that together they make a powerful combination of negative forces for these boys.' (Cooper, 1993: 56)

A mark of successful intervention at all stages of the 'challenging' behaviour continuum is a recognition that social interactions can both determine and negate individual development, and that the individual has to be understood in context.

For young people with profound disabilities and challenging behaviours the use of touch as a therapeutic medium, or the incorporation of a variety of sensory approaches which include touch, sounds, lighting and imagery, has been found to be an effective method of intervention especially in reducing self-injury (Withers and Ensum, 1995; Hegarty and Gale, 1996). In recognition of the importance of empathy in intervention strategies, Cragg (1997) describes the concept of engagement for staff working with people with learning disabilities as

'. . . giving the person as much help as needed to participate in useful/ valued activity. Engagement can be: either in whole or part of a task/ activity/interaction. Either continuous or "stop-start". Either in the lead role or as an active spectator. Includes proximity, attention, and communication.' (Cragg, 1997: 9)

When an individual with learning disabilities does not use speech to communicate, avoids eye contact and becomes easily frustrated, it can be all too easy to leave them alone and make little effort to provide stimulation. The notion of 'engagement' offers a positive intervention to help make the daily quality of life more meaningful and interesting to people who may not seek engagement of their own volition.

The vexed issue of physical restraint for challenging behaviours is one which concerns service providers and guidelines are available to staff working in residential settings. Harris *et al.* (1996) offer a series of valuable case studies, including the example of Russ, a young man with few social skills who becomes very agitated by any changes to his routine. When he first visits a new building or a room which has been rearranged he is likely to become distressed, making whining noises and banging his head with his fist and attacking other people. In the past, this reaction to new surroundings significantly reduced Russ's quality of life as his carers were wary and tended not to introduce new experiences if possible. Staff now recognise that if they can help Russ to overcome his distress when confronted with a strange environment, he very quickly settles down. The most effective method of doing this is for a member of staff to sit on either side of Russ and hold his arms firmly by his side. After two or three minutes Russ will relax and begin to look carefully at his surroundings. After another five minutes or so he is relaxed enough to wander around without physical contact although staff remain close by and offer reassurance through physical contact when necessary. For Russ and other people like him, fear and anxiety about trying new experiences has inhibited quality of life. Physical intervention has been necessary to create new learning opportunities.

This offers a positive example of physical intervention which is used to support a more interesting experience of daily life. Unfortunately, physical intervention has sometimes been used in a punitive and intimidating manner or been employed by stressed staff without consideration of other methods of more positive engagement. McGill *et al.* (1994) give an example of a young woman with learning disabilities and challenging behaviour who was moved out of a long-stay hospital into a community home at a time of staff shortages. As in the case of Russ, she was distressed with changes and her challenging behaviour increased just at a time when there were few staff to support her needs. As a consequence, she was moved back into long-term institutional provision because she gained a label of being too disturbed to cope. The delicate process of change and adaptation to new demands requires intensive staff attention, understanding and empathy.

One valuable intervention strategy for people who may have limited means of communicating their specific needs is to provide the necessary procedures for each individual in written form, including the details of how they like to be dressed, what food they enjoy and the kinds of tasks that can be expected of them. The disability arts group, *Acting Up*, has used multimedia technology to help people with learning disabilities present themselves as they wish to be seen through video and photographic imagery, working in collaboration with service users and providers (Crowhurst, 1995). The gradual shift towards an increased level of engagement and empathy in service provision reflects the impact of the self-advocacy movement over the last few years.

Drug intervention in the treatment of young people with learning disabilities and mental health problems has been particularly controversial and much concern has been voiced about the use of Ritalin to treat ADHD. Whilst some teachers record remarkable improvements in behaviour and capacity to learn, others express anxiety at the effect which the drug has upon personality and its side effects of weight loss and drowsiness. Some parents have been found to give children increasing doses of Ritalin according to their child's prevailing mood, risking drug overdose and drug dependency. Various drugs have been used to treat children with autism but Trevarthen *et al.* (1996) suggest that no 'magic bullets' have been found, which was unsurprising given the heterogeneous manifestations of the disorder and its complex pathophysiology. They concluded that such fundamental ways of intervening with brain activity could not replace the need for psychological and empathetic forms of treatment. One delicate area in which drug intervention has been found of value is that of treating people with learning disabilities who sexually abuse others. Murphy (1997) gives the example of a young man with Asperger's syndrome who took a sexual interest in children. He was given lithium treatment for his bipolar mood disorder and received social skills training to help him to cope better with his sexual feelings. He was discharged to a group home shared with just one other resident and was closely supervised. Under these conditions, he was considered at very low risk of offending. In a social climate where 'care in the community' initiatives have been much criticised for the high risk to the general public which seems often to occur, it is clearly valuable if a combination of drug and behaviour modification intervention can help to support someone in a community placement.

The development of social skills is seen as most important in programmes for autistic children, using games to encourage them to explore their emotions. Attwood (1998) describes the kinds of games which can be helpful for young people with Asperger's syndrome to assist them in expressing their emotions and recognising the feelings of others. Young people with Asperger's syndrome can often say inappropriately unkind things or laugh when they are distressed, creating difficulties in social interaction. Attwood found that the verbal expression of feelings was often extremely difficult for them but written expressions could be far more emotional and powerful. This observation indicates why the intervention termed 'facilitated communication' has become so popular in the treatment of autism, particularly in Australia and the USA. A research team led by the US researcher, Biklen, described 'facilitated communication' as the 'hand-over-hand or hand-on-forearm support of students as they point to pictures, letters or objects to augment communication' (Biklen *et al.*, 1991: 163). They provide a positive example in a middle school student, Abdul, who made noises rather than using verbal language:

'The speech therapist asked him to focus on the computer screen . . . She then typed "Trees lose their leaves in . . ." The student typed "F" and then tapped his hand on the computer screen. He banged the table hard and vocalized again. The speech therapist asked him to "Finish it", to which he typed, "GFALL" . . . To the next statement, "I have run out of . . . for the razor", he typed "BLADES". Less than a month and a half later, this student was still hitting people and himself and was making noises in the classroom. The fact that he was communicating with facilitation had not "cured" him of his many behaviours associated with autism . . . Over time he had become more able to or interested in sitting at the computer or language board to communicate.' (Biklen *et al.*, 1991: 172)

The example given by Biklen *et al.* shows that facilitated communication for autistic children can offer them a more user-friendly means of expression than an exclusive reliance upon verbal language. However, there are critics of this approach, one of them being Diane Twachtman-Cullen, who has described detailed case studies of children who appeared to be placed under considerable pressure and tension whilst working with a facilitator. She has questioned the extent to which autistic individuals may be struggling to please their facilitators rather than being true to themselves, observing conflict and tensions which the facilitator appeared to ignore or over-rule. She asks, 'Could it be that the highly touted alleged synchrony between facilitator and client occurs *only* when the client is performing in the manner that is intended by the facilitator? If so, the following question must be asked: What price does conditional synchrony exact?' (Twachtman-Cullen, 1997: 94). Her misgivings raise important ethical issues in relation to those young people whose combined experiences of learning disability and mental illness make them vulnerable to exploitation and abuse. A priority in any intervention should surely be to treat everyone with respect and dignity.

There is much rhetoric in current literature on the importance of empowerment for people with learning disabilities if they are to be acknowledged as active citizens (e.g. Ramcharan *et al.*, 1997). This means respecting difference and not forcing people into a form of behaviour which may damage their identity. As Jordan (1990) says of intervention with autistic children,

'At a humane level, many children with autism appear to derive comfort—if not pleasure—from their obsessions, and it would seem unnecessarily cruel to deprive them of this without good reason . . . It should not be forgotten that we all have behaviours that we would not necessarily indulge in at work, or even in public, but which are perfectly acceptable in the privacy of our own homes. As children who are autistic seldom get granted the privilege of privacy, we should be careful not to burden them with abnormal and unnecessary constraints.' (Jordan, 1990: 56–57)

Her wise words offer valuable baseline guidance for those who work on intervention programmes. Many young people who experience a combination of learning disability and mental illness have developed social behaviours which are deemed inappropriate. Whilst it is necessary to prepare them to live as adults in a society which is largely intolerant of differences, it is also important to respect their individuality and their right to be themselves. As I observed in residential self-help programmes for young people who experienced multiple disabilities,

> 'Before we offer the concept of "choice" we have to support these students in their inner search for identity: they must know *who they are* before knowing *what they are about*.' (Corbett, 1989: 158)

Often intervention programmes can become impositions of 'normal' behaviours which fail to challenge racial, sexual and class stereotypes.

El-Hadi (1996) considers the particular dilemmas inherent in some therapeutic interventions which are offered to young people from ethnic minorities. He suggests that certain types of therapeutic intervention may fit the child and family better than others. His experience as a consultant adolescent psychiatrist has led him to feel that individual psychotherapy is less acceptable in non-Western cultures where the family is perhaps more central. Task-setting and behavioural focal therapy are usually better understood by Asian families than insight-giving therapy. Detailed note-taking early on in the therapy may also appear intrusive to families who may have had negative experiences of institutions where such procedures are common. He suggests that structural family therapy, which focuses on issues of authority, boundaries and rules, is more suitable for non-individualistic societies (for example, some African ones) which are quite hierarchical and where the kinship group may be more significant than the individual. The practical role of intervention is recognised when he says that,

> 'In my practice I do write letters to the housing department or to the social security department to help them with their benefits . . . I think it is important to recognise the relative power and authority which the therapist/helper or expert has, and to be prepared to use it on behalf of the family to gain their confidence before any therapy can take place.' (El-Hadi, 1996: 103)

The approach he takes demonstrates both care and vision in relation to this professional role. It is a form of intervention which may be appropriate for those working with young people who have complex disabilities in the twenty-first century in which 'widening participation includes the sharing of skills and rich learning experiences by the transfer of ideas between different countries' (Corbett, 1998: 77). Central to this flexible, receptive approach is an understanding that there are many different ways to respond to individual needs and that no one method is intrinsically superior.

SUMMARY: PRIORITIES FOR INTERVENTION AND RESEARCH

The key priority for intervention and research is that of quality of life. The focus over recent years has tended to be upon the normalisation of people with learning disabilities, to make them acceptable within the *status quo* of their society. This has sometimes led to their being severely inhibited and expected to conform to a pattern of behaviour which is rigidly conventional. At the end of the twentieth century, such narrow conformism is unacceptable and incompatible with current visions of active citizenship. The focus is now much more likely to be upon developing the capacity for meaningful relationships, participation in a rich social life and enjoying living within the local community, rather than merely upon the daily living skills required to run a home. There is increased recognition that people with dual disabilities may have very different priorities which reflect their gender, ethnicity and sexuality, and that real empowerment means listening to them and treating their views with respect. There needs to be a balance between providing the level of support which enables these young people to live in the community and being intrusive and prescriptive in their daily decision-making.

As residential long-stay provision has changed to encourage small group homes in the community, there are new risks attached to young people whose behaviours may become a cause for public concern. Intervention and research has to monitor the progress of initiatives which support community living, such that neither the individuals themselves nor the general public are exposed to unnecessary dangers. This requires realistic staffing levels and acknowledgement of where the specific risks are located. An integral part of the new role for young people with complex disabilities is that they are encouraged to take responsibility for their own actions, where they have sufficient capacity to understand the implications, and to learn to accept that this is the other side of having increased choice. A positive approach to intervention is one which sets 'quality of life' as a key target to be achieved.

REFERENCES

American Psychiatric Association (1987) *Diagnostic and Statistical Manual of Mental Disorders*, 3rd edn (revised). Washington, DC: American Psychiatric Association.

Attwood, T. (1998) *Asperger's Syndrome: A Guide for Parents and Professionals*. London: Jessica Kingsley.

Biklen, D., Winston Morton, M., Saha, S., Duncan, J., Gold, D., Hardardottir, M., Karna, E., O'Connor, S. and Rao, S. (1991) I AMN NOT UTISTIVC ON THJE TYP ('I'm not Autistic on the Typewriter'). *Disability, Handicap and Society*, 6(3), 161–180.

Bowley, B.A. and Walter, E. (1992) Attention deficit disorders and the role of the elementary school counsellor. *Elementary School Guidance and Counselling*, 27, 39–46.

Burgoine, E. and Wing, L. (1983) Identical triplets with Asperger's Syndrome. *British Journal of Psychiatry*, 143, 261–265.

Carvel, J. (1998) Schools Face 'Apartheid'. *The Guardian*, Tuesday 6 January, 6.

Churchill, J., Brown, H., Craft, A. and Horrocks, C. (Eds) (1997) *There Are No Easy Answers: The provision of continuing care and treatment to adults with learning disabilities who sexually abuse others*. Nottingham: Department of Learning Disabilities.

Cooper, P. (1993) *Effective Schools for Disaffected Students*. London: Routledge.

Corbett, J. (1989) The quality of life in the 'Independence' curriculum. *Disability, Handicap and Society*, 4(2), 145–163.

Corbett, J. (1998) *Special Educational Needs in the Twentieth Century: a Cultural Analysis*. London: Cassell.

Cragg, R. (1997) *Getting Engaged*. Kidderminster: British Institute of Learning Disabilities.

Crowhurst, G. (1995) Giving 'invisible' people voices: multimedia technology. *Community Living*, 9(2), 14–15.

El-Hadi, A. (1996) The management of emotional problems of children from ethnic minorities. In V. Varma (Ed.) *Managing Children with Problems*. London: Cassell.

Finlay, M. (1995) Tourette's syndrome and challenging behaviour: a case study. *British Journal of Learning Disabilities*, 24(2), 80–83.

Gillberg, I.C. and Gillberg, C. (1989) Asperger syndrome—some epidemiological considerations: a research note. *Journal of Child Psychology and Psychiatry*, 30, 631–638.

Gillberg, C., Steffenberg, S. and Schaumann, H. (1991) Autism: epidemiology: is autism more common now than 10 years ago? *British Journal of Psychiatry*, 158, 403–409.

Gray, P., Miller, A. and Noakes, J. (1994) *Challenging Behaviour in Schools*. London: Routledge.

Harris, J., Allen, D., Cornick, M., Jefferson, A. and Mills, R. (1996) *Physical Intervention: A Policy Framework*. Kidderminster: British Institute of Learning Disabilities.

Hegarty, J. and Gale, E. (1996) Touch as a therapeutic medium for people with challenging behaviours. *British Journal of Learning Disabilities*, 24(1), 26–32.

Howe, K. and Miramontes, O. (1992) *The Ethics of Special Education*. New York: Teachers College Press.

James, D., Mukherjee, T. and Smith, C. (1996) Schizophrenia and learning disability. *British Journal of Learning Disabilities*, 24(3), 90–94.

Jordan, R. (1990) The years between 6 and 12. In Ellis, K. (Ed.) *Autism: Professional Perspectives and Practice*. London: Chapman and Hall.

Kanner, L. (1973) *Childhood Psychosis: Initial Studies and New Insights*. Washington, DC: V.H. Winston and Sons.

Kanner, L. and Eisenberg, L. (1956) Early infantile autism: 1943–1955. *American Journal of Orthopsychiatry*, 19, 55–65.

Kiernan, C. and Kiernan, D. (1994) Challenging behaviour in schools for pupils with severe learning difficulties. *Mental Handicap Research*, 7, 117–201.

Mansell, J. (1994) Challenging behaviour: the prospect for change. *British Journal of Learning Disabilities*, 22(1), 2–5.

McGill, P., Emerson, E. and Mansell, J. (1994) Individually designed residential provision for people with seriously challenging behaviours. In E. Emerson, P. McGill and J. Mansell (Eds) *Severe Learning Disabilities and Challenging Behaviours*. London: Chapman and Hall.

Menninger Clinic (1969) *Disturbed Children*. San Francisco: Jossey-Bass.

Moss, S. (1997) Assessing and Responding to the Mental Health Needs of People with a Learning Disability. Keynote address in 1997 British Institute of Learning Disabilities International Conference, Manchester, 14–17 September.

Murphy, G. (1997) Treatment and risk management. In J. Churchill, H. Brown, A. Craft and C. Horrocks (Eds) *There Are No Easy Answers*. University of Nottingham: Department of Learning Disabilities.

Peagam, E. (1994) Special needs or educational apartheid? The emotional and behavioural difficulties of Afro-Caribbean children. *Support for Learning*, 9(1), 33–38.

Prasher, V. and Clarke, D. (1996) Case report: challenging behaviour in a young adult with Down's syndrome and autism. *British Journal of Learning Disabilities*, 24(4), 167–169.

Qureshi, H. (1994) The size of the problem. In E. Emerson, P. McGill and J. Mansell (Eds) *Severe Learning Disabilities and Challenging Behaviours*. London: Chapman and Hall.

Ramcharan, P., Roberts, G., Grant, G. and Borland, J. (Eds) (1997) *Empowerment in Everyday Life*. London: Jessica Kingsley.

Robertson, M. (1994) Annotation: Gilles de la Tourette syndrome—an update. *Journal of Child Psychology and Psychiatry*, 35(4), 597–611.

Rogers, B. (1994) Teaching positive behaviour to behaviourally disordered students in primary schools. *Support for Learning*, 9(4), 166–170.

Russell, P. (1997) Don't forget us! Messages from the Mental Health Foundation Committee's Report on Services for Children with Learning Disabilities and Severe Challenging Behaviour. *British Journal of Special Education*, 24(2), 60–65.

Slee, R. (1995) *Changing Theories and Practices of Discipline*. London: The Falmer Press.

Steffenberg, S. (1991) 'Neuropsychiatric assessment of children with autism: a population-based study. *Developmental Medicine and Child Neurology*, 33, 495–511.

Trevarthen, C., Aitken, K., Papoudi, D. and Robarts, J. (1996) *Children with Autism: Diagnosis and Intervention to Meet Their Needs*. London: Jessica Kingsley.

Twachtman-Cullen, D. (1997) *A Passion to Believe: Autism and the Facilitated Communication Phenomenon*. Boulder, Colorado: Westview Press.

Withers, P. and Ensum, I. (1995) Successful treatment of severe self injury incorporating the use of DRO, a Snoezelen room and orientation cues. *British Journal of Learning Disabilities*, 23(4), 164–167.

Wodrich, D. (1994) *Attention Deficit Hyperactivity Disorder*. Baltimore: Paul H. Brookes.

Part III

SPECIAL CONTEXTS AND SETTINGS

Chapter 10

The Mental Health of 'Looked After' Young People

Juliet Koprowska and Mike Stein

Any examination of mental health issues relating to looked after young people raises a complex and diverse set of issues. First, looked after young people are by no means a homogeneous group. For example, they are ethnically diverse, and young people of mixed heritage are over-represented in the 'care' system (Rowe *et al.*, 1989). Some young people come into the care system quite briefly, because their family cannot manage temporarily; others come into care 'for longer periods because of abuse, neglect, chronic social difficulties or severe be-havioural problems' (Wolkind and Rushton, 1994: 252). Young people also enter the care system at different ages, with or without their siblings, and with varying contact with their family of origin (Wolkind and Rushton, 1994). Some are 'accommodated' with foster families, others with relatives, and others in residential establishments. Legislation, policy and practice all have an impact on the admission of young people into care, and on the nature of the care they receive.

When it comes to mental health, the picture is also complex. A multitude of factors have an impact on people's mental health, and some individuals are more 'resilient' than others, for reasons which are not yet fully understood (Rutter, 1985). Genetic inheritance, temperament, quality of relationships, life experiences and social circumstances all have a part to play (Rutter, 1985; Newton, 1988). Moreover, some of the conditions which can make people vulnerable to mental health problems overlap with the conditions that can lead to entry into the care

Young People and Mental Health. Edited by P. Aggleton, J. Hurry and I. Warwick.
© 2000 John Wiley & Sons Ltd.

system. It is widely accepted that, as Utting *et al*. (1997: 68) put it, 'Looked after children especially those in residential care are identified as a group whose mental health needs are known to be greater than those of the general population of the same age.'

In this chapter we will begin by exploring the research evidence on the mental health of looked after young people. This will be drawn from two main sources: first, the very few specific mental health studies; and second, the more general studies concerning the 'care' of young people. We will then go on to discuss the risk factors and health promoting behaviours including those in families and substitute care. We will conclude by considering effective interventions for primary and secondary prevention, and by identifying directions for future research.

RESEARCH EVIDENCE

Young people who are looked after by local authorities constitute a very small proportion of all young people in the country: approximately 0.5% (Wolkind and Rushton, 1994). They are a group who are much researched yet, to our knowledge, there has been only one study conducted in the UK which is exclusively dedicated to discovering the prevalence of mental disorder in looked after young people (McCann *et al*., 1996). The young people involved were 'in care' in Oxfordshire. The results of this study certainly support Utting's statement, and arouse deep concern. McCann and colleagues found that 57% of young people in foster care and 96% of those in residential care had some form of psychiatric disorder: a combined total of 67%. The comparison group of young people living with their families had a rate of 15%. The figures for conduct disorder (28%), overanxious disorder (26%) and major depressive disorder (23%) were startlingly higher than the comparison group: 0%, 3% and 3%, respectively. They also identified a number of young people (8%) with a psychotic disorder, in contrast to none in the comparison group. They concluded that 'a significant number of adolescents were suffering from severe, potentially treatable psychiatric disorders which had gone undetected' (McCann *et al*., 1996: 1530). One of the implications of this study is that reliance upon referral to psychiatric services as an indicator of the mental health needs of young people in care is not adequate. The authors do not say, however, whether any of the young people in their study were attending psychiatric or psychological services.

It is worth noting that none of the other studies cited above make reference to the presence of psychotic disorders. Schizophrenic disorders often emerge in late adolescence (Wing, 1978; Werry and Taylor, 1994). There is good evidence that there is a genetic component in schizophrenic disorder (Werry and Taylor, 1994), and also that stressful life events precede schizophrenic breakdown (Brown and Birley cited in Werry and Taylor, 1994). It is also likely, though the authors have not been able to establish any figures, that some young people in care will have a parent with a schizophrenic disorder, as it is a mental disorder which can, at least intermittently, make it difficult for a parent to care for a child. What is more, young people in care are undoubtedly subject to stressful life events, such as moving into independent accommodation at an early age (Stein, 1993, 1997). Whilst the numbers are likely to be very small (for each 100 000 people in the total population of England, there are between 10 and 15 new cases of schizophrenic disorder each year (Wing, 1978)), the presence of schizophrenic and psychotic disorder in looked after young people appears to be a neglected area that warrants further research and intervention.

A recent study of the health needs of 48 young people leaving care found that 17% had long-term mental illnesses or disorders, including depression, eating disorders and phobias, but this represented nearly all the females (87%) within the sample. Just over a third of the total sample had deliberately harmed themselves since the age of 15 or 16, either by cutting, overdosing, burning, or by a combination of two or more of these means. Nearly two thirds of the young people had thought about taking their own lives and 40% had tried to when aged between 15 and 18, at the time they were leaving care (Saunders and Broad, 1997).

There are numerous studies of young people in care, and the degree of attention paid to their mental health needs varies considerably from study to study. On the one hand, it is clear that many aspects of young people's needs can be overlooked or underestimated, including their mental health needs (Rowe et al., 1984; Simms and Halfon, 1994; McCann et al., 1996). On the other hand, one North American study has shown that young people in foster care are high users of mental health services (Halfon et al., 1992). The children constituted less than 4% of the child population eligible for Medi-Cal,[1] yet they accounted for 49% of the utilisation of mental health services funded by this medical programme. Young people aged 12–17 used services more than younger children. There are dangers in assuming that US studies would yield similar results here in the UK, however, as there are many differences between the two systems and between the populations living in care. There is a greater tendency to 'medicalise' emotional and social problems in the USA than in the UK, and another study suggests that some young people may not need the services to which they are referred (Garland et al., 1996). Garland's team found a tendency to refer young people who had been sexually abused, even when they displayed no symptoms to cause concern. Nonetheless, Halfon's study is worth citing in the light of the Oxfordshire research. Even if the take-up of child and adolescent psychiatric services is much lower in the UK (and figures are not available), this could simply indicate a failure to identify mental health problems and a consequent absence of appropriate referral.

While few studies take psychiatric disorder as a central focus, many look at behaviour and social adjustment, and seek to account for the presence of the difficulties they identify. Comparisons between studies are hard to make, as their purposes, parameters and definitions vary. The child welfare systems in the USA, Europe and the UK differ, and the reasons for young people entering the care system and the kind of care provided for them are influenced by geography and history. Research instruments used vary, as does research design. Nonetheless, there are common themes which can be drawn out. Table 10.1 identifies some of these studies and delineates some of the differences between them to illustrate this point. The list is by no means exhaustive.

Four of the studies concern adults brought up by people other than their family of origin. The studies were conducted for a variety of purposes. For example, the purpose of Triseliotis and Russell's (1984) study was to try and establish whether the disadvantage common amongst the families of children entering the care system would be 'transmitted' to their offspring, even if they were brought up outside the family. Quinton et al. (1984) also looked at transgenerational processes. They aimed to discover whether women brought up in institutions had more difficulty in parenting their own children than women brought up in their family of origin. Cheung and Buchanan (1997) were looking at the tendency towards depression in adulthood for people brought up in care. Dumaret et al. (1997) looked at the impact of a stable foster home on young people who had had adverse childhood experiences.

Triseliotis and Russell's study compared adoptees with children brought up in residential care. The two groups differed in a number of ways at the outset; principally, the adoptees had spent less time with their family of origin, entering both the care system and their final placement at an earlier age, and coming more frequently from younger mothers who were single. Before final placement, more of the adoptive children had 'moderate to severe emotional problems' and three were referred for psychiatric help, in contrast to none of the residential children. By the time they left school, however, the situation had reversed, with a significantly higher proportion of the residential children showing emotional and behavioural problems and being referred for psychiatric help. The adopted children had happier memories of their upbringing, and described more benign and less punitive regimes than members of the residential group. Both groups improved upon the living circumstances of their family of origin, but there was a difference between those coming from 'very "disturbed" backgrounds'. The adoptees did as well as those from less disturbed families, while the residential group did not. These were the people who were likely to have psychiatric problems. Whilst the study concluded that social disadvantage was not 'transmitted' from one generation to the next, it showed that, through a complex interplay of factors, children and young people brought up in residential care were disadvantaged.

Quinton et al. (1984) compared women brought up in institutions for extended periods with women brought up in their family of origin. Overall, nearly a third of the women from institutions showed good parenting, in contrast to almost half of the comparison group. However,

Table 10.1 Selected research studies

Authors	Population	Instruments	Comparison	Results
Triseliotis and Russell, 1984 Scotland	40 adults who had been adopted, and 44 adults who had grown up in residential homes All in their 20s	Case records, interviews with the population, questionnaires and self-rating scales	Children who had grown up in foster care	Adoptees had happier upbringings, were more successful and were better adjusted. People brought up in residential care fared worst
Rowe et al., 1984 England	200 young people, aged 4–19, in foster care for at least 3 years, of whom 145 were fostered with unrelated people, and 55 were fostered with relatives	Case records, interviews with foster children, foster parents, natural parents and social workers. Rutter A scale with foster parents	None	At placement, 40–80% had at least one problem; 1–4 year olds had the most problems. At foster-parent interview, 67–74% had at least one problem; 7–9 year olds had most
Quinton et al., 1984 England	94 women aged 21–27 brought up in institutions	Interviews with the population	51 women aged 21–27 from the same area of London, brought up in their own families	Women from institutions fared worse: 31% psychiatric disorder (5%) 25% personality disorder (0%) 31% good parenting (48%) 20% good overall outcome (63%)
St Clair and Osborn, 1987 England	Data from the Child Health and Education Study when children aged 5, 7 and 10 Children who were or had been in care, and adoptees	Rutter Scales	Children who had been separated from mother	Those in residential care most likely to have antisocial behaviour at age 10
Stein et al., 1994 Canada	248 young people aged 4–16	Standardised Clinical Information System Questionnaires completed by young people over 7, care takers and teachers	Normal population and clinical group	41–63% had a disorder
McCann et al., 1996 England	88 young people aged 13–17	Achenbach child behavioural checklist and youth self-report questionnaires Interviews with high scorers	Matched young people from same school class or GP practice	67% psychiatric disorder in care group (96% in residential care, 57% in foster care), 15% in comparison group
Cheung and Buchanan, 1997 England	Data drawn from the National Child Development Study At age 23, 66 people (22 men, 44 women) At age 33, 38 people (23 men, 15 women)	Malaise Inventory	People never in care, both socially disadvantaged and not disadvantaged	Those in care likely to have higher Malaise scores. Worse for men as they get older
Dumaret et al., 1997 France	59 adults reared for at least 5 years by foster families; 23 years old or more at time of study	Semi-structured interviews with 45 subjects Additional information about 14 siblings not interviewed	None	56% well integrated 12% average integration 20% partially integrated 10% in situations of failure

40% of them showed poor parenting, in contrast to only 11% of the comparison group. Nearly a third of the women brought up in institutions had a psychiatric disorder, and a quarter had personality disorders (5% and 0% in the comparison group, respectively). Even so, a fifth of the women from institutions had a good overall outcome; Quinton's team noted that the most important protective factor was a stable relationship with a 'non-deviant' husband or partner.

Cheung and Buchanan (1997), and Dumaret *et al.* (1997) examined the psychosocial adjustment of adults who had previously been in care. They used very different methods: Cheung and Buchanan re-analysed results from two 'sweeps' of the National Child Development Study, at ages 23 and 33, while Dumaret *et al.* interviewed adults who had been fostered. Cheung and Buchanan compared people who had been in care with people who had experienced 'severe social disadvantage' and people who had not experienced 'severe social disadvantage'. They used the Malaise Inventory, which indicates a tendency towards depression. Those who had been in care had a risk of higher scores, but there were significant gender differences. Women in each group were at risk for higher scores than men in the same group, but the risk for all women lessened as they grew older. It increased for men who had been in care. Although they offer some tentative suggestions about why these changes occurred, more research is required to understand them. Dumaret's team found a rather more hopeful picture than Quinton's. More than half of their respondents were 'well integrated', and 68% were well integrated or average. These are people raised in foster homes rather than institutions and they have received specialist support from a dedicated fostering agency.

Rowe *et al.* (1984) looked, by contrast, at young people still in long-term foster care, and looked at their psychosocial development across a broad range. Many of the children had problems at the time of joining the foster family. The most common problems reported by foster parents were 'attention-seeking behaviour or being withdrawn, sleeping difficulties, temper tantrums and lack of concentration' (Rowe *et al.*, 1984: 91). During the course of the placement, only six of the 145 children had no problems. The most commonly reported problems were lack of concentration and temper tantrums, with antisocial behaviour being more common than 'neurotic' symptoms. Boys were more prone to problems than girls. There were 37 black children in the study, all of whom were fostered with white families. There were no differences in adjustment between the black and white children.[2]

St Clair and Osborn (1987), and Stein *et al.* (1994) also considered children currently in care, but whereas Stein *et al.* were primarily interested in prevalence of psychiatric disorder, St Clair and Osborn looked at educational and behavioural outcomes. Stein *et al.* found that the girls in care had significantly higher rates of 'externalising' behaviour than the girls in the community sample; their scores were equal to those of the boys in care. In the community sample, the boys' scores were higher than the girls'. Many of the young people, especially the boys, showed developmental delays.

RISK FACTORS AND HEALTH PROTECTING BEHAVIOURS

'Health, not illness, is the norm of society; resistance, not capitulation, to mental disorder is the norm; adaptation and recovery from stress, and not breakdown, is the way of the majority.' (Garmezy, 1987: 164)

There are no simple explanations for the presence of mental health problems in some people and not others. There is no clear mechanism of cause and effect. A multi-factorial approach has to be taken, and there is still insufficient knowledge to provide an adequate predictive tool. This is, in part, because studies identifying risk factors, for instance, can show the likelihood of the development of mental health problems in a certain number of individuals, but cannot identify which particular individuals will be affected. Risk factors are aspects of the individual or their circumstances that increase the likelihood of developing a psychiatric disorder. Protective factors are aspects of the individual or their circumstances which reduce that chance in the face of stressors. There appears to be a complex interaction between the two, and no single risk or protective factor operates in isolation.

Some of the major risk factors for childhood psychiatric disorder were identified by Rutter in his influential study of children in the Isle of Wight and in London. Cited in Garmezy (1987), these were: '(1) severe marital distress, (2) low social status, (3) overcrowding or large family size, (4) paternal criminality, (5) maternal psychiatric disorders, (6) admissions of children into foster home placement' (Garmezy, 1987: 165). The study showed that one risk factor on its own made little difference, two risk factors increased the likelihood of a psychiatric disorder by four times, and four factors increased the risk by ten times.

Indeed, in their study of 2500 children admitted to care, Bebbington and Miles found that prior to being looked after, only a quarter of children were living with both parents, three quarters of their families were in receipt of income support, over half were living in 'poor' neighbourhoods and only one in five lived in owner occupied housing. Other factors contributing to a greater likelihood of admission to care were overcrowding, linked to large family size, young parenthood and a child's parents being of different ethnic origins. The cumulative effect of these deprivation factors in terms of the probability of admission to care is dramatic (Figure 10.1)—from odds of 1 in 7000 for Child 'A' to 1 in 10 for child 'B' (Bebbington and Miles, 1989).

Wedge and Phelan (1988a, 1988b) found that social workers cited disrupted family relationships as a contributory factor in over half of all admissions to care, and Bebbington and Miles (1989) indicate that

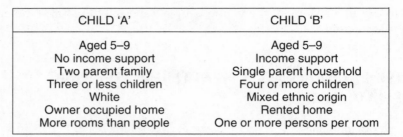

CHILD 'A'	CHILD 'B'
Aged 5–9	Aged 5–9
No income support	Income support
Two parent family	Single parent household
Three or less children	Four or more children
White	Mixed ethnic origin
Owner occupied home	Rented home
More rooms than people	One or more persons per room

Figure 10.1　Probability of admission to care

'broken family' was the single factor most highly correlated with entry to care. In addition to social deprivation and family breakdown, we need to add the impact of damaging intra-family relations including physical, sexual and emotional abuse, or neglect, and the consequences of these experiences for primary socialisation, including emotional and cognitive development (Stein, 1994).

The study by Rowe *et al*. (1984) identifies very similar problems in the backgrounds of fostered children. Dumaret *et al*. (1997) found that those with the most severe problems in adulthood had experienced more adversity in childhood, in the form of family disruptions and repeated trauma. They also found a link between severe and prolonged emotional deprivation and clinical disorder in adulthood. The young people in the study by Stein's team (1994) in Canada had also experienced many psychosocial problems, with substantial numbers of the adults caring for them having problems with alcohol or substance use, criminal or psychiatric histories, and the experience of themselves being in care as a child. Ninety-two per cent of the children had been maltreated.

Rutter (1985) has drawn together a wealth of research evidence about the nature of risk factors, protective factors, and the interaction between them. He makes a strong case for using the concepts with caution, and makes it clear that risk factors do not simply accumulate until breaking point is reached. He highlights a number of important issues concerning interactive processes. He examines, for example, the impact of certain kinds of risk factor, such as separation from one's primary caregiver, early parental loss as a predisposing factor in depression, and having a parent with a mental disorder. In each case, it is important to recognise that the individual qualities of the child, the state of the family as a whole, and the wider environment can interact in ways that protect the child.

Timing affects the impact of certain experiences. Separation from one's primary carer, for example, on admission to hospital, is likely to be a more stressful experience for pre-school children than for infants of four months or for older children, as pre-school children have formed 'selective attachments' to people from whom they are to be separated, and yet have not the cognitive maturation to comprehend that the situation is temporary.[3]

The age of the child is not the only important factor. In addition, children who are securely attached and who have had 'previous happy separations, or who have been well prepared for the experience are less likely to show distress' (Rutter, 1985: 602). The temperament of the child plays a part, as does a supportive relationship. Rutter cites a study by Main and Weston underlining the importance of a secure attachment to one parent, which can alleviate the effects of an insecure attachment to the other. He concludes: 'What seems important for protection is a secure relationship with someone' (Rutter 1985: 603).

In addressing the impact of early parental loss on predisposition to depression, Rutter (1985) makes it clear that it is not the loss in isolation which is responsible, but the changed family circumstances to which the loss can give rise. If parental loss leads to 'inadequate care of the children and to lack of emotional stability in the family', then it predisposes to depression. It can also start a chain of events which combine to predispose to depression. 'Self-esteem and self-efficacy makes coping more likely' (Rutter 1985: 603), and coping reduces the chance of making the kind of choices which predispose to depression. He cites a study by Parker which shows that a good marital relationship protects against depression. Rutter's own study (see Quinton *et al.*, 1984) gave similar results, but found that women brought up in institutions were less likely than the general population to make a harmonious marriage.

In considering the risks associated with having a parent with mental disorder, Rutter maintains that the main risks come from the family discord to which such a disorder tends, and the risks are highest when the child is directly involved in the quarrelling. Protective factors are that the other parent is mentally healthy, that the child maintains a good relationship with one parent, and that the family returns to a harmonious state. Boys are more at risk than girls, and the child's temperament again plays a part, with a child deemed 'difficult' being at higher risk, probably because such a child is more likely to be the subject of parental hostility. Experiences beyond the home environment have their impact too. The women brought up in institutions who had had some good experiences at school (such as good relationships with their peers, achievement in sport, music, and, less commonly, academic work) made more harmonious marriages. It is also important to note that adverse situations provide opportunities for young people to acquire responsibilities (in caring for a sick parent or younger siblings, say) which can increase self-esteem. Overall, an easy disposition, and a good relationship with a supportive adult, whether one is a young person or a grown up, seem to be key features in contributing to resilience.

This important paper (Rutter, 1985) brings together a number of complex issues that throw light on the difficulties faced by those trying to ameliorate the circumstances of looked after young people. Substitute care should, as a minimum, aim to compensate young people for what is deemed to be missing in their family background. However, recent research studies have highlighted the large variations in the quality of care (Sinclair and Gibbs, 1996). Many children's homes are badly managed, unstable, lack agreed goals and are characterised by a delinquent culture in which young people are often bullied and sexually harassed by other young people. The young residents are likely to run away and get into trouble through involvement in crime, prostitution or being a victim after going to live there. Many of these young people, not surprisingly, are very miserable and 40% have thought about killing themselves. A majority of young people living in children's homes have already 'broken down' in foster care. They have experienced disruption and movement during their time in care, and a weakening of links with their families, friends and neighbourhoods. These experiences combined with incomplete information, separation and rejection may contribute to identity confusion often amplified for black and mixed heritage young people brought up in a predominantly 'white' care system. Commenting upon the movement of looked after young people, Stein (1993: 239) has argued:

> 'Such an objective description as "multiple placement" cannot capture the emotional impact upon young people of changing carers, friends, neighbourhoods, schools on several occasions with little constancy in their life. Neither, despite the resilience of young people, can it capture the emotional energy and strength required by these young people to meet changing expectations derived from new relationships and different social situations—those very same young people whose own developmental stages have been impaired or damaged by their pre-care experience. A rare convergence of sociological and psychiatric perspectives would conceive being in care under these conditions as an assault on personal identity.'

Research studies have also documented their poor educational performance, their feelings of being stigmatised and their variable preparation for leaving care. And on leaving care at between 16 and 18 years of age, paradoxically far younger than many other young people leave home, loneliness, isolation, unemployment, poverty, homelessness and 'drift' feature significantly in many of their lives.[4] Such young people's transitions to adulthood are thus both compressed and accelerated compared to others (Biehal *et al.*, 1995). The demands this places upon them may constitute a severe psychological burden, as captured by focal theory (Coleman and Hendry, 1993).

Recent research studies of care leavers have also identified stability, continuity and maintaining family links as protective factors. For those young people who do achieve stability, this is clearly linked with positive outcomes both whilst living in care, in settling down, going to school and not running away, and on leaving care, particularly in respect of relationship skills and good education and employment outcomes. Closely connected to stability is the importance of looked after young people being offered a through care experience that maintains continuity of support, particularly between carers and social workers. In regard to family links, Biehal *et al.* (1995) found that the opportunity to explore personal histories—their story—was closely connected with a positive self-concept for young people leaving care. Even where family relationships remained poor, a knowledge and sense of family offered a symbolic reassurance to young people and engendered a sense of belonging. Conversely, those who remained confused about their past found life out of care more difficult to manage, had lower self-esteem, and had difficulties managing relationships (Biehal *et al.*, 1995).

PREVENTION

It is probably clear that, since the factors which influence mental health interact in complex ways, prevention is likely to be a complex process. How can policy makers or clinicians decide upon strategies or interventions when there are so many variables to be considered? And how can the relatively small group of young people at risk for admission to care, and at risk for mental health problems, be identified so that their circumstances can be influenced?

Before attempting to answer these questions, primary and secondary prevention need to be defined. For some writers, primary prevention aims to reduce *incidence* of a disorder, i.e. the number of new cases in the population, whereas secondary prevention aims to reduce *prevalence*, i.e. the severity and persistence of a disorder in those who already have some symptoms. A third approach called tertiary prevention is the reduction of the impact of acquired disability (Catalano and Dooley 1980; Graham, 1994). Newton (1988), rather than using these terms, distinguishes between a disease model for prevention and one based on a health perspective. A disease model identifies the factors which contribute to the causation of a disorder, and takes as its focus people suffering from a disorder; a health model looks at those factors which prevent disorder from developing, and looks at those people who are free from the disorder. Newton argues that both a disease model and a health model are important in prevention. It is immediately plain that Newton's perspective is related to the concepts of risk factors and protective factors. It also contains some of the same notions as the distinction between primary and secondary prevention, in that a health model, often linked with health promotion strategies, aims to reduce incidence, and the disease model is associated with the reduction of prevalence.

Primary Prevention

'The quality of family relationships plays an overriding part in determining the risk of disturbance in a child.' (Graham, 1994: 817)

The quality of family relationships are themselves influenced by many factors. Graham (1994) cites a number of studies showing that living in accommodation where there is nowhere safe for children to play, and where parents become more prone to depression, increases the risk for developmental delay and emotional and behavioural problems. He argues that high rise flats and hostels for the homeless are not suitable places in which to raise children. Employment is also a factor which protects adults (and teenagers) from mental health problems. Given that parental mental disorder and deprivation factors associated with poverty, such as living on income support, have already been identified as risk factors for children being admitted to care, government action to improve employment prospects could play a part in reducing the number of children who enter the care system.

Preventive efforts can be directed at parents who are identified as at risk in a number of ways. In practice, most of these interventions seem to be aimed at mothers and mothers-to-be. Although this may be pragmatic, in that women remain the primary carers of children in Britain today, the importance of helping fathers to parent their children well should not be underestimated.

Depression in mothers can give rise to poorer parenting (Cox and Rutter, cited in Rutter, 1985). Both Graham (1994) and Newton (1992) suggest that mothers and mothers-to-be who are depressed should be identified and treated early. It is not clear, however, what either author here means by the term 'treatment'. The circumstances that give rise to depression are multi-factorial, and while both anti-depressant medication and cognitive behavioural therapy are known to be effective (Paykel, 1992), a confiding relationship is also an important feature in the lives of women less prone to depression (Brown and Harris, 1978), and this is not so easily provided.

Since psychiatric disorder in parents is known to make it more likely that there is marital discord, which in turn has an adverse impact on children, there is undoubtedly a case both for treating ill parents and helping partners to maintain a good relationship with them and with their children.

Graham (1994) and Newton (1992) both discuss attempts to improve the pre- and post-natal care of women who are likely to have babies with low birth weight, or babies likely to be born early, or babies likely to be neglected or abused. Graham cites a study by Olds *et al.* in which women at high risk were selected. They were young or single or on low incomes, or had a combination of these attributes. The study showed that home visiting by a trained nurse led to improved birth weight and fewer pre-term births in the under 17 year olds, and post-natal visiting led to a reduction in child abuse. Newton discusses the work of Ounstead *et al.*, who set up a service in Oxford whereby midwives could refer any woman about whom they had concerns, particularly when their concerns were about mother–infant interactions. Cases of serious abuse appear to have been reduced, although seven children (out of 5356 screened) who had not been identified as at risk did experience abuse or neglect (Newton, 1992).

The Homestart and Newpin organisations (Newton, 1988, 1992; Frost *et al.*, 1996) are schemes in which mothers of young children are befriended by a volunteer mother. The two schemes are organised in somewhat different ways, but share many similarities. In the Homestart scheme, the volunteer helps the referred mother to make use of local resources, such as toy libraries and playgroups. Newpin also has a house which serves as a 'drop-in' for all the mothers, facilitating the making of friendships in the wider group. There are crèche workers, and regular educational and psychotherapy groups are held. Newpin members can go on to train to become befrienders themselves. The Newpin research, which is extensively summarised by Newton (1992), indicates that the women made more friends, had better relationships with their families of origin, and reported reduced behavioural problems in their children. For women who attended continuously, their levels of depression were also reduced. These examples of statutory and voluntary endeavours show encouraging results, and suggest that child abuse, neglect, poor family relationships and, therefore, the likelihood of children coming into care, can be influenced by early intervention.

Secondary Prevention

'[S]omething more than "normal" family life and "normal" parental interest are required to overcome the effects of early deprivation: average inputs are not enough for children with above-average needs.' (Colton and Hellinckx, 1994: 567)

Children and young people showing signs of mental health problems need to be identified more accurately and sooner. The NHS Health Advisory Service (1995) has recommended the creation of a 'primary mental health worker' for children and adolescents. The role is a specialist one, to work with primary care workers such as general practitioners, health visitors, teachers, school nurses and medical officers, child care social workers, family aides and other support workers. The main tasks of the specialist worker are to help primary care workers consolidate skills and acquire new knowledge and skills relevant to the mental health of children and young people, help them to recognise disorders and refer young people where appropriate, and assess and treat some individuals who do not need a more specialised service. They suggest that the primary mental health worker is a role which could be occupied by a variety of people at different times or on a shared basis. Suitable occupants for the role are qualified professionals with mental health training, such as psychologists, mental health trained social workers, community psychiatric nurses, senior occupational therapists and senior registrars and clinical assistants.

Clearly, a 'primary mental health worker' for children and adolescents could be of great value to social workers with responsibilities both for looked after young people, and for young people living in difficult family situations where being looked after could perhaps be avoided if suitable help were available. Foster carers and residential social workers could also benefit.

Simms and Halfon (1994) highlight the need for the thorough assessment of children when they enter the care system. They say that there is little continuity of health care for foster children in the USA. They found that records were often not adequate, and even if social service departments were successful in piecing them together, there was often no one to interpret them. They also found that foster parents were inadequately trained to recognise health care needs. Similar problems in the British system have been identified.

The recent introduction of the *Looking After Children Assessment and Action Records* in the UK as a system for planning, decision making, reviewing and monitoring the day to day care of children looked after by local authorities has the aim of improving the standard of care provided for looked after children and thus giving them a better chance of achieving their full potential (Parker *et al.*, 1991; Ward, 1995; Department of Health, 1996b). The materials cover six different age groups and ask questions on seven dimensions of development: health, education, identity, family and social relationships, emotional and behavioural development, social presentation and self-care skills. Although it is recognised that all seven dimensions may be relevant to the promotion of mental health in the widest sense, the main dimensions of emotional and behavioural development that are covered in the Assessment and Action Records reflect the most common socio-emotional difficulties of childhood and adolescence. These dimensions are: feelings distressing to the young people themselves (emotional problems, including anxiety and depression); overactivity and inattention; problems relating to adults (attachment and related problems); quality of relationships with peers (pro-social behaviour); and behaviours unacceptable to others (oppositional/defiant and conduct problems). These dimensions have been validated by a very substantial amount of research being derived from well established questionnaires including the Rutter Scales for parents and teachers and similar instruments, and thus provide an internationally accepted grouping of common problems (Rutter *et al.*, 1970, 1994; Goodman, 1994; Rutter and Hay, 1994). The emotional and behavioural development sections of the Assessment and Action Records have the potential to serve several purposes. They provide an opportunity for carers and young people to record strengths and difficulties, and therefore to assess needs and work on them. They provide for a systematic assessment of the young person's development and outcomes over the time they are looked after. And, finally, they provide the opportunity to compare approaches to ameliorating problems among the looked after children and young people (Quinton, 1996).

Colton and Hellinckx (1994), in their review of residential and foster care in the European Community, point out the value of both specialist foster care services, and specialist, small scale, residential services for adolescents with severe difficulties. The use of 'mentors' to young people in care has also been suggested (Department of Health, 1996a). Perhaps these services can provide the special relationship which Rutter (1985) identifies as a crucial protective factor in the lives of young people.

PRIORITIES FOR INTERVENTION AND RESEARCH

The important contribution of family support services in protecting children from abuse has been recognised by the Department of Health in a major report (Department of Health, 1995). In the context of reviewing the findings from 20 research studies the Report concludes:

> '. . . at the time the research was undertaken, the balance between services was unsatisfactory. The stress upon child protection investigations and not inquiries, and the failure to follow through interventions with much needed family support prevented professionals from meeting the needs of children and families.' (Department of Health, 1995: 55)

Political support, financial resources and professional commitment are required for preventive action, so that fewer children and their parents have to endure the misery of poor parenting and separations. If, however, children are experiencing difficulties and do have to be looked after, then early detection of mental health problems through multi-disciplinary assessment and good liaison between health, education, social services and the specialist child and adolescent mental health services to make suitable interventions are required. Supportive relationships with reliable adults need to be promoted, whether those adults are the young people's own parents or relations, foster carers, teachers, child care workers or mentors. Schools also have a contribution to make in preventive mental health, for example, through the curriculum, in reducing bullying and in promoting meaningful activities for young people by which they can enhance their self-esteem (Graham, 1994; see also Thompson, Chapter 12, in this volume).

Despite the wealth of information about looked after young people, more empirical knowledge is needed in order to underpin interventions. There are major gaps in our knowledge about gender and ethnicity. Even though the reasons for young people being looked after change over time, and policies and practice will continue to transform, it is possible to identify significant themes and make meaningful comparisons. Longitudinal studies are required to inform transformations in policy and practice. We do not currently know how many looked after young people are referred to the child and adolescent mental health services, how many go on to enter the adult mental health services, how many suffer major mental disorders in adult life, including psychotic disorders, nor how many of them commit suicide. In sum, there is a need for ongoing research into mental health needs and services which identifies starting points, processes and outcomes for looked after children and young people, and which is able to compare those with samples of 'non-care' young people. In this way, we will be able to build up a far greater knowledge and evidence base of problems, protective factors and what works with this highly vulnerable group of young people.

ENDNOTES

1. California's Department of Health Services Medicaid programme, providing access to medical care for people who are uninsured or on a low income.
2. Similarly, recent research into the experiences of young people leaving care found that '[t]here was little perceived difference between the black/mixed heritage and white young people in relation to their degree of self esteem, knowledge of their background and general sense of purpose. For the black young people their sense of ethnic identity changed over time and their identification with a particular group was strongly related to their identification with or rejection of family members' (Stein, 1997: 39).
3. Rowe *et al.* (1984) note that the children aged between one and four at time of placement had the most problems.
4. See Stein (1997) for a review of leaving care research studies.

REFERENCES

Bebbington, A. and Miles, J. (1989) The background of children who enter local authority care. *British Journal of Social Work*, 19, 349–368.

Biehal, N., Clayden, J., Stein, M. and Wade, J. (1995) *Moving On, Young People and Leaving Care Schemes*. London: HMSO.

Brown, G. and Harris, T. (1978) *Social Origins of Depression*. London: Tavistock.

Catalano, R. and Dooley, D. (1980) Economic change in primary prevention. In R.H. Price, R.F. Ketterer, B.C. Bader and J. Monahan (Eds) *Prevention in Mental Health*. Beverly Hills and London: Sage, pp. 21–40.

Cheung, S.Y. and Buchanan, A. (1997) Malaise scores in adulthood of children and young people who have been in care. *Journal of Child Psychology and Psychiatry*, 38, 575–580.

Coleman, J.C. and Hendry, L. (1993) *The Nature of Adolescence*. London: Routledge.

Colton, M. and Hellinckx, W. (1994) Residential and foster care in the European Community: current trends in policy and practice. *British Journal of Social Work*, 24, 559–576.

Department of Health (1995) *Child Protection Messages from Research*. London: HMSO.

Department of Health (1996a) *Focus on Teenagers*. London: HMSO.

Department of Health (1996b) *Looking After Children, Reader*. London: HMSO.

Dumaret, A.-C., Coppel-Batsch, M. and Couraud, S. (1997) Adult outcome of children reared for long-term periods in foster families. *Child Abuse and Neglect*, 21, 911–927.

Frost, N., Johnson, L., Stein, M. and Wallace, L. (1996) *Negotiated Friendship, Homestart and the Delivery of Family Support*. Leicester: Homestart UK.

Garland, A.F., Landsverk, J.L., Hough, R.L. and Ellis-MacLeod, E. (1996) Type of maltreatment as a predictor of mental health service use for children in foster care. *Child Abuse and Neglect*, 20, 675–688.

Garmezy, N. (1987) Stress, competence and development: Continuities in the study of schizophrenic adults, children vulnerable to psychopathology, and the search for stress-resistant children. *American Journal of Orthopsychiatry*, 57, 159–174.

Goodman, R. (1994) A modified version of the Rutter parent questionnaire including extra items on difficulties and strengths: A research note. *Journal of Child Psychology and Psychiatry*, 35, 1483–1494.

Graham, P. (1994) Prevention. In M. Rutter, E. Taylor and L. Hersov (Eds) *Child and Adolescent Psychiatry: Modern Approaches*, 3rd edn, pp. 815–828. Oxford: Blackwell.

Halfon, N., Berkowitz, G. and Klee, L. (1992) Mental health utilization by children in foster care in California. *Pediatrics*, 89, 1238–1244.

McCann, J.B., James, A., Wilson, S. and Dunn, G. (1996) Prevalence of psychiatric disorders in young people in the care system. *British Medical Journal*, 313, 1529–1530.

NHS Health Advisory Service (1995) *Child and Adolescent Mental Health Services: together we stand*. London: HMSO.

Newton, J. (1988) *Preventing Mental Illness*. London and New York: Routledge and Kegan Paul.

Newton, J. (1992) *Preventing Mental Illness in Practice*. London: Routledge and Kegan Paul.

Parker, R., Ward, H., Jackson, S., Aldgate, J. and Wedge, P. (1991) (Eds) *Assessing Outcomes in Child Care*. London: HMSO.

Paykel, E.S. (1992) Recognition and management of depression in general practice: consensus statement. *British Medical Journal*, 305, 1198–1202.

Quinton, D. (1996) Emotional and behavioural development. In *Looking After Children, Reader*. London: HMSO.

Quinton, D., Rutter, M. and Liddle, C. (1984) Institutional rearing, parenting difficulties and marital support. *Psychological Medicine*, 14, 107–124.

Rowe, J., Cain, H., Hundleby, M. and Keane, A. (1984) *Long-Term Foster Care*. London: Batsford Academic and Educational.

Rowe, J., Hundelby, M. and Garnett, L. (1989) *Child Care Now*. London: Batsford/BAAF.

Rutter, M. (1985) Resilience in the face of adversity: protective factors and resistance to psychiatric disorder. *British Journal of Psychiatry*, 147, 598–611.

Rutter, M. and Hay, D. (1994) (Eds) *Development Through Life: A Handbook for Clinicians*. Oxford: Blackwell.

Rutter, M., Tizard, J. and Whitmore, K. (1970) *Education, Health and Behaviour*. London: Longmans.

Rutter, M., Taylor, E. and Hersov, L. (1994) (Eds) *Child and Adolescent Psychiatry: Modern Approaches*. Oxford: Blackwell.

Saunders, L. and Broad, B. (1997) *The Health Needs of Young People Leaving Care*. Leicester: De Montfort University.

Simms, M.D. and Halfon, N. (1994) The health care needs of children in foster care: a research agenda. *Child Welfare*, 73, 505–524.

Sinclair, I. and Gibbs, I. (1996) *The Quality of Care in Children's Homes: short report and issues*. Working paper 3, Social Work Research and Development Unit, York, University of York.

St Clair, L. and Osborn, A.F. (1987) The ability and behaviour of children who have been 'in-care' or separated from their parents. *Early Child Development and Care*, 28, 3, Special Issue.

Stein, E., Raegrant, N., Ackland, S. and Avison, W. (1994) Psychiatric disorders of children 'in care': methodology and demographic correlates. *Canadian Journal of Psychiatry*, 39, 341–347.

Stein, M. (1993) The abuse and uses of residential care. In H. Ferguson, R. Gilligan and R. Torode (Eds) *Surviving Childhood Adversity*. Dublin: Social Studies Press.

Stein, M. (1994) Leaving care, education and career trajectories. *Oxford Review of Education*, 20, 349–360.

Stein, M. (1997) *What Works In Leaving Care?* London: Barnardos.

Triseliotis, J. and Russell, J. (1984) *Hard to Place*. London: Heinemann.

Utting, W., Baines, C., Stuart, M., Rowlands, J. and Vialva, R. (1997) *People Like Us: The report of the review of the safeguards for children living away from home*. London: The Stationery Office.

Ward, H. (1995) (Ed.) *Looking After Children: Research into Practice*. London: HMSO.

Wedge, P. and Phelan, J. (1988a) The impossible demands of child care. *Social Work Today*, 19(35), 9–11.

Wedge, P. and Phelan, J. (1988b) Moving towards a wider range of foster homes. *Social Work Today*, 19(39), 18–19.

Werry, J.S. and Taylor, E. (1994) Schizophrenic and Allied Disorders. In M. Rutter, E. Taylor and L. Hersov (Eds) *Child and Adolescent Psychiatry: Modern Approaches*, 3rd edn, pp. 594–615. Oxford: Blackwell.

Wing, J.K. (1978) *Reasoning about Madness*. Oxford: Oxford University Press.

Wolkind, S. and Rushton, A. (1994) Residential and foster family care. In M. Rutter, E. Taylor, and L. Hersov (Eds) *Child and Adolescent Psychiatry: Modern Approaches*, 3rd edn, pp. 252–266. Oxford: Blackwell.

Chapter 11

Young People, Mental Health and Homelessness

Davina Lilley

'Home is where one starts from. As we grow older the world becomes stranger, the pattern more complicated . . .'

T.S. Eliot (1940) *East Coker*

'All people must have a room to "realise themselves freely as human beings, to exercise their identities". Our homes are "an inseparable element of our human identity. Deprived of all aspects of his home, man would be deprived of himself, of his humanity".'

V. Havel (1992) *Summer Meditations*

Homelessness is a growing problem, and it is increasingly visible in many of our major cities. It may be caused by a number of factors including housing shortages, acute poverty, physical and emotional disabilities and changes in family structure (Shlay and Rossi, 1992). While some individuals may personally be more vulnerable to homelessness than others, changes in the housing market, in employment opportunities and in welfare policy undoubtedly also have a role to play. Among adults in the USA, alcohol and substance abuse (Smith *et al.*, 1991), mental and physical illness (Interagency Council on the Homeless, 1992) and criminal convictions have been shown to be strongly associated with homelessness (Wolch *et al.*, 1998). But what of the situation for young people in Britain?

Before it is possible to answer such a question it is necessary first to define what homelessness means. The definition to be adopted here stresses the absence of permanent accommodation. A person is homeless when they have no place or space that they can call their own. Such a definition encompasses the street homeless, as well as those living in

Young People and Mental Health. Edited by P. Aggleton, J. Hurry and I. Warwick.

temporary accommodation such as bed-sits, hostels and squats, which can be susceptible to sudden termination (Ruxton, 1996). It may be extended to include the notion of 'psychological homelessness', i.e. those who lack a sense of belonging, stability and social ties. The relative invisibility of this latter group of people means that their needs frequently go unacknowledged.

In mid-1998, the UK Government's Social Exclusion Unit published findings which suggested that between 30 and 50% of people sleeping rough suffer from mental health problems. The majority of those with mental health problems had these, however, before becoming homeless (Social Exclusion Unit, 1998). Of the 167 homeless young people interviewed in an earlier study entitled *Off to a Bad Start*, two thirds had classifiable mental health problems (Craig *et al.*, 1996). It is not always a simple matter to classify the mental health problems of homeless young people using the conventional typologies and classifications. Not only may the young person be experiencing some of the 'normal' pressures associated with growing up, she or he may be having to deal with hunger, exposure to the elements, depression, drug and alcohol abuse and the effects of being sexually or physically abused. While it is important to recognise that not all homeless people have mental health problems, the focus in this chapter will be on the very many that do.

YOUNG PEOPLE AND HOMELESSNESS

Homelessness among young people is not a recent phenomenon. In 1876, Dr Barnardo estimated that over 30 000 young people in London were homeless. With the introduction of compulsory education and fewer opportunities for child labour, there was a decline in youth homelessness and the phenomenon did not become widely visible again until the 1960s and 1970s. A number of factors have since combined to contribute to an increase in homelessness among older as well as young people. In the UK, these include greater social and geographical mobility which has weakened traditional local support structures; greater instability and change within family relationships; marked increases in unemployment, particularly youth unemployment; and changes to welfare and housing benefits introduced as part of the previous Government's efforts to reduce public expenditure and enhance self-reliance.

Elsewhere in Europe, it has been estimated that up to four million people may be homeless, of whom one million are under the age of 21 (Ruxton, 1996). In Denmark, it is estimated that the number of young homeless people doubled between 1976 and 1989 (Ruxton, 1996). More recently, France has reported an increase in homelessness from 20% to 50% among young people leaving care (Ruxton, 1996). A recent study in Belgium reported that 61% of young homeless people were from institutional settings, and 18% had previously been imprisoned (Ruxton, 1996).

In the USA, recent studies suggest that up to 1.3 million young people may be homeless in any one year, and there is evidence that the numbers are increasing. About a third of young homeless people in that country report leaving home because of physical abuse, and about a tenth have experienced sexual abuse (Robertson, 1991). A recent report by the National Coalition for the Homeless (NCH) Project found that homeless young women aged 13–15 years of age were more than 14 times as likely to become pregnant as their non-homeless peers, and that almost one in three homeless girls between the ages of 16 and 19 becomes pregnant (NCH, 1998). Black young people outnumber whites in urban areas, while the opposite is true of rural areas (Daly, 1996).

In Britain, a recent enquiry by the Housing Campaign for Single People entitled *We Don't Choose to be Homeless*, showed that 250 000 under 25 year olds experienced homelessness in the UK in 1996 (Evans, 1996). Nationally, about 20% were from black and minority ethnic backgrounds, and the greatest increase over previous years was among under 18s. An estimated 26 000 young homeless people were living in inner London alone (Evans, 1996). With respect to educational background, 50% of the residents of the St Mungo's Association in London (a provider of accommodation and resettlement services for the homeless) had academic qualifications, one in ten had been educated to Advanced level, and a further 10% had a degree (cited in Evans, 1996). Outside of London, there was strong evidence of increasing homelessness among young people. In 1994, for example, the Portsmouth Single Homeless Project noted that two thirds of the people approaching them were under 18 years of age, and Leeds City Council saw a threefold increase in young homeless people between 1990/1 and 1994/5 (cited in Evans, 1996).

It is widely accepted that upwards of a third of young homeless people in the UK are care leavers, that is young people leaving institutional or foster care settings. A recent report has suggested that of the 8000 young people leaving care each year a quarter have no support (cited in Evans, 1996). Centrepoint in London report that a third of their young homeless clients seeking refuge have backgrounds in care (Strathdee and Johnson, 1993)

MENTAL HEALTH ISSUES FOR HOMELESS YOUNG PEOPLE

The development of young people can be looked at in a variety of ways and encompasses a variety of dimensions including physical, cultural, social and psychological aspects. There is clear evidence from both the USA and the UK to suggest that homeless young people experience a variety of mental health problems. A recent study of the mental health problems and educational attainment of homeless young people in shelter in Los Angeles showed that 47% had receptive vocabulary delay, 39% had delayed reading, 37% had depressive symptoms and 28% had significant behavioural problems (Genovese, 1996). The fact that these difficulties were seen among 6–12 year olds highlights the seriousness of the problem and the need for early intervention. Forty-two per cent of the young people in this same study had been witness to serious violence.

In the UK, Craig *et al.*'s (1996) study for the Mental Health Foundation found that 55% of the 167 16–21 year old young homeless people interviewed, 55% had experienced physical abuse, 50% had run away from home or from being looked after by a local authority, 66% suffered from a psychiatric disorder, and 33% had made at least one suicide attempt. A more recent but smaller scale study found that of 48 hostel users interviewed, 25% had been looked after by local authorities, 35% had a drug or alcohol-related problem, 31% had received some kind of psychiatric treatment, 17% had committed an act of self-harm, and 21% had attempted suicide (Just Ask, 1997).

What are the principal mental health issues affecting young homeless people? In order to identify these it is first necessary to distinguish the normal developmental challenges associated with 'adolescence' and growing up. Psychologists, psychotherapists and counsellors agree that the period between puberty and adulthood is, for many young people, a time of turbulence, creativity and rapid development. It is a period of hope and a time to build and develop strengths. Yet it is also a period when some can feel immensely vulnerable. Young people may be struggling with physical and psychological changes, increased sexual and perhaps aggressive drives, the desire to understand and find out who they are, and the need to become autonomous and establish their position in the world.

In Western industrialised societies, the transition from childhood to adulthood often involves growing separation from parents and family, concurrent with establishing an autonomous position in relation to peers. The challenges associated with successfully making such a transition may be compounded by extremes of mood and the re-awakening of earlier unresolved conflicts. The role of the environment is critical in enabling young people to successfully negotiate such transitions. The transition from childhood to adulthood may be easier when the environment is relatively stable, non-intrusive and non-abusive, and when the young person can challenge parents and other authority figures but not succeed in destroying them.

According to many writers (Winnicott, 1990), the containment of these issues requires a safe space, one without dangers and one which the young person can call their own. A young person may need to feel safe psychologically (internally) as well as physically (externally) if they are to cope well with the challenges that confront them. According to Winnicott (1986), 'space', both physical and psychological, can act as a container for highly charged emotions, a vehicle of exploration and a support for change. Recognition of young people's need for space (in both of these senses) needs greater acknowledgement by those working with young people. A young homeless person is unlikely to have this space and may be seeking it. Somewhat paradoxically, often the street is initially attractive because it represents an escape from a lack of psychological space. It is seen as offering a safer option in comparison with the home or institution the person has left (Just Ask, 1998).

As stated earlier, many young people become homeless as a result of sustained abuse, either physical, mental or sexual, and unresolved family conflicts. Among the accounts given by young people interviewed in recent research are:

'Growing up was painful. Things were not going well when I was thrown out of home at 19 by my parents.' (cited in Evans, 1996)

'I was in care, I had no support, no accommodation and no family.' (Just Ask, 1996)

'I left home at 14 years because my stepfather abused me and my sister.' (Just Ask, 1996)

In reality, however, the street is not a safe space and life on it can present the young person with added difficulties. So, for young homeless people, there are not only the challenges of becoming an adult to be faced, but also the added problems of physical and mental survival—finding shelter, food and money; avoiding pimps and being attacked; and resisting substance abuse as a means of coping with the situation. That said, it is important to stress that for perhaps a minority of young people, being homeless and living on the street can be an expression of independence. These young people may see street life as a community and a stepping stone into adulthood.

As a consequence of this complexity, young homeless people will often present with a variety of complex problems. Mental health problems may include the effects of isolation, feelings of lack of self-confidence and low self-worth, anxiety and fear, the after effects of trauma, abuse and emotional neglect, depression, substance abuse, self-harming behaviour and suicidal ideation (Sibthorne et al., 1995; Diaz et al., 1997). In the UK and other countries, young homeless people not infrequently fall between gaps in services. Are their problems the province of social services, the police or professionals working in medical and psychological services? It is often non-statutory services that have to deal with the day to day issues, and then often without adequate resources and support.

The complex sets of mental health issues that young homeless people face often cannot be given the kind of discrete label that might lead to a concrete response. Not infrequently, diagnostic terms such as 'personality disorder' may be used to try to give some semblance of meaning to the complex picture presented. Often the young person faces multiple problems and their self-generated solutions may include substance use, criminal activity and selling sex. These practices may in turn bring further difficulties of a physical and psychological nature. The complexity of the situation is perhaps demonstrated in the following three case studies of individuals recently in contact with the *Just Ask* service in London.

Jo was in her teens, a runaway, homeless and unemployed. She had experienced a long history of family sexual abuse. She suffered from extreme anxiety and depression, and was only able to express herself and deal with feelings through painful self-harming behaviour. Following contact with the agency, she was found a room in a short-stay hostel run by a housing charity. The hostel, although it represented a safer space for her, was not without its problems. Jo found it difficult to identify with other members of the group, particularly in relation to the drug use that took place there. Throughout her stay in the hostel and the later tenancy of a flat, she received long-term counselling. The work involved exploring her deep emotional pain and conflict. The process was very slow, and her self-destructive behaviour often impeded the work. Underpinning the work was close collaboration with a range of agencies and professional bodies. This meant better support and a more coherent approach to meeting Jo's needs. After about a year, her efforts at self-harm were significantly reduced.

Susie was in her late teens and had been street homeless for two years. She was currently sleeping rough with no access to benefits because of her age. She had been abused while with foster parents, was depressed, and had a history of substance abuse and prostitution as a means of survival. She requested somewhere to talk about her feelings. It was difficult for her to keep appointment times, however, so the service had to be flexible in this respect. She described her life on the streets and the constant harassment she received from the pimps by whom she was trapped. She lied about her age in an attempt to access benefits to which she was not entitled. She spoke of hoarding some tablets under a bridge which she planned to use when life became too intolerable. She had been in care since the age of six and subsequently fostered. At the end of one session, she told the counsellor that her life story would soon appear in the news media. After this happened, she did not return for counselling.

Stuart was in his teens and of mixed ethnic origin. His parents had divorced when he was eight. At the age of 15 he had several encounters with the police and arguments with his mother and brothers which eventually led to him being excluded from the family home. He used drugs heavily for a period of two years, then he was encouraged to seek help. Prior to coming for this he had been attending a drug rehabilitation centre, and was currently living in a hostel. He came to the service because a close friend had just died from a drug overdose and he was afraid he would resort to using drugs again. He was offered long-term counselling which he accepted. He began to come to terms with the problems from which drug use had provided an escape:

his depression, his lack of confidence/self-esteem, and uncertainties about his sexual identity. He is now beginning to want to be more independent, to be less reliant on his family, and to make new relationships.

RISK FACTORS AND HEALTH PROTECTING BEHAVIOURS

Before discussing the various risk factors associated with mental health problems among homeless young people, it is important to stress that homelessness is most usually a symptom of underlying difficulties. While it may contribute to, and exacerbate, certain mental health problems, many of these have their origins in the cluster of variables that led the young person to become homeless in the first place. We therefore need to be sensitive to multiple levels of causation with respect to homeless young people's mental health. A number of safety nets need to be put in place to help prevent young people becoming homeless and thus decrease the likelihood of mental health problems developing.

Poverty

The role of poverty in social disadvantage is a contentious issue bedevilled by problems of definition. Harker (1997) among others has identified a recent increase in the proportion of the population affected by poverty. He estimates that between 1979 and 1993 there was an increase from 10% to 32% in the proportion of the population living in poverty. Approximately 1.0 million young people may live in poverty in Britain today (Harker, 1997). The effects of this are many but include social exclusion, dismay and despair, alongside an increase in criminal activity and drug taking. Over the same period, there has been a 52% increase in the number of crimes committed by young people aged 10–13, and an increase in suicide among young men from 23 per 1000 (in 1981/32) to 49 per 1000 (in 1991/3).

The health problems associated with living in poverty can be severe. For young people in poverty, there is a four times higher risk of their experiencing serious mood disturbances, suffering serious injury, becoming drug users and dying before the age of 20 (Harker, 1997). Poverty can also mean that young people have fewer life chances and are excluded from experiences and activities available to mainstream families such as going on holiday, being able to participate in school trips, and having access to the cultural 'badges' of their peer group. It is important to address issues of poverty so that children are not excluded from the social and cultural life of the community, and thereby become vulnerable to homelessness and mental health problems.

Education

While it would not be fair to say that all homeless young people have had educational difficulties, there is evidence to suggest that a significant number of young people coming into contact with homelessness agencies in the UK have experienced some kind of problem at school (Evans, 1996). These problems are very diverse, however, and may include difficulties in learning, problems with school attendance, bullying and other kinds of abuse.

It is within the education system that the first signs of psychological homelessness may become evident, and the school has an important role to play in preventing later physical homelessness. However, education and training may be needed for teachers to recognise the early signs of vulnerability. Without such knowledge it is easy to misinterpret early warning signs such as bullying, being bullied, persistent absence, withdrawal, excessive daydreaming and deteriorating schoolwork. There needs to be greater discussion of the emotional issues that contribute to school failure and the contribution that counselling and other forms of support can make in such cases.

Counselling also has a particularly important role to play at crisis points in a child's and young person's life. These may include bereavement, family breakdown, the re-marriage of a mother or father, physical or mental illness in a parent, and abuse. Such issues, if not dealt with at the time, may become the causes of future homelessness. Trained counsellors could have an important role to play within the school system, providing support to adults and young people alike. They may be able to assist other professionals in identifying and helping with young people's problems, support staff who are faced by challenging behaviours and parents under stress, provide counselling and support for teachers, and offer counselling for young people with difficulties.

Employment

A number of reports have shown a clear link between unemployment, homelessness and mental health problems (Harker, 1997). Young homeless people not infrequently leave school with few or no educational qualifications. As employment opportunities for the unskilled have decreased, more young people become unemployed and are attracted to larger cities in search of work. Often arriving with little money and no accommodation and contacts, many may be forced to live rough on the streets. Employment also has an important psychological role to play in people's lives. A job can provide an individual with a sense of worth, self-esteem and independence. Without the opportunity to work, a young person can become hopeless and despairing, and may resort to other means, including criminal activities, in order to obtain money.

The link between homelessness and unemployment underlines the importance of initiatives that provide housing alongside training for employment. These include special projects and day centres for the homeless as well as the Foyer movement which originated in France but which has been further developed in the UK. Staff working in Job Centres may need additional training to help them better understand the practical and emotional difficulties faced by homeless young people in their search for employment.

Welfare Benefits

The withdrawal of housing benefits from young people aged 16–17 in 1989 resulted in a substantial increase in youth homelessness in the UK (Strathdee, 1992). The solution to this problem is not straightforward since to re-introduce benefits is likely to be neither politically acceptable nor necessarily efficacious. Instead, a greater diversity of sources of support is needed for young people wishing to leave home. This might include the creation of a range of 'half way house' situations between the home and the outside world. All of these would need to address young people's psychological and emotional needs as well as their physical needs.

Young People Being Looked After

At stated earlier, young people who have been looked after by local authorities have an especially high risk of becoming homeless. The Utting Report, *People Like Us* (1997), details clearly some of the effects of being looked after in local authority homes, with foster parents, or at boarding school (Utting, 1997). Several areas of significant disadvantage were identified including educational under-achievement, unemployment, homelessness and criminality. Four in ten young prisoners and one in four adult prisoners, for example, have been looked after by local authorities.

While the number of young people being looked after is declining, the risk of harm or abuse is not. Closer links are needed between educational authorities, social services departments and counselling services so that individual programmes of education and training in social skills can be developed alongside support for psychological and emotional development. While such action calls for additional resources in the immediate term, its longer-term benefits are likely to be substantial.

INTERVENTIONS FOR PREVENTION

Central to the success of interventions to prevent the occurrence of homelessness among young people, and associated mental health problems, is collaborative work between different agencies. Organisations working in isolation will be less effective in helping the young person, since a fragmented approach will enhance confusion and isolation. Wherever possible, statutory and non-statutory organisations need to work together as an interdisciplinary team. Change can then be more easily facilitated, consolidated and sustained. Interventions that have proven successful in preventing psychological and physical homelessness need to occur in several different fields.

Preparation for Adulthood

The age of maturity and adulthood is no longer clearly defined in UK society. There are several ages at which young people can come to understand themselves as adult—the age 16 for (hetero)sexual relationships; 18 in order to vote, marry without parental consent and purchase alcohol in a bar; and the age of 21 still hold symbolic significance in many people's minds. It is important to note that emotional maturity is not inevitably linked to any of these milestones.

Education for adulthood is conspicuous by its absence in perhaps the majority of schools, and many teachers feel unsure about how to undertake such work. That said, schools have a potentially important role to play in helping young people learn about processes of development, the role of parents, characteristics of 'good' and 'bad' parenting, and social and emotional relationships including marriage. While the National Curriculum sets limits on the time available for a consideration of issues such as these, it is important not to ignore them.

A 'half way' house, such as that traditionally provided by university education, may be valuable for young people who are not academically inclined. Systems of community living in which young people have access to counselling and support (both formal and informal) may have a valuable role to play. They may be able to offer young people the opportunity to gain a measure of independence, to learn to live with others and to cater for themselves in a context physically and psychologically separate from their family of origin.

Preparation for Pregnancy and Parenthood

There is now a considerable body of evidence to suggest that cycles of deprivation and disadvantage can be perpetuated within families across the generations (Marrone, 1998). Poor housing, poverty, lack of healthy food, lack of emotional support and the parent's own psychological development and history will all have an effect on offspring. It is important to help would-be parents to recognise the need to be with their child(ren) emotionally, to contain their anxieties, to respond to needs and to tolerate the inevitable frustrations. If it is to be successful, this kind of education may need to be offered in several different environments, and tailored to the sometimes different interests and needs of young women and young men. Schools, youth services, community health centres and sexual health services need to work in partnership if good progress is to be made.

Young homeless women may have special needs in relation to safeguarding their sexual health, including the avoidance of unwanted pregnancy. Some may lack the knowledge, experience and emotional maturity to cope with a baby, and access to appropriate support in the homeless context. Education in sex, sexuality and relationships needs to be provided in ways attuned to their needs, and those of their male sexual partners, so as to prevent pregnancy when such is not desired, and to enable young homeless women with children to access relevant services.

Other Areas for Intervention

Once a young person has become homeless, however, a range of further interventions may be needed. In order to identify the package of support best suited to the individual, a thorough assessment of needs should first be carried out. This should be done in such a way as to ensure that the young person concerned is fully involved in devising and monitoring the care and support programme to be implemented (Cohen *et al.*, 1991). Different agencies may need to be involved including general practitioners, mental health workers, substance abuse workers and counsellors. Access to shelter and housing, perhaps through a hostel or other arrangements, will need to be provided. As stated earlier, Foyers offering both residential and training facilities may be found helpful by some young people. Provision for longer-term counselling and support may need to be made. This will offer a stable reference point throughout what, hopefully, will be the transition to a more secure set of living arrangements, including education and employment. Regardless of context, services need to be accessible, flexible and non-stigmatising in the manner in which they are provided.

CONCLUSIONS

Homelessness among young people and its relationship to mental health issues presents us with a complex and bewildering picture. What is clear is that homelessness is not going to disappear, and is likely to grow unless action is taken. There are pointers to homelessness and mental health issues present in an individual's life from a very early stage. These provide opportunities for intervention of a kind which in the longer term can prevent the young person becoming homeless and at greater risk. Teachers, other professionals, carers and the family need help in identifying what these early signs may be, and in taking appropriate action. While trauma and crises in young people's lives can contribute towards homelessness, they also represent windows of opportunity for counselling and other kinds of help.

REFERENCES

Cohen, E., Mackenzie, R. and Yates, G. (1991) HEADSS: a psychosocial risk assessment instrument: implications for designing effective intervention programs for runaway youth. *Journal of Adolescent Health*, 12, 539–544.

Craig, T., Hodson, S., Woodward, S. and Richardson, S. (1996) *Off to a Bad Start*. London: Mental Health Foundation.

Daly, G. (1996) *Homeless*. London: Routledge.

Diaz, T., Dusenbury, L., Botvin, G. and Farmer-Huselid, R. (1997) Factors associated with drug use among youth living in homeless shelters. *Journal of Child and Adolescent Substance Abuse*, 6, 91–110.

Eliot, T.S. (1963) East Coker. *Collected Poems 1909–1962*. London: Faber and Faber.

Evans, A. (1996) *We Don't Choose to be Homeless*. London: CHAR.

Genovese, B.J. (1996) And God will fill the bullet holes with candy. *British Medical Journal*, 313, 7072, 1583–1587.

Harker, P. (1997) *Young People, Poverty and Health*. Bristol: University of Bristol.

Havel, V. (1992) *Summer Meditations*. Toronto: Knopf.

Interagency Council on the Homeless (1992) *Outcasts on Main Street: Report of the Federal Taskforce on Homelessness and Severe Mental Illness*. Washington, DC: Interagency Council on the Homeless.

Just Ask (1996) *A Transitional Space*. London: Just Ask.

Just Ask (1997) *Hostels—A new future for the homeless*. London: Just Ask.

Just Ask (1998) *A Space to Think*. London: Just Ask.

Marrone, M. (1998) *Attachment and Interaction*. London: Jessica Kingsley.

NHC (1998) National Coalition for the Homeless Fact Sheet—http://nch.an.net/edchild.

Robertson, M.J. (1991) Homeless women with children. *American Psychologist*, 46, 11, 1198–1204.

Ruxton, S. (1996) *Children in Europe*. London: NCH Action for Children.

Shlay, A. and Rossi, P. (1992) Social science research and contemporary studies of homelessness. *Annual Review of Sociology*, 18, 129–160.

Sibthorne, B., Drinkwater, J., Gardner, K. and Bammer, G. (1995) Drug-use, binge drinking and attempted suicide among homeless and potentially homeless youth. *Australian and New Zealand Journal of Psychiatry*, 29, 248–256.

Smith, E., North, C. and Spitznagel, E. (1991) Alcohol, drugs and psychiatric comorbidity among homeless women: an epidemiologic study. *Journal of Clinical Psychiatry*, 54, 82–87.

Social Exclusion Unit (1998) *Social Exclusion Unit Report.* Government White Paper CM4045. London: HMSO.

Strathdee, R. (1992) *No Way Back.* London: Centrepoint.

Strathdee, R. and Johnson, R.M. (1993) *On the Streets.* London: Centrepoint.

Utting, W. (1997) *People Like Us.* London: HMSO.

Winnicott, D.W. (1986) *Home is Where We Start From.* Harmondsworth: Penguin Books.

Winnicott, D.W. (1990) *Deprivation and Delinquency.* London: Routledge.

Wolch, J., Dear, M. and Akita, A. (1998) Explaining homelessness. *Journal of the American Planning Association*, 54, 443–453.

Chapter 12

Bullying and Harassment in and out of School

David A. Thompson

Until about ten years ago, researchers tended to see bullying as too complex a phenomenon to commit much research energy to. They were also usually dissuaded from learning more about bullying by the emotionally sensitive nature of the problem—even now, many schools resist the suggestion that bullying is occurring inside their walls, and many who are involved as victims keep their stresses to themselves. However, since the mid 1980s there has been a rapid expansion of research in the field, largely catalysed by a small group of Scandinavian (Olweus, 1978, 1980) and English researchers (Lowenstein, 1978).

Olweus himself and Arora and Thompson (1987) made the breakthrough when they accepted that the best research strategy for getting to grips with the issue of the definition of bullying and the problems of estimating the incidence of bullying, the first of the researchers' questions, was by adopting the strategy of asking the children themselves if they were being bullied or were engaged in bullying others. This could be done either by directly asking the children how frequently they were being bullied, and hoping that the children would be able to consistently use the researcher's definition of bullying included on the questionnaire (Olweus, 1978, 1991); or by asking questions about the specific behaviours which were experienced in school and then asking, as a subsequent question, 'If this happened to you would you call it bullying?' (Arora and Thompson, 1987).

From this early work it became clear that children could indeed respond appropriately to such questions, and also that when this initial problem of definition and assessing incidents had been tackled, there

Young People and Mental Health. Edited by P. Aggleton, J. Hurry and I. Warwick.
© 2000 John Wiley & Sons Ltd.

was a great public interest in the topic. This has resulted in an explosion of material on this issue over the last ten years. There is growing international interest in the topic in spite of the fact that many languages do not have a single concept which would be translated by the English word 'bullying'. Apart from the Scandinavian work, the first international perspectives came from O'Moore and Hillery (1989, 1991) from Eire, followed by research interest in Australia (Rigby and Slee, 1993) and Canada (Pepler *et al.*, 1993). American researchers have tended to concentrate on peer aggression and victimisation generally, rather than on bullying processes specifically (see, for example, Perry *et al.*, 1990).

Much of the energy behind the subsequent research came from the public response to the issue, and in particular to a number of tragic case histories of children being very badly affected by being bullied which have appeared in the press. Clearly for some children at least, being bullied causes very significant mental health problems of chronic anxiety and fear of school.

DEFINING BULLYING

There are wide variations between what different individuals consider the key characteristics of bullying. In academic research, there have been four major criteria for defining any particular interactions as bullying. Three of these are widely subscribed to, but the fourth has its roots in Scandinavian conceptions of bullying and is less widely accepted in Britain. All studies see bullying as being essentially a type of aggressive behaviour, involving a systematic abuse of power, and occurring over a prolonged period of time. Scandinavian researchers would also add that it is characterised by a group of people bullying a single individual. Some British researchers would disagree with this, claiming that if one individual exercises the systematic abuse of power over another individual, then this should also be seen as bullying.

A useful definition of bullying that is easily intelligible by children who can read is that used by Smith and Sharp (1994). Translated and amended from that used by Olweus (1991), it reads:

> 'We say a young person is being bullied, or picked on, when another young person or group of young people, say nasty or unpleasant things to him or her. It is also bullying when a young person is hit, kicked or threatened, or locked inside a room and things like that. These things may take place frequently and it is difficult for the young person being bullied to defend himself or herself. It is also bullying when a young person is teased repeatedly. But it is not bullying when two young people of the same strength have the odd fight or quarrel.'

Types of bullying interactions are usually divided between those that are primarily verbal and those that include an element of physical assault. Some researchers also make a distinction between direct verbal or non-verbal bullying on the one hand, where there is a specific interaction between the bully and the victim, and indirect bullying characterised by threats mediated through the wider social group which may not involve such direct interaction. Examples of the latter would include, for example, social exclusion or spreading rumours.

The definition of bullying is quite important, because it is linked to the range of reported incidents of bullying. In general, studies that take a more general and broadly based definition of bullying tend to report a much higher incidence of bullying than those studies that take a tighter definition. So, for example, many telephone help lines such as Childline report that as many as 60% of children experience bullying at one time or another (MacLeod and Morris, 1996). Studies using a tighter definition of bullying, often behaviourally based, suggest that 20–30% of children of primary school age and 10–20% of children of secondary school age report being bullied at some time. Approximately 3–6% of children report being bullied for more than a year.

As presented here, these figures are very much approximations because of the variations reported between different studies. There are three reasons for these sometimes large variations. The first is that different definitions are often used, the second that the incidence of bullying shows a gradual drop as children move from primary age to secondary school age, and the third that there are large variations between different schools in similar circumstances in the amount of bullying reported by children. For example Smith and Sharp (1994) reported differences in incidence between both primary schools and secondary schools of the order of two and a half times, such that one secondary school may have an incidence reported of say 7–8%, and another secondary school of apparently similar characteristics of size, general intake, and academic attainment of approaching 20%. It is accordingly almost impossible to give a figure which represents a generally accepted incidence of bullying. It has to be qualified by the age of the children or young person concerned, the definition of bullying adopted, and most importantly by the specific institution in which the bullying is measured.

Because of this huge variation due to particular institutional factors, some researchers (e.g. Arora 1994, 1996a, b) have advocated that intervention studies should be focused on particular institutions rather than be local education authority wide, as the task for interventions is to reduce the incidence of bullying in particular schools and colleges. The second radical proposal she makes is that the term bullying should not be used at all, as it is so amenable to misinterpretation. Instead, schools and researchers should concentrate on the incidence of specific behaviours which can then be categorised as being of a 'bullying type', and focus estimates of incidence and evaluations of the effectiveness of interventions on specifically defined interactions, rather than on a generic term 'bullying'. This last suggestion is almost certainly one which will not be taken up by either the academic or the practitioner professional communities, because a large part of the concern of the general public and parents who support anti-bullying work comes from the use of the term itself and the universal condemnation which bullying activities attract.

What can be said without any shadow of doubt is that in all schools at least 5–10% of children of all ages experience long-term persistent bullying which actively interferes with their mental health and success in achieving educational and social goals. This is true even in schools where anti-bullying policies are in place (Sharp *et al.*, 1998). The anti-bullying policies only have the effect of helping to reduce bullying towards the lower end of this range. In practice, the important information needed by practitioners of all types relates to their own particular institution, so the question is not, 'What is the general incidence of bullying?', but 'What is the incidence of bullying in this particular school or college, with these particular students, and this particular management approach?' It is only on the basis of information of this degree of specificity that effective intervention programmes can be launched and their success be monitored.

BULLYING AND OTHER FORMS OF HARASSMENT

Bullying as a description for certain kinds of behaviour often overlaps with more general forms of harassment, such as racial or sexual harassment. In each of these instances, a specific aspect of interpersonal behaviour is used to express a bullying relationship (either through gender and sexual relationships, or relationships between different ethnic groups), and many of the same social dynamics apply. With respect to both sexual and racial harassment, however, there is a much larger proportion of people in the community concerned who, while possibly not supporting such harassment, would not feel themselves to be particularly influenced or affected by it, and so would be less likely to take a clear stand against it than they would against bullying *per se*. From the research to date, it is not safe to assume that reductions in sexual harassment and racial harassment would flow naturally from the implementation of an anti-bullying policy (see, for example, Gillborn, 1990, and Drouet, 1993). However, in their general mental health effects, the results of racial and sexual harassment are likely to be similar to those of bullying, that is with many individuals learning how to deal with them successfully, but with a small but significant minority suffering genuine and long-lasting mental health problems as a result.

ROLE OF EQUAL OPPORTUNITY POLICIES

In recent years, schools have been encouraged to set up general equal opportunities policies, with multiple aims including reducing discrimination against members of minority ethnic groups, against gender groups, and against people with special needs (Sharp and Thompson, 1997). Whole school policies have been developed on a number of these issues to help achieve the schools' aims in these areas, and when well drawn up and well implemented are thought to go some way towards avoiding the kinds of institutionalised racism and sexism that lead to the marginalisation of certain children.

However, in all these areas, to be effective policies need to include clear definitions and clear procedures for changing or monitoring practice. They also need to be clearly understood and actively supported by all those in school to be effective. Generally speaking, top-down, broadly based policies do not usually have the specificity of definition and procedures necessary for change. They also often lack understanding and support from the school community. Anti-bullying policies are thought to work better by those involved when they are separately formulated and implemented, and not included in a more general 'behaviour policy' or 'equal opportunities policy' (Smith and Sharp, 1994). When schools do develop multiple whole school policies, they need to plan carefully to avoid working from overlapping and sometimes contradictory definitions and procedures (Thompson and Sharp, 1994).

MENTAL HEALTH CONSEQUENCES OF BULLYING

Research to date enables us to be fairly specific about the kind of problems resulting from bullying. Being a victim can result in significant problems, resulting from the way the individual reacts to the chronic stress of being consistently involved in predictable aggressive and humiliating situations. This stress may exacerbate pre-existing tensions or conditions in, for example, the child who stammers. Mooney and Smith (1995), following a questionnaire survey of adult stammerers, reported that 82% of respondents were bullied at some period in their school lives. Of these, 59% reported having been bullied at least once a week. Sixty-five per cent of those responding reported that their existing social difficulties were made considerably worse by being bullied, including increased speech difficulties, increased general anxiety and shyness, loss of confidence and self-esteem, and increased difficulty in forming friendships. While not all children who were bullied and who had speech dis-fluency felt that the bullying at school had influenced their adult personality, some 27% did, including a 22 year-old respondent who reported 'I became suspicious of all people and constantly scared of ridicule. I am now a nervous wreck before parties and other social occasions and tend to drink to calm me down. I still do not feel I can trust people: I tend to be paranoid.'

As well as exacerbating already existing difficulties, bullying can itself be associated with common health symptoms in primary school children. In a large-scale semi-structured interview study of nearly 3000 children, Williams *et al.* (1996) reported an association between children reporting being bullied sometimes or more often, and not sleeping well, bed wetting, feeling sad, experiencing headaches and having tummy aches. Increased frequency of bullying was significantly related to an increasing risk of symptoms for all the reported health symptoms. These same authors conclude that 'health professionals seeing primary school children who present with headaches, tummy aches, feeling sad or very sad, bed wetting, and sleeping difficulties should consider bullying as a possible contributory factor' (Williams *et al.*, 1996: 18). Studies of truancy from school (Reid, 1989; Pervin and Turner, 1994; Balding *et al.*, 1996) also show that the fear of being bullied at school and the actual experience of being bullied are significant causes of chronic absenteeism.

In terms of the severity of the results of bullying, the most severe and dramatic reaction is undoubtedly found in the comparatively small number of children who attempt or commit suicide when being severely victimised at school. For these children, and probably others as well, the inhibitions felt about talking to others about the experience of being bullied are undoubtedly one of the most severe features of the process of being bullied.

General Self-esteem and Self-confidence

Several school studies have included survey questions about self-esteem, self-confidence, and the prevalence of feelings of anxiety and insecurity amongst students who are persistently bullied. Rigby and Slee (1993) found that students who were being bullied at least once a week reported a significantly greater incidence of general depression, suicidal thoughts and somatic complaints than those who were not. In a similar study, Haselager and Van Lieshout (1992) found that students who were bullied were more likely to show signs of physical complaints, mood changes linked to signs of depression, and tended to give themselves more negative self-evaluations than children who were not bullied. The victimised children were also more likely to be shy and withdrawn compared with their classmates, and were less likely to be chosen as friends.

Olweus (1980), in a large-scale questionnaire survey in Scandinavia, found that students who were frequently bullied reported low levels of self-esteem, had negative self-concepts, felt ignored by their schoolmates, and scored more highly on questions indicating anxiety and insecurity than other non-bullied students. Balding *et al.* (1996), following a large survey of secondary school children, reported that about a quarter of children in Year 8 described themselves as being afraid of being bullied, to the point that they were sometimes afraid to go to school. These students described themselves as being ill and being more anxious to a greater extent than their non-bullied peers. Pervin and Turner (1994) reported similar findings, as did Boulton and Underwood (1992) in a large-scale interview study of primary school children.

There is some evidence for gender effects also in relation to self-esteem and victimisation. The same general findings of lower self-esteem amongst victimised students also holds good for all-girls' schools (Neary and Joseph, 1994), and in an earlier study by Rigby and Slee (1991), the authors reported that both boys and girls who were persistently bullied showed significantly lower self-esteem than non-bullied students, and also that variations in self-esteem were more highly associated with gender than with victimisation.

Sharp (1995, 1998), in a detailed and comprehensive study of the impact of bullying on children and on their capacity to manage stress in general, replicated many findings above, demonstrating that,

1. Within the group of students who had been bullied, those with high self-esteem scores reported significantly less stress than those with low self-esteem scores.
2. Students who had been bullied reported a continuously increasing incidence of specific negative mental health reactions which correlated with increasingly low measures of self-esteem.
3. The most common reactions to being bullied were irritability, repeated memories, feeling panicky or nervous, and inability to concentrate.
4. Students with low self-esteem were more likely to respond to bullying either passively or aggressively than students with high self-esteem, in other words in a relatively uncontrollable way.

There is, in addition, some evidence that simply witnessing bullying, especially amongst younger children, can also produce feelings of being upset, anxiety, and avoidance. For example, Eslea and Smith (1995), in a large questionnaire study of primary schools, found that 32% of children reported feeling upset when other children were bullied. Hazzan (1991), in an interview study of six year olds, likewise found that of those students who could effectively verbalise their feelings of stress, about 40% said they felt upset when they saw other children being hurt. This did not seem to be specifically related to identification with the children being bullied *per se*, but more to the feeling that 'their turn might come next'.

One of the aspects of bullying often overlooked is the length of the 'bullying relationship' inside which some children live their lives as victims. These can easily last six months or a year, and in a significant number of instances in excess of a year (Cole, 1977; Sharp *et al.*, 1998).

One of the few long-term studies which followed up known bullies into adulthood was that of Olweus (1993). He reports research on the stability of aggressive behaviour over time, as school students move into young adulthood. Specifically, he identified a group of pupils who had been identified whilst at school as persistently bullying others. By the time of follow-up, at age 24, 60% of these students had received criminal convictions.

From the above, it can be seen that the experience of being bullied causes large numbers of children to experience a wide range of usually relatively minor psychological problems. A smaller proportion of these children experience significantly more major problems, sometimes of a psychosomatic nature, sometimes of a psychiatric nature, and sometimes related to social isolation and rejection. These can lead to longer term maladaptive patterns of personal interaction.

RISK FACTORS AND HEALTH PROTECTING BEHAVIOURS

It is popularly perceived that the victims of bullying are physically smaller and less aggressive than bullies. Victims are seen as having the tendency to be socially isolated from their classmates or other friendship groups, and to have some physical idiosyncrasy such as being very tall or very short, or very fat or very thin.

Findings from research only support these latter characteristics as being associated with social isolation, and a tendency to be less aggressive. 'Physical idiosyncrasy' is not generally a defining characteristic of victims, and seems to be more a product of children using any convenient descriptor to label children who have already become the victims of bullying. For example, another 'physical idiosyncrasy' sometimes used by children when asked why they bully someone in particular, is 'they're not wearing the right gear', which demonstrates how victims are chosen for reasons of relative social exclusion, rather than actually possessing any particular physical idiosyncrasy.

The most generally useful protective factor for bullying is the reduction of social isolation combined with efforts to ensure that children have the social skills to integrate into their social groups, and have groups of friends in most or all the social situations they find themselves in—the playground, going to or from school, or in other activities at the evenings and weekends—this is likely to protect against bullying.

The other major health protecting behaviour is for the children to learn to demonstrate an appropriate level of assertiveness. In a recent major study of the stress felt by victims of bullying and the coping mechanisms that they evolved to defend themselves, Sharp (1998) says 'Students who are more emotionally resilient, have higher self esteem, and are more assertive may be more effective at managing their relationships. They may be able to de-escalate potentially bullying situations in their earlier stages, or avoid becoming enmeshed in long-term bullying relationships.' She also identifies a general tendency for students to learn more strategies to avoid bullying as they get older, and this relates to the general reduction in the incidence of bullying observed by other researchers as children progress through the primary school years into early and middle adolescence.

INTERVENTIONS TO REDUCE BULLYING

Most research on bullying has been directed to assessing incidence and identifying effective means of minimising bullying. There are four levels of intervention to minimise bullying and to be maximally effective probably all four should be used.

First, efforts need to be made to help all children develop good social relationships. This can take place via the activities found in some pastoral curricula or in periods of tutorial work or personal social and health education. Unfortunately, with the advent of the National Curriculum in schools, and with increasingly greater emphasis on time spent on raising academic attainment, many schools have reduced their teaching of this type.

Second, schools need to establish whole school anti-bullying policies. To be effective, these need to be developed through consultation with all school staff and pupils, as well as parents, governors and other interested parties. They also need to be clearly related to the school's discipline system so that bullying is included as a behaviour which is thoroughly disapproved of, but where the normal sanction system is modified to use group based sanctions of the type specifically developed to deal with bullies. (See, for example, Pikas, 1989, and Maines and Robinson, 1994.)

Third, support groups can be valuable for victims of bullying themselves, or for individuals perceived as being vulnerable to victimisation due to their relative social isolation. Arora (1991) offers an early description of the use of victim support groups, and direct work with victims of bullying has since developed through the use of peer group counselling (Cowie and Sharp, 1996). This has the advantage that it can be implemented using the skills and knowledge of senior pupils in secondary schools in addition to the staff time that may be available.

A fourth area of work is directly with children identified as bullies themselves, or who from time to time bully others. As mentioned above, this is best carried on within an agreed framework as part of a whole school anti-bullying policy, and is best done using some of the 'no blame' approaches (Sharp and Smith, 1994).

One of the main researchers in the field, Olweus (1993) found that the most effective arena in which to approach bullying is that of the school class. Here, the local implications of whole school anti-bullying policies can be worked out, general group work for all students or specific group work to support vulnerable children can take place, and teachers are likely to have the most detailed knowledge of the bullying taking place.

In all anti-bullying activities, the support and involvement of parents is very important. This is particularly so for the establishment of whole school policies which are effective in encouraging children to let someone know if they are being bullied, and in some forms of group work as a sanction to influence children who tend to bully others (see, for example, Foster and Thompson, 1991). In all school-based work, specific staff training is usually central to the success of the project. Areas of training most often needed concern group work with children on emotional issues, child counselling skills and project management (Thompson and Smith, 1991).

A recent finding relates the level of bullying in classes to the general level of training and performance of teachers in creating effective learning environments (Roland, 1998). This links success in managing a class of students to increase their level of attainments to an improved standard of behaviour in those classes, and hence a reduction in the bullying reported by the children in those classes.

PRIORITIES FOR INTERVENTION AND RESEARCH

There has been much activity to encourage schools and youth services to create anti-bullying policies over the past five years. Very many have done so, and many are actively monitoring changes in levels of bullying from year to year. However, the evidence we have as to the long-term effectiveness of such anti-bullying policies is somewhat depressing. In one recent study of the long-term implementation of anti-bullying policies at a secondary level, in four out of the five secondary schools concerned the policy had been implemented less and less thoroughly over the two years since the end of the actual intervention project itself. The policy had not been reviewed effectively since the end of the intervention project, and the levels of bullying in the schools were rising again to their original level. In the fifth school, however, due to clearly defined continuous implementation of the anti-bullying policies and the induction of new staff and students into their use, the level of bullying had continued to decrease over the two years since the end of the intervention project (Thompson, 1995).

This highlights one urgent area for research which, due to its longitudinal nature, is difficult to encompass in the usual style of research projects. Research has clearly demonstrated that anti-bullying policies and their associated group work can reduce bullying in the short term (see, for instance, Smith and Sharp (1994) and Arora (1994, 1996a)). However, we know far too little about how to ensure that policies continue to be implemented over time. These processes are bound up with the general management of whole school policies in schools and how they are influenced by changing personnel and educational priorities. There has been very little longitudinal research around these issues, although there has been some discussion of them (Thompson and Sharp, 1994).

A further set of issues needing conceptual clarification and further research is that of the effects of sexual harassment, and of racial harassment on children, and of the relationship between bullying processes and these other forms of harassment. Because much of the work on bullying to date has been done in schools, there is an increasing awareness that research into different aspects of bullying in the community and bullying between adults is needed (Randall and Donohue, 1993; Randall, 1996). Because of the dependence of the bullying process on more general social attitudes as well as the particular activities of individuals, it is likely that research in these areas will be difficult to do. Bullying in the workplace, however, is an area of research attracting increasing interest.

CONCLUSIONS

Bullying is a widely occurring activity which many people and children experience, and from which a significant minority of children and adults suffer serious effects. Bullying is amenable to intervention if that intervention is taken up by significant social institutions such as schools or work places. The major challenge to minimising bullying lies in the creation of sufficient social will to intervene decisively over long periods of time. Because the relevant institutions are those with which most of us have some contact, there is some hope that increasing social awareness of bullying and its effects will in itself lead to less tolerance of bullying wherever it occurs.

REFERENCES

Arora, C.M.J. (1991) The use of victim support groups. In P.K. Smith and D.A. Thompson (Eds) *Practical Approaches to Bullying*. London: David Fulton.

Arora, C.M.J. (1994) Is there any point in trying to reduce bullying in secondary schools? *Educational Psychology in Practice*, 10(3), 155–161.

Arora, C.M.J. (1996a) A longitudinal survey of secondary school pupils' perception of the definition, incidence and processes of bullying. Unpublished PhD Thesis, Department of Educational Studies, University of Sheffield, UK.

Arora, C.M.J. (1996b) Defining bullying—towards a clearer general understanding and more effective intervention strategies. *School Psychology International*, 17, 317–329.

Arora, C.M.J. and Thompson, D.A. (1987) Defining bullying for a secondary school. *Educational and Child Psychology*, 4(3/4) 110–120.

Balding, J., Regis, D., Wise, A., Bish, D. and Muirden, J. (1996) *Bully Off; Young People that Fear Going to School.* Exeter: Schools Health Education Unit.

Boulton, M. and Underwood, K. (1992) Bully/victim problems amongst middle school children. *British Journal of Educational Psychology*, 62, 73–87.

Cole, R.J. (1977) The bullied child in school, an investigation. Unpublished Thesis for MSc (Educational Psychology), Department of Educational Studies, University of Sheffield, UK.

Cowie, H. and Sharp, S. (Eds) (1996) *Peer Counselling in Schools—A Time to Listen.* London: David Fulton.

Department for Education (1994) *Bullying—Don't Suffer in Silence. An anti-bullying pack for schools.* London: HMSO.

Drouet, D. (1993) Adolescent female bullying and sexual harassment. In D. Tattum (Ed.) *Understanding and Managing Bullying.* Oxford: Heinemann.

Elliott, M. (Ed.) (1991) *Bullying—A Practical Guide to Coping for Schools.* Essex: Longman.

Eslea, M. and Smith, P.K. (1995) Attitudes towards bullying in primary school pupils and parents. Paper presented at the Annual Conference of the British Psychological Society, University of Warwick.

Foster, P. and Thompson, D.A. (1991) Bullying—towards a non-violent sanctions policy. In P.K. Smith and D.A. Thompson (Eds) *Practice Approach to Bullying.* London: Fulton, pp. 13–24.

Gillborn, D. (1990) *Race, Ethnicity and Education—Teaching and Learning in Multi-ethnic Schools.* London: Unwin Hyman.

Haselager, G.T. and Van Lieshout, C.F.M. (1992) Social and affective adjustment of self and peer reported victims and bullies. Paper presented at the Fifth European Conference on Developmental Psychology, Seville.

Hazzan, K. (1991) Is bullying upsetting? An investigation of stresses in infant school children. Unpublished MSc Thesis, Department of Educational Studies, University of Sheffield.

Lowenstein, L.F. (1978) Who is the Bully? *Bulletin of the British Psychological Society*, 31, 147–149.

MacLeod, M. and Morris, S. (1996) *Why Me? Children Talking to ChildLine about Bullying.* ChildLine: London.

Maines, B. and Robinson, G. (1994) *A No Blame Approach.* Bristol: Lame Duck Publishing.

Mooney, S. and Smith, P.K. (1995) Bullying and the child who stammers. *British Journal of Special Education*, 22(1), 24–27.

Neary, A. and Joseph, S. (1994) Peer victimisation and its relationship to self concept and depression among school girls. *Personality and Individual Differences*, 16(1), 183–186.

Olweus, D. (1978) *Aggression in the Schools: Bullies and Whipping boys.* Washington, DC: Hemisphere.

Olweus, D. (1980) Familial and temperamental determinants of aggressive behaviour in adolescent boys. *Developmental Psychology*, 16, 644–660.

Olweus, D. (1991) Bully/victim problems amongst school children: basic facts and effects of a school-based intervention programme. In D. Pepler and K. Rubin (Eds) *The Development and Treatment of Childhood Aggression*. Hillsdale, NJ: Erlbaum.

Olweus, D. (1993) *Bullying at School: What we Know and What we Can Do*. Oxford: Blackwell.

O'Moore, A.M. and Hillery, B. (1989) Bullying in Dublin schools. *Irish Journal of Psychology*, 10, 426–441.

O'Moore, A.M. and Hillery, B. (1991) What do teachers need to know? In M. Elliot (Ed.) *Bullying: A Practical Guide to Coping for Schools*. Harrow: Longman.

Pepler, D., Craig, W., Zeigler, S. and Charach, A. (1993) A school based anti-bullying intervention—preliminary evaluation. In D.P. Tattum (Ed.) *Understanding and Managing Bullying*. Oxford: Heinemann Educational.

Perry, D.G., Williard, J.C. and Perry, L.C. (1990) Peers—perceptions of the consequences that victimised children provide aggressors. *Child Development*, 61, 1310–1325.

Pervin, K. and Turner, A. (1994) An investigation into staff and pupils' knowledge, attitudes, and beliefs about bullying in an inner city school. *Pastoral Care in Education*, 12(3), 16–21.

Pikas, A. (1989) The common concern method as the treatment for mobbing. In E. Roland and E. Munthe (Eds) *Bullying: An International Perspective*. London: David Fulton.

Randall, P.E. (1996) *A Community Approach to Bullying*. Stoke-on Trent: Trentham Books.

Randall, P.E. and Donohue, M. (1993) Tackling bullying as a community. *Child Education*, 70, 78–80.

Reid, K. (1989) Bullying and Persistent School Absenteeism. In D. Tattum and D. Lane (Eds) *Bullying in Schools*. Stoke-on-Trent: Trentham Books.

Rigby, K. and Slee, P. (1993) Dimensions of interpersonal relating among Australian school children and their implications for psychological well-being. *Journal of Social Psychology*, 133(1), 33–42.

Roland, E. (1998) School influences on bullying. Unpublished PhD Thesis. School of Education, University of Durham, UK.

Sharp, S. (1995) How much does bullying hurt? The effects of bullying on the health, happiness and educational progress of secondary aged students. *Educational and Child Psychology*, 12(2), 81–88.

Sharp, S. (1998) Bullying in schools: A study of stress and coping amongst secondary aged students who have been bullied. Unpublished PhD Thesis, Department of Educational Studies, University of Sheffield.

Sharp, S. and Smith, P.K. (Eds) (1994) *Tackling Bullying in your School—A Practical Handbook for Teachers*. London: Routledge.

Sharp, S. and Thompson, D.A. (1997) The Establishment of Whole-school Policies. In G.A. Lindsay and D.A. Thompson (Eds) *Values into Practice in Special Education*. London: Fulton.

Sharp, S., Thompson, D.A. and Arora, C.M.J. (1999) How long before it hurts? An investigation into long-term bullying. *School Psychology International* (in press).

Smith, P.K. and Sharp, S. (Eds) (1994) *School Bullying: Insights and Perspectives*. London: Routledge.

Tattum, D. (Ed.) (1993) *Understanding and Managing Bullying*. Oxford: Heinemann Educational.

Thompson, D.A. (1995) Two years on: problems in monitoring anti-bullying policies in schools and their effect on the incidence of bullying. Paper presented at the European Conference on Educational Research, September 1995, University of Bath, British Educational Research Association, UK.

Thompson, D.A. and Smith, P.K. (1991) Effective action against bullying—the key problems. In P.K. Smith and D.A. Thompson (Eds) *Practical Approaches to Bullying*. London: Fulton.

Thompson, D.A. and Sharp, S. (1994) *Improving Schools—Establishing and Integrating Whole-School Behaviour Policies*. London: Fulton.

Williams, K., Chambers, M., Logan, S. and Robinson, D. (1996) Association of common health symptoms with bullying in primary school children. *British Medical Journal*, 313, 17–19.

Index